THE LENTEN MOON

BOOKS BY VON GOODWIN

The Egg Moon

The Hunter's Moon

The Hitching Post of the Sun

VON GOODWIN WEBSITE

www.vongoodwin.com

This website contains additional products,
services, resources and links.

THE LENTEN MOON

LIVING THE QUESTION

VON GOODWIN

BALBOA.
PRESS

A DIVISION OF HAY HOUSE

Balboa Press books may be ordered through booksellers or by contacting:

Balboa Press
A Division of Hay House
1663 Liberty Drive
Bloomington, IN 47403
www.balboapress.com
1-(877) 407-4847

Because of the dynamic nature of the Internet, any web addresses or links contained in this book may have changed since publication and may no longer be valid. The views expressed in this work are solely those of the author and do not necessarily reflect the views of the publisher, and the publisher hereby disclaims any responsibility for them.

The author of this book does not dispense medical advice or prescribe the use of any technique as a form of treatment for physical, emotional, or medical problems without the advice of a physician, either directly or indirectly. The intent of the author is only to offer information of a general nature to help you in your quest for emotional and spiritual well-being. In the event you use any of the information in this book for yourself, which is your constitutional right, the author and the publisher assume no responsibility for your actions.

Any people depicted in stock imagery provided by Thinkstock are models, and such images are being used for illustrative purposes only. Certain stock imagery © Thinkstock.

ISBN: 978-1-4525-3344-5 (sc)
ISBN: 978-1-4525-3345-2 (e)

Printed in the United States of America

Balboa Press rev. date: 4/14/2011

In memory of:

Myrna Sue

August 15, 1941 – March 28, 2002

PREFACE

*Many of us crucify ourselves between two thieves -
regret for the past and fear of the future.*

Fulton Oursler

Regret makes a wilderness of the past robbing one the benefit of experience. And orchestrations based on fear predestines the future to be the same; a recurring theme of more regret. It is easy to sit in a position of self-judgment and critique an experience that has ultimately led one to a higher level of enlightenment. And yet, that higher level of consciousness does not permit judgment. One is where one needs to be at the exact moment that is required for disclosure.

Incidents that are often self-defined as struggles and setbacks are necessary tutorials in living. Most of us, from time to time, complain about these happenings. And playing the part of a victim of circumstance temporarily satisfies one's needs; needs that support an existence that is based on fear and self-loathing. Ignoring these occurrences as opportunities, however, is to turn a blind eye and a deaf ear to guidance; guidance that is often as subtle as apparent coincidence. And this unawareness compounds one's confusion and complicates one's life. And yet, this too is an experience and a lesson to be learned.

Listening to that small voice that often manifests itself as an intuitive feeling is profound intelligence. There is an energy that exists that permits the interaction of human intent with natural forces to permit creation. And what we feel as humans affects what happens in the world around us. Nature, in fact, is a type of mirror, in that what one projects is what one receives. There is no sitting this one out; everyone dances to this cosmic fugue – everyone co-creates.

This book, *The Lenten Moon*, is the first of thirteen writings. It chronicles a tragic time in the life of my sister and me. One we refer to as the source of all of our questions. Regret and fear filled our lives and is chronicled with our intent to hold selected individuals accountable for acts of eternal consequence. It seems to be dark and self-serving. Colleagues have commented on its extreme detail. The detailed accounting was necessary to demonstrate the magnitude of pain and confusion both my sister and I experienced.

The Egg Moon, the second book of the series describes what the spiritually unconscious would describe as simple coincidence. These were happenings that were strewn before us in the most unusual places and circumstances. Within a ten year period there were times when these incidents were obvious, and then there were times when the meaning remained concealed until we were ready to understand. And there are still gleanings of wisdom from these experiences that are made aware to us in dreams, life and living.

To learn from experiences, particularly those that have come at such a high price, is the source of wisdom. *The Hunter's Moon* lists events in the lives of my sister and me when the application of the enlightenments proved beneficial to others. It is one thing to know something, and quite another to use that knowledge. In fact, true enlightenment manifests itself as a need to serve others. The remaining books of the Moon Book series provide writings of deeper experiences in living life as a participant. And the thirteen books provide a primer for defining wisdom. Wisdom is not what one knows, wisdom comes from: Living the Questions.

THE WORST DAY

Slowly the moon is rising out of the ruddy haze,
Divesting herself of her golden shift, and so
Emerging white and exquisite; and I in amaze to
See in the sky before me, a woman I did not know
I loved, but there she goes and her beauty hurts my heart;
I follow her down the night, begging her not to depart.

D. H Lawrence

The full moon lit the countryside with a luminosity that made the shadows become an extension of the night; framing the trees with a ghostly aura as if nature was caught between a world of reality and one of my making. The silver orb peered through the branches and made its presence known to me in a way that was most unusual. Having been a source of wonderment and pleasure on many occasions this evening was far different. For tonight the Lenten Moon rose in the east; a celestial event marking the beginning of a time on introspection for the ancients as they mourned the murder of Christ at the hands of the Romans. And it marked a time of reckoning for me as I contemplated the death of my mother at the hands of those whose character is as murky as night. The date was Thursday, March 28.

The night air was so cold that one could hear it; a faint tinkling timbre that seemed to suggest a cleanness, a purity; a consciousness that there is more to living than simply existing. It hurt to take a breath. The cold burned my lungs as if to remind me I am not worthy of its benefits; an unseemly mixing of that which is pure with that which is contemptible. One is either alive, or not; quick or dead. And often the difference in the two involves a simple answer to an unasked question. And the demon that haunts me tonight is the realization that I have not been a good steward of life; I did not ask the right questions. As a result, my world came to an end today; I no longer felt that I deserved any of life's benefits.

My lodging is the lower level of my brother's home – a typical basement domicile that was furnished with left-over furniture and knick knacks; an intermediate step for possessions before being exiled to the thrift store. A game room for billiards and darts, a small claustrophobic bedroom and bathroom, and a media room provided the bare essentials that I needed. It had the look of a do-it-your-self project.

Some parts were incomplete and others were professionally done. All in all, it was perfect for what I required; a place to hide and reflect, to sort things out. For the day, this day had been one that I will never forget; it will forever hold a place in my mind of one of great loss. To have something that means so much to me taken away. And to have someone's memory scattered about as so many leaves in the park was distressing. The weight of my despair was more than I could bear.

I sat on the futon and wrapped myself in a blanket; a quilt made by artisans of Gees Bend, Alabama. The pattern of the quilt had interlocking rings of multi colored pieces of cloth; scraps of material made into a piece of art. The room was decorated with a southwestern color scheme and the walls held vacation artifacts ranging from the Hopi of Arizona to the Mayans of the Yucatan. Books bulged from the shelving with subjects ranging from mutual funds and string physics to reincarnation and the paranormal. On a casual visit, there were enough stimuli to hold my attention for hours, but tonight was different. My mind was not geared toward stimulation; on the contrary it had been overly taxed by the day's events, and it simply wanted rest. One object did catch my eye and removing it from the bookshelf I saw that it was a photo album. Opening it to the first page I saw a picture of my mother helping my brother and me open Christmas gifts.

The picture was old, I was so small. It seem as though it was a different lifetime and, yet I remembered the smallest of detail. It was a Christmas in the early 60's, before Kennedy's assassination. My childhood unlike most of my friends was benchmarked by historical events; not birthdays or vacations. That was the environment in which I was raised; pre-Kennedy assassination, post-Kennedy assassination, Pre-Woodstock, post-Woodstock, my life as a child was rich with information and learning. My parents, however, struggled to make ends meet. My brother and I did not realize then that times were difficult, mother always made things better and protected us from the unpleasant. This Christmas, I suppose, was leaner than some. My dad worked as a carpenter and when jobs were scarce, he would pull a shift, or two, at the pipe shop – a factory where cast iron tubing was made. Mother, on the other hand, tried to be a stay-at-home mom. Sometimes, the need for additional money would require her to work as a waitress at the Ponderosa; a drive-in restaurant located near our home on Fifteenth Street. I remember her discussing with my dad her fear in servicing certain drive-up customers; children are the best eavesdroppers. I remember that fear was manifested as anger in my mother; she would not let it get the best of her. My brother and I would miss her and even though our dad would attempt to stand-in for her, it was not the same. Although, in retrospect he could not afford it, dad would surprise her by taking my brother and me to the restaurant for a milkshake, and to see mother.

Looking closely at the picture, the gifts that were opened were modest and creative. My brother sat near the Christmas tree and played with small, plastic model cars that he pushed through a maze of soft drink bottle caps. I do remember that. Dad had collected bottled caps from the store at the corner of our street and mother had painted them various colors. They hid this labor of love from my brother and me. And when the giant box was opened, there were hundreds of brightly painted metal caps, the limits of which were bounded only by our imagination; streets, buildings, cities – whatever a child's mind could concoct.

In the background of the picture, I could see the kitchen. The table had four place settings. In the center of the table were three bowls, the contents of which were unknown – that detail escapes me. But, I do remember the weekly trip to the grocery store. The name of the store escapes my memory, as well. The sign bearing the name was in disrepair with missing lettering; it looked like a foreign language. I do remember the emblem. It was a black bear with a red bowtie.

Assisting mother with loading the cart was my job; bread, milk, eggs and cheese was her responsibility, can goods was mine. At that time, can goods were marked using a paper label; a loose wrapping whose ends were glued together. Often, the labels would separate from the can and the contents were then anyone's guess. These unmarked cans were placed in large wire baskets and sold for pennies; a bargain that was too attractive to pass - actually, economics forced mother to purchase the unmarked cans. She sheltered her children from the harsh realities of life and without any complaints she made a game of selecting the unmarked canned goods. I would pick up a can and shake it, this feels like green beans. Good! Throw it in the cart. This one sounds like cream. No, we have cream. That was my job and I thought I did it well; I made my contribution.

Mother always knew what to do, she protected us, she taught us, she cared for our bodies and she nourished our souls – I am but a fraction of what she wanted me to be. And even with my shortcomings, I have done well – I see further than she only because I stand on her shoulders. And for me to forget her and what she has done for me would be for me to deny the existence of everything good and decent. I can't let this day end as it has; I will find my answers to the unasked questions.

I placed the photo album on the table and pulled a bottle of pinot noir from the wine rack. I poured a glass, the first glass and stared at it as I thought of my day; the worst day of my life.

PART I

The Trial

*Dare any of you, having a matter against another, go to
law before the unjust, and not before the saints?*

1 Corinthians 6:1

CHAPTER 1

Voir Dire

Jury duty [is] a bog of quicksand on the path to justice.
Sidney Bernard

The attorneys representing the Plaintiff and the Defendant positioned themselves before the judge to establish the rules of engagement. These rules came in the form of motions. Information that may be, or may not be, allowed into evidence as testimony. Many were basic, compulsory items that were as much a house-keeping chore as creative legal maneuvering. The exceptions were two hard-hitting setbacks for the Plaintiff. The first motion denied the opportunity to enter into the court record the relationship the expert witnesses for the Defense had with the Defendant. They both were insured by the same malpractice insurance company. I was concerned that force could be brought to bear and the witnesses would adjust their 'medical best-practice standards' to support the defendant. This relationship could certainly compromise the credibility of the witnesses with respect to conflict of interest issues. Also, to compound the problem the Defendant's counsel is a staff attorney for the malpractice company. Secondly, a motion to deny as a charge against the Defendant the Informed Consent to Treatment clause that had been added after the initial filing of the law suit – a breaking of legal protocol. Fifteen minutes into the trial and I was not feeling well.

The Defendant's attorney, Damian Goretti, did not show any satisfaction in winning the critical motions. In fact, he was well rehearsed in the theatrics of the courtroom having been in many battles and, as rumor had it, undefeated in all legal wars. His tall Gregory Peck-like demeanor certainly had a calming effect for his client and the opposite for me – I avoided eye contact. Scuttlebutt has it that he is named for two Saints: St. Damian – the patron saint of physicians and St. Goretti – a saint who forgave murders. The irony is more than coincidental; an attorney who champions doctors and absolves those who kill; a macabre twist on typecasting.

The reputation of his legal firm is one of not settling out of court – all suits are to be tried. This group of attorneys is considered bullies in the profession of practicing law. *Deep Pockets* have been words used to describe to what extent this group would go to, to win – out spend, out last and outsmart their opposition. After all, this is their primary focus – their only focus – defending malpractice claims. Truly a well oiled machine and it showed.

The courtroom was an intimate setting. The opponents sat within close proximity - so close that whispers could be heard despite efforts to keep them confidential. Wood veneer lined the walls. Overstated, wooden desks and uncomfortable pews that made ones back hurt throughout the day agitated the tension of the participants. Opposite the jurors box on the Defendant's side of the courtroom was a large projection screen. This screen would facilitate the presentation of evidence and support material. The Bench was elevated to place the judge in a position of authority and above that was the Great Seal of Alabama. Flanked on either side of the Bench were the flags of the United States and Alabama. Behind the Bench was a door where the judge would appear and retire. And beyond the door one could see bookshelves lined with legal journals. Frosted windows reached to the ceiling on one side of the courtroom. The windows served to remind me life goes on with sounds from the street below, even though for the next few days time for me would stop and focus on the last thirty one days of a life.

Ms. Santiago served as the court secretary and she managed the comings and goings of the jury, the opposing parties and climate control of the courtroom. Her job was simple enough, count the jurors with her extended index finger and a total of less than fourteen require her to search and fetch the missing. The official announcement that a session was about to start began with her asking both parties, 'defense ready?', 'plaintiff ready?' and with affirmation from both her response would be, 'alright then, I'll get the judge'. My heart would skip a beat each time she uttered this phrase – the uncertainty of the immediate future created a high level of anxiety, as if riding a roller coaster in the dark and not having the ability to anticipate the next rise or fall, bend or curve.

Ms. Santiago announced the arrival of the jurors. We rose; standing in honor, of those that staffed the jury pool as they entered the courtroom in three groups of twelve. One group occupied the jury box and the remaining groups sat on the first two rows on either side of the visitors section. Thirty six men and women, young and old, representing many walks of life found their seats as the selection process began. I looked closely at each person and was careful not to stare. What physical characteristic or facial expression would indicate their desire to be conscientious? Each juror would be paid ten dollars per day and ten cents per mile for travel. So, money could not be their motivation. Had their parents taught them to take important things seriously? Had their adult experience in living created wise souls? Who wanted to be there, who didn't? I answered my question with, 'no one wanted to be there!'

Judge Kent addressed the jury pool by thanking them for their sacrifice in serving as a juror and that this is what makes our judicial system unique in the world. He then asked each juror to stand and give their name and profession, their spouse's name and profession and their place of residence - *voir dire* had begun. Adding to my quick assessment of physical characteristics were the juror's voice intonation, where they lived and if they could remember and respond to the questions that were asked of them. I found myself over-analyzing the responses. For some the profession was not favorable – medically related – perhaps too sympathetic to the defense. For others the place of residence was not good – too rich or too poor – I wanted real, middle-class people with similar experiences in living as I have had.

The attorneys were permitted to ask questions of the group or to an individual. Each side looked for reasons to strike, or to remove a juror. Questions were extremely straight-forward. Do you know the Plaintiff or Defendant, do you have previous experience as a juror, and have you ever sued anyone, extremely simple questions. However, this was not an enlightened group of individuals. One juror when asked if he could follow the judge's instruction regarding deliberating the evidence and setting aside personal prejudice answered that he could not comply. The same questions was asked again, with slightly modified wording, and he answered the he could comply. So, which is it, I wondered? Similar disheartening responses were given by other jurors. One slept throughout the process and was eventually selected. In fact, it was arguably the worst collection of warm bodies the Plaintiff's attorney had ever experienced.

Jurors with opinions and prejudices that did not show a propensity to return a favorable decision for their client were placed on lists by each attorney. This list was used to rank the least favored jurors. Each juror was identified by number. Each side took turn beginning with the Plaintiff's attorney announcing the number of a juror that would not be retained until the pool had been reduced to fourteen jurors - twelve jurors and two alternates. My emotions were up and down with each juror that was excused. Glad for one, saddened by another. This was in my mind a key moment in the trial.

I realized at this point the difficulty in winning a case with complex issues. I remembered leaving the hospital the day of my mother's death – with many more questions than answers. Years of investigative research into the causes of her condition and sleepless nights of reliving decisions rushed through my head. Had I done all that I could do? How would the jurors understand the relationship of a drop in a blood platelet count with a doctor's reason for prescribing a specific care-plan? How could the jurors grasp the concept of standard-of-care when many looked as if they could not balance a check book? How should the case be made that Informed Consent is central to a patient's right to know? The final verdict would be in the hands of the jury – in many ways this did not seem like justice – it seemed more like a lottery. Did I feel lucky? These questions and many more bore heavily on my optimism as the morning court session broke for lunch.

The Plaintiff's attorney was not encouraged by the selected jurors and knew this compromised his ability to win. Grasping for the only straw that was available, he made a motion to the judge to excuse the entire jury because of a racial imbalance. Too few African-American jurors had been selected. The judge granted the motion and the jury selection process was repeated with thirty six new jurors. My enthusiasm grew because of the cleverness of the Plaintiff's attorney - my attorney - and the hope of selecting a more intelligent group of twelve.

This bold move was performed by Reynard Laurence. Mr. Laurence had been researching the complex medical details of the case for five years. His confidence in the exactness of the evidence was overshadowed by several hard truths. No one had ever won a malpractice case against Mr. Goretti's firm, most people are averse to lawsuits in general and people don't want to believe that doctors can be less than honorable. Shaking the god-like persona that people place on their doctors and a Biblical verse in the Book of Corinthians that suggest lawsuits are unrighteous, the holy war to decide arrogance versus ownership had been waged.

With the new jurors in place, Judge Kent instructed the jury to not discuss the case with anyone, do not conduct any independent research and focus on the evidence and not the opinions of the attorneys or the witnesses. As I sat there my concern was not with the jurors discussing the trial or with them conducting independent research, it was their ability to comprehend and recall the evidence. The evidence was straightforward, the jurors were suspect, and I was scared. With the second jury in place and the legal maneuvering scorecard essentially even, court was adjourned with instructions to reconvene at 8:30 AM the following day.

CHAPTER 2

A Tale of Two Patients

*It was the best of times, it was the worst of times, it was the age of wisdom,
it was the age of foolishness, it was the epoch of belief, it was the epoch
of incredulity, it was the season of light, it was the season of darkness, it
was the spring of hope, it was the winter of despair, we had everything
before us, we had nothing before us, we were all going direct to heaven,
we were all going direct the other way - in short, the period was so far like
the present period, that some of its noisiest authorities insisted on its being
received, for good or for evil, in the superlative degree of comparison only.*
Charles Dickens

I wandered the hallways of the Jefferson County Courthouse waiting
for the morning session to begin; avoiding inappropriate contact
with jurors and wrestling with nervousness that at times make me
ill. I had not slept well the night before thinking of the events of the
first day. This will become overwhelming if I allow the emotions to
pile onto me. After a single day my role in this epic had diminished
greatly. Although I spent years researching the medical detail for the
case, mentoring the legal team in technicalities, it was now not my
game to play and my place was on the bench. I have an attorney and
a team of experts. They are in control, which meant I was not. This is
what troubled me, the most. No control of what will happen, when
it will happen or how it will happen. The realization aggravated my

sense of independence and at that moment I was *told* to enter the courtroom and be seated, I was *told* where to sit. Control yourself, I thought.

The jurors had taken their places in the jury box. The attorneys were arranging their files and exhibits. The court reporter was setting up her equipment and organizing the tapes to record the session's narrative. Everyone knew their role in this judicial theater and as if on cue Ms. Santiago stepped onto center stage and asked, 'Defense ready?', 'Plaintiff ready?', and in unison both attorneys answered, 'Yes Ma'am'. Her response, 'Alright then, I'll get the judge'.

Judge Kent entered through the door behind the Bench and everyone rose in respect for the court and his position to preside over it. With that, Judge Kent took his seat and read the charge. Although I had previously secured a copy of what was being read and was very familiar with the text, the impact of the words seemed very different. A robed man that was anointed by our customs sat in a position of ultimate authority – the venue was intimidating. As he read the document the words did not simply float around as motes of dust, they were aimed with pinpoint precision at a person – the defendant. One could not help but sense a pheromone of fear as it wafted about, this was truly a humbling experience. It is quite different to be tough and unyielding when you are in the comfort of one's friends and allies and different still to stand toe-to-toe in an arena of competition with an adversary – at this point, blinking was not an option. His wife nervously listened, rubbing her hands as if to wipe away some invisible stain. I felt some pity for the Doctor. Why couldn't he have been less arrogant and sought experienced advice from a colleague before taking a course of action for which he was ill-prepared and ill-equipped? Why didn't he fully confide in me prior to the surgery? What in heaven's name made him think he could 'pull this off'? At that moment my attention was diverted to Judge Kent as he prepared the jury for the Plaintiff's opening remarks.

Mr. Laurence's stature was not as impressive as Mr. Goretti's. What he lacked in height he compensated with bark – a gifted and quick-witted orator. Perfectly dressed with a blue suit, fashionable green tie and cuff links, he looked the part – could he walk the walk?

His voice was strong – no problem hearing his rhetoric. When he was successful in delivering a hard blow to the defense, the corner of his lips would curl to display a slight smile – he enjoyed confrontation. I settled in and positioned myself so that one eye could watch his performance and the other could watch the juror's reactions. This was the time to capture the court's imagination.

Plaintiff's Opening Remarks by Mr. Laurence

Mr. Laurence's mannerisms were exaggerated; nervously jumping about from one thought to another and from one place to another. This nervous jumping-about was not a result of fear as much as it was an issue of capacity - an impatient need to tell it all and tell it now. He believed in the merits of the case. His enthusiasm, however, more than compensated for his winding path to the truth; a trip that often took several attempts.

"May it please the Court, ladies and gentlemen of the jury? On March 28th, 2002, a lady named Myrna Sue Carroll, who was 60 years old, died while undergoing open-heart surgery at Oak Mountain Hospital. She died when the heart-lung machine that her blood was flowing through during the surgery completely clotted off. Now, why did this happen? We will prove to you that she died because of the negligence and the inattention of her Doctor. And to fully understand what happened in this case, we need to start about a month earlier, when she entered Oak Mountain Hospital with some chest pains, and they found out that she had had a mild heart attack. They ran some tests on her, and they decided that she needed to have triple bypass surgery, a common surgery. During the surgery on March 4th, they introduced and gave her a lot of the drug called Heparin. And you will hear a lot about that in this case. Heparin is used to thin the blood during the surgery. The only problem is that a lot of people develop a fairly severe allergy to Heparin."

"After her first surgery, she started displaying all of the signs and all of the symptoms that should be a red flag to the physician. She started displaying all of the signs and symptoms of this allergy, and they didn't catch it. They let her go from the hospital. She had to have a number of different blood checks and the results showed that her blood was very unstable. See, the symptoms of the allergy is a hyper coagulation of the blood or a hyper clotting of the blood. Two weeks after her surgery, she had to be readmitted to the hospital, and they found out that all three vessels that they had bypassed during the first surgery were completely clotted. You'll hear the evidence that this is an extremely rare occurrence, when all three blood vessels clot and that this is a sign and symptom that should have been recognized as a Heparin allergy. But they didn't recognize it. They continued to treat her with the very drug that was causing these problems. They gave her Heparin."

"After a couple more days in the hospital, they didn't really know what to do. They decided that they were going to schedule another surgery. The problem with this decision was, tests were performed the day before surgery that indicated a setback - they found out she was allergic to Heparin. Instead of postponing the surgery, instead of giving her reversal drugs that would undo the signs and the symptoms of this allergy, they decided to plow ahead with the surgery. There's one complication, though. This surgery has to be done with blood thinners, and they couldn't use the blood thinner Heparin. They had to use a substitute. The substitute requires a completely different technique in the monitoring of the blood during surgery. It requires different machines, different techniques, and different technology. And the doctor that had decided to perform the surgery on her, Dr. Zopyros, was not trained on how to do this type of surgery with Hirudin, the substitute drug. In fact, he had never read about it. Never read about it, never been trained about it, never watched a video about it, and never observed it being done. None of his team had ever seen it done. None of his team had ever researched it. But they decided to try it anyway. And it cost Ms. Carroll her life."

"You see, what happened was, they decided to move forward with this substitute drug, and the literature that you will see during this trial indicates that the monitoring of the blood during the surgery requires the use of a machine that monitors how quickly your blood is clotting, to make sure that the heart-lung machine doesn't clot up. They didn't have this machine at the hospital. And so they tried to use the same method that they used to monitor the blood with Heparin. They tried to use that on the substitute drug, and it didn't work. And during the surgery, the machine completely clotted up, and she died."

"Now, you'll hear evidence that it is the doctor's responsibility to formulate a plan to keep her blood from clotting up during the surgery. And he failed to do it. Now, before we go through all of the facts and all of the evidence and all of the medicine in this case, I want to introduce you to the parties. First of all, we have Vicki Anderson, who's from Houston -- and you were introduced to her a little bit yesterday -- and you have Vaughn Goodson. These are the children of Myrna Sue Carroll. Myrna Sue Carroll was 60 years old at the time that she died. And you can take a look at a picture of her from the summer before she passed away. She's at the Grand Canyon. She was full of life, a happy woman going into the golden years of her life when she underwent this surgery. Who else are the parties? We have the defendant, which is Dr. Andrew Zopyros. He's a cardiothoracic surgeon that works at Oak Mountain Hospital for the Vulcan Clinic. The Vulcan Clinic is also a party because that entity is the employer of Dr. Zopyros. We're claiming that the Vulcan Clinic and Dr. Zopyros are responsible for Ms. Carroll's death. So what is this case going to be about? What do we have to prove?"

"Well, you'll see on the screen that we have to prove to you that there was a violation. We'll prove to you that there was a violation of what's called the standard of care, or basically the rules that you're supposed to follow when you're a doctor. There are doctors all across the country that follows a certain standard of care, and we'll prove to you that the breach of this standard of care cost Ms. Carroll her life. Before we get into that, though, there are a lot of medical terms that are very difficult to understand. It's not words that we normally have in our day-to-day life. In fact, I had to learn a lot when we started this case. So what I'm going to do, I'm going to take a little bit of time to try to introduce you to some of the medical terms so that, hopefully, we can understand the terminology when I say things like "thrombocytopenia" or "ECT machine" or things like that. Hopefully, we'll have a little bit of a background to it. So, first of all, I want to go over some of the blood terminology."

"You will hear in this case that the blood has both red blood cells and platelets, and that they are flowing through the veins. And so let's take a look at what platelets actually look like. Platelets are these round things that are basically shaped like plates that are floating through the body in the veins. You will hear that one of the signs of this allergy to Heparin is a reduction in the platelet count. So when you hear the term "platelet," think of these round plates flowing through the blood. There are a couple of other pictures we have of platelets. The typical flow of platelets goes through the veins and gets pumped around just like the blood through the heart and out of the heart, and to the rest of the body – and keeps on going. All right, next, we have – let's go to the next screen. In addition to platelets, we're going to go over the term 'antibody' or allergy. Sometimes when the body has an agent introduced to it, it can form an allergy. We all have an understanding of what that means, and we all have allergies more or less from time to time. During the spring, if we sniff pollen or smell pollen, it causes your body to have an allergic reaction. The way your body has an allergic reaction is it starts formulating what's called antibodies."

"Antibodies, if we'll take a picture of it, are like particles that form in the blood that -- that begin to have a reaction in your blood. So when you hear about a Heparin allergy or Heparin antibody, think of an agent being introduced into the blood that's going to interact with the platelets, like we see here."

"Go to the next one, Laine."

Laine assisted Mr. Laurence by organizing evidence, exhibits and pre-trial testimony utilizing a laptop computer. As the attorney requested a document, Laine would retrieve the information and then project the image onto the screen. Laurence constantly made requests for data and Laine responded in kind.

"The antibodies that you just saw in that picture will bond with the platelets, and the bonding with these platelets can cause what's called clotting, or thrombosis. We're all familiar with what a blood clot is. But I want you guys to understand through the medicine what we're talking about. Because a hyper clotting or a rapid clotting - an abnormal clotting is what we're going to be dealing with in this case. And we'll prove to you that the reason why she died is because she had a hyper clotting of the blood that was an allergic reaction to this medicine."

"Keep going, Laine."

"The clotting formulates when the platelets bond with the antibodies, and then they start forming granules like suction cups and stick to the wall of the vein. And we'll prove to you that because of the Heparin that she was given, she actually formed these antibodies. We know because of a test that was done. The tests show that she had a Heparin allergy."

"We're dealing with what's called an open-heart surgery. That's something that we have all been exposed to or are familiar with. But I want to go over the basics of an open-heart surgery so that if we go through it during the case and we ask the doctor about it, then we'll be familiar with what happens. First of all, we have the heart. We all know what the heart is. It's the muscle in the body - a muscle in the body that actually pumps the blood around our body. It pumps -- there are chambers in it. The blood comes in one side, it goes in the different chambers, and then it's pumped out to the rest of our body."

"Sometimes the vessels that are running in the heart become clogged. That's why they tell us not to eat bacon and cholesterol - things that will cause us to have a clogged artery. So what happens is that in order for the heart to get the blood it needs, they take a vein from the leg and that I'll show you -- let's go to the next picture. They will take a vein from your leg, and they will remove that vein, they will clean it out, and they'll make sure that it has good flow. And then what they will do is, they will go to the heart, and they will basically plug the vein in where there's not a clot, and they will bypass the clot or the clotting, and they will infuse the vein into where the blood can come in, flow through the bypass, and flow out. It's just like, for example, Interstate 459 down here. If there's clogged traffic on I-59, there's a bypass on I-459 where you can get from I-20 to I-59, no traffic jam. You can bypass the traffic. It's just like that; except they do it with a vein that they take from your leg.

In this case, we will be dealing with a triple bypass, where they took three different sections of vein, and they had three different clots that they bypassed. So that's what I'm talking about when we say 'open-heart surgery' and 'bypass'.

"During bypass surgery, we use -- or they use what's called a heart-lung machine. The heart-lung machine basically, during surgery -- and if I'm in your way, y'all let me know. During surgery what happens is, they stop the heart and completely bypass the heart so that the surgeon can perform the bypass grafting. While that is happening, oftentimes they will have a heart-lung machine. Sometimes they do the surgery with what is called an off-pump surgery. Off-pump means they do not utilize a heart-lung machine. An on-pump surgery, they use a heart-lung machine. And what happens is, during the surgery, the body continues to need the oxygenated blood. And so what they'll do is, they'll plug the body into the machine, and the blood will flow out. As it will come back toward the heart and it will then flow out into the machine. It will become oxygenated through the machine. It's a very complex, very detailed machine, very expensive machine, and high-tech. The machine then oxygenates the blood, and then it pumps it back into your body. And they have the heart-lung machine plugged into the veins that take the blood away from your heart. So it comes into the heart, it gets oxygen, and it goes back into your body. That allows the surgeon to perform the surgery and your body to continue to receive the oxygen."

"Let's go to the next screen, Laine."

"This is what it looks like during the surgery. The heart-lung machine is placed beside the patient. The patient will be lying on the table. And as you can see from the arrows here, the blood will come up towards the heart, go into this machine that's beside the bed, get oxygenated, and then flow away. This is the very machine that clotted up during the surgery on March 28th. That's not supposed to happen."

"Let's go to the next screen, Laine."

"During the open-heart surgery, if the blood is pumped into the heart-lung machine without a blood thinner, it will clot. It forms a reaction with the lining of the tubing, and it starts to stick to the tubes, and it will clot. So, therefore, there has been the development of what we know as Heparin and other drugs that are blood thinners that help the blood to not clot during surgery, and it allows the heart-lung machine not to clot and stop during the surgery. It's very important that you administer the correct amount of Heparin so that the blood remains thin. There's a catch with Heparin, though. Heparin is a product from the mucous of a pig lung. I didn't know that until this case. It's either the mucous from a pig lung or the mucous from a cow lung. Now, that sounds dirty. It's a product that they make from that mucous that naturally causes the thinning of the blood. But the problem with that is there are a significant amount of people that receive Heparin and have a reaction to it. They're allergic to it, like some people are allergic to peanut butter. People are allergic to different things. There are people in the world that when they get Heparin, they develop an allergy or an antibody to the drug. Some people who develop the allergy never have any symptoms. They just develop the antibody, and nothing happens. The antibodies do not form in such rapid progression that it causes the blood to clot. So somebody can get Heparin, have open-heart surgery, and never have any reaction to it. However, some people -- let's go -- let's go to the next one. Some people can develop what is known as the Heparin allergy."

"Keep moving, Laine."

"When you develop the Heparin allergy, there are a number of signs and symptoms that -- that people look for, that doctors look for in order to determine whether or not you're having this allergic reaction: One is a drop, a massive drop in the number of platelets that are in your blood; another is massive clotting. Sometimes patients have both a massive drop in the platelets and clotting at the same time. And we'll go over that in a little bit more detail in just a minute. Up on the screen are the words Activated Clotting Time machine, or an ACT machine. Go to the next screen. During the open-heart surgery - go back one - go to - go to the next one. No, go back to the surgery picture. Yeah, that's it. During the surgery, what will happen is, there are professionals that work with the cardiovascular surgeon called the perfusion team. Perfusionists are those professionals that actually monitor the blood. They're the ones that thin the blood. You'll hear evidence that the doctor is responsible for this team. He's responsible for introducing the plan, making the determination as to what to do. They just are carrying out the plan during the surgery. You will hear that during the surgery, while on the heart-lung machine, the way they monitor the blood to make sure that the heart-lung machine does not clot is they use different monitoring machines and different lab work. And they will take a sample of the blood that's coming through the machine, and they will test it. When you're using Heparin, they use what's called an ACT machine. It's called the Activated Clotting Time machine. And so ACT is just a short version of that. And the purpose of the ACT is; they put the blood into a little bowl or dish, and they measure how quick the blood is contracting, the stickiness of the blood, so to speak. And by determining how much time it takes for the platelets to clog together, they're able to come up with a value that shows them how thick the blood is."

"The reason why this is extremely important is because, based on those numbers, you can tell when the blood is about to clot. And so you can determine whether you have to give them a little bit more medicine or whether you need to lay off the medicine. If the blood is not clotting at all, it may be too anticoagulated, or too thin. Or if it's too thick, then they inject another bolus or another dose of the drug Heparin. Let's go to the next screen."

"We talked a little bit earlier -- let's go to the next one -- about a Heparin allergy. The Heparin allergy forms when the body receives Heparin. There is an antibody, and there is an agent called PF4, which is very detailed. Basically, it's part of the platelet that has a catcher's mitt on it. It's a receptor, and it catches the antigen. And what it does is - when it catches it - it causes another antibody to stick to it. And all of the blood vessels -- I mean, all of the platelets start to clot, to stick together, and it prevents the blood from flowing through the vessels."

"Let's go to the next one, Laine."

"Many years ago, back -- I guess I would say in the '70s and '80s, the doctors that were using Heparin began to see the same signs and symptoms showing up in patients after the administration of Heparin. And initially what they saw, and the first thing that clued them into the fact that there may be a Heparin allergy, was a drop in the platelet counts. The big word that you see on the screen is called thrombocytopenia. Thrombocytopenia is a way to describe the number of platelet cells and the fact that it's too low. If you have low platelets, that's called thrombocytopenia. And that term has been around for a long time. If you have a platelet below, some say 130,000 platelets per milliliter – others say 100,000 - that is defined as thrombocytopenia. As the doctors began seeing the drop in the platelet counts, they termed it an allergy to Heparin, Heparin-induced thrombocytopenia. There have been a lot of studies. There have been books written, actually. And one author has put together a number of different papers in a booked called <u>Heparin-Induced Thrombocytopenia</u>. And what you'll learn in the course of this trial is, although the allergy took on this name, Heparin-induced thrombocytopenia is just a broad term used to describe all kinds of conditions. It is not just meant to describe a drop in platelet count. Heparin-induced thrombocytopenia has been reduced to HIT. So if you hear us say HIT or HIT 1 or HIT 2, you may understand that we are talking about a Heparin allergy. With the Heparin allergy, you can have, one, a drop in the platelet counts; or, two, you can have a severe clotting disorder, or you can have both. Any of those terms -- I mean, any of those conditions can be used to describe the Heparin allergy, and they're all symptoms of them."

"Let's move on, Laine."

"What happens, as I've described to you here - I've have an illustration of it - is that as the platelets and the red blood cells move through the veins, and the Heparin is introduced, it sticks to the platelets, and it sticks to the wall of the vessel. I just wanted to illustrate it for you so that you could -- you could visualize the process. Let's move to the next one. Now, as I mentioned to you earlier, there are a number of different signs and symptoms that are involved. But in this book and in other articles, they've developed a table. And this is written in high medical terms, so it's hard for me to even read. But what it shows in this table is what's called the Four

Ts; The Four Ts. And this is a chart that you can look at -- and there are other ones out there, but this one the author has formulated to show what someone's pretest probability of having a Heparin allergy is. And by 'pretest probability' what I mean is, you can take a sample of the blood, do a lab test on it, and know with a hundred percent certainty whether or not there's an antibody in there or whether or not there's an allergy."

"The doctors are supposed to look for signs and symptoms of this allergy so that they will know what to do. They'll know whether or not to even test for it. And what the Four Ts chart is, it's a tool so that one can use it to see whether or not there is thrombocytopenia. And they've assigned a point scale. And we'll go over this during the trial. You'll either have a two point rating if you fall into this category or one point rating if you fall into this category. You look at the number of platelets. Then you look at when the platelet fall occurs. For example, in most Heparin allergies, the platelet fall will not start right away. It will be between days five and ten after you've been administered Heparin. So you look to see if there is a platelet count drop, you then look to see whether or not the platelet count drop occurs within days five and ten. Then you'll see whether or not there are any other symptoms, like a thrombosis or a clot. Then you look to see whether or not there are any other causes of thrombocytopenia. We'll go over this chart in just a little bit more detail as we review the medical records. But I wanted to introduce you to it now. But there is basically what is called the Four Ts. And it just describes the symptoms that one might look for, basically what I would describe as the red flags of the body."

"Let's move on. I told you earlier that we have to prove to you that the doctor violated the standard of care in this case. And so I wanted to take just a minute to introduce you to what we will prove to you is the standard of care that a doctor must follow if he realizes or recognizes that there is a Heparin allergy. And I don't think that this will be disputed in this trial. The standard of care will require the doctor to immediately discontinue all Heparin. The body has an allergy to it. If you continue receiving the Heparin, then it will just increase the symptoms, and it can be fatal. If you have a Heparin allergy and you keep receiving Heparin, then it can often times be fatal, if it goes untreated. So the first thing that you do is stop all of the Heparin."

"Next, it requires - the standard of care requires - that you give a reversal drug. There is a product or there are products that are called direct-thrombin inhibitors. That's a long term basically to describe a drug that is like Heparin, but it doesn't cause the same chemical reactions that your body has had to Heparin, and it inhibits, or stops, the production of what's called thrombin. That's what causes your blood vessels -- I mean your blood platelets to stick together. So there's a reversal drug or drugs that are called direct-thrombin inhibitors. So you stop the Heparin, and you give a reversal drug. One of the drugs that we're going to be talking about a lot during this trial is the direct-thrombin inhibitor called Hirudin."

"The next thing, if you have a Heparin allergy you cannot continue the treatment of the symptoms of that allergy with Coumadin. Coumadin is also - I think we talked about it yesterday in opening statements - I mean, in voir dire, a drug that will thin your blood. For those patients that have a Heparin allergy or a Heparin reaction, Coumadin will also have an adverse effect on the body and on the blood chemistry. I don't know why. I don't know how to explain it, but the literature and the doctors will tell you that if a patient has a Heparin allergy, then they shouldn't be getting Coumadin either. So the standard of care is, if you find out or if you suspect that a patient has an allergy, you immediately stop all Heparin, you give a reversal drug, and you do not treat the symptoms with Coumadin."

"Now, I already went over the direct-thrombin inhibitor. I mentioned to you that one of them is named Hirudin or Refludin. That's like saying Ibuprofen and Advil. It's the same thing. One's just a marketing brand name for the drug. Hirudin is the drug. Refludin is the brand name that you'll see that shows up in this chart. That's a reversal drug - it's a direct-thrombin inhibitor. Now, Hirudin also comes from an animal. I know you are all familiar with the story about the medical use of leeches on George Washington. Well, Hirudin comes from the spit of a leech, basically. It's a secretion of a leech. And what it does is it prevents clotting. So when I was growing up, all of the stories that I read about people using leaches, I thought they were insane. They really weren't. They knew what they were doing."

"Let's move on, Laine."

"If a patient has to have open-heart surgery, and they have a Heparin allergy, they cannot have Heparin. So you have to use a substitute. If you're doing a substitute surgery, a Hirudin-use surgery, then the monitoring device that is used to monitor Heparin does not work. The books will say, the literature will say that the method that's used for Heparin is not accurate for Hirudin. Basically, when they drop the blood into the little bowl and they inject the chemical that makes it clot - one can then time the clotting rate. The chemical that works for Heparin doesn't work with Hirudin. It doesn't react with Hirudin. So it's basically having no monitoring at all at high doses. At low doses, you can get some sort of reading from it. But at high doses that you need during open-heart surgery, it's not accurate. So what they have found is that there is a device called the Ecarin Clotting Time machine, or ECT machine. And the literature says that if you are doing an open-heart surgery with Hirudin, you need to have an ECT machine. Because there are so very few surgeries with Hirudin, not everybody has an ECT machine. The evidence will be that this hospital didn't have one. But the evidence will also be that you can call the manufacturer and have one delivered within three to five days. So when you're listening to the evidence, the ECT machine is what is used to monitor the Hirudin. The ECT machine -- let me describe to you for just a second how it works. They take the venom from a pit viper snake and they mix it in the blood, and it reacts with the leech spit, and it makes the blood clot. And for some reason, whatever time that it takes for that blood to clot, they're able to monitor the coagulation and calculate the rate of clotting; that is an interesting fact about the ECT machine. We have all of these animal products that I didn't know about before this case."

"Keep going, Laine."

"We have to prove to you - and it's our responsibility - that Dr. Zopyros failed to follow the standard of care in treating Ms. Myrna

Sue Carroll. We also have to prove to you that Ms. Myrna Sue Carroll's death was probably caused by the defendant's failure to follow the standard of care. And the standard of care is defined as the level of reasonable care, skill and diligence as other similarly situated cardiothoracic surgeons in the same general line of practice usually follow in the same or similar circumstances. So let's take a walk through the medical records and through Ms. Carroll's treatment to see whether or not there was a violation of the standard of care."

"First of all, what you'll see is that she was admitted into Oak Mountain Hospital. She was admitted into Oak Mountain Hospital on the 26th of February. She had some heart pains; normal coronary artery disease or normal clogging of the vessels. A lot of people have that as they get older. And what they did was, they decided, after doing some tests, they decided to perform surgery. One of the tests they did was a blood test, and they measured the amount of platelets that were in her blood. We looked at platelets earlier, all of those round things that are in your blood. They count those to tell them a number of different things. And on February 27th, they had a platelet count of 311,000. When it shows just the 311 that means 311,000. The reason why this is important is because they take the high platelet count prior to the administration of Heparin, and they use that as a baseline in order to determine whether or not there's been a large drop in the platelets. So with that being said, after they do some of the blood tests, they decide to go ahead and perform the surgery, a triple bypass surgery, on March 4th, 2002. During the surgery, they use Heparin. I meant to tell you this - when she was first admitted on February 26th and they noticed that she's had a heart attack, they began giving her Heparin at that time in lower doses."

"During surgery, she receives a massive dose of Heparin in order to allow the open-heart surgery to work. After her surgery on March 5th, she ends up having - go ahead and open that up - they end up having a platelet count run. They didn't do one the day of surgery, which is unusual. But they did one the day after her surgery, on March 5th, and she had a platelet count that was 163,000. And what the evidence will show and what the math shows is that

that is a platelet count drop of 48 percent. A lot of the literature that deals with heparin-induced thrombocytopenia talks about a relative platelet count drop of approximately 50 percent. A lot of the literature just describes it as a 50 percent drop. It's not a hard, fast number as to whether or not you have the allergy or not. If you drop 49 percent, you don't have it; if you drop 50 percent, you do. That's not true. If you have relative, an approximate, 50 percent drop that can be a significant sign that you may have a Heparin allergy. However, the evidence will also show that after open-heart surgery; a lot of people have a large platelet drop. That, in and of itself, is not a red flag. A lot of people have a platelet drop because there are fluids infused into the body during the surgery. And so what you do is, if you have a platelet drop like that, you monitor it, and then you look to see whether or not there are any other signs or symptoms that may indicate that you're having a problem."

"One of the things you look for is thrombosis, or clotting. So let's take a look at what happened next in her time line. On that very same day - actually, the morning of the 6th the chart listed that she developed the signs and symptoms of this on the night of the 5th; the development of what's called a DVT, which is a deep vein thrombosis of the leg. And what they did is they ran a test because she got up, and her leg was blue, and it was very swollen. It was twice the size of the other leg. So the family members got concerned, they called the doctor in, and they did a check. And what they did is, they did a Doppler survey and they looked and examined the legs. And they were able to tell that there were three large vessels in the left leg that were completely clotted. That's not normal. And so now what you have is a 48 percent drop in the platelet count and another red flag. You've got three vessels that have completely clotted out of nowhere in her left leg. You'll hear the evidence from the literature and from the doctors showing you that those people who have a Heparin allergy, the most common place in the formation of thrombosis or clots is the left leg, the deep vein thrombosis. That's exactly what she had."

"So, now that she has thrombocytopenia, basically a 48 percent fall in platelet count from this chart that we looked at earlier - and if you go back to the 26th of February as the first day that she had the Heparin, then you can count seven days before there was approximately a 50 percent fall. Here is where you see that it was between five and ten days we discussed earlier. And she had a new thrombosis, a new clot. So when you look at the table listing the Four Ts she had the signs and symptoms showing that she was at high risk for having a Heparin allergy. Even the defendant's expert witness in his deposition admitted that when you apply her condition at Oak Mountain to this chart she met the conditions. What do they do? They continued her on Heparin. And then they started giving her Coumadin, two things that you're not supposed to do if you're at high risk for having a Heparin allergy. Instead of performing the simple blood test that would have told them whether she had this allergy, they just continued her on the drugs that were causing her problems. Her platelets did go back up before they discharged her. But when they discharged her, the evidence will be that her blood was having serious problems."

"There is a test called the INR. When you're receiving Coumadin, the INR test, or basically the INR value, is a number that you get measuring the coagulation effect of the Coumadin. Her INR value was extremely high. It meant that her blood was not stable on the Coumadin. They discharged her. During the time that she was discharged, you will see that she had INR values that were abnormal. She was going to her primary care physician at the Black Warrior Clinic. And she wasn't actually seeing the doctor but she was going over there, and she was getting her INR tested. She was not on Heparin at this time. When she left the hospital, they stopped the Heparin. But they continued her on Coumadin to treat the condition of the DVT. She was going to the clinic, they were taking a lab value, they were measuring her INR, and they were faxing the results to Dr. Zopyros. Now, you'll see and hear evidence that the normal value of 2.5 to 3.5 is what you would expect in a patient that was receiving Coumadin. If the value is below that it means that your blood is way too thick, especially if you're on a blood thinner. If your value is above that, that means that your blood is way too thin, and you need to back off the medicine. And as you can see, the values, they go all over the board. The INR values initially, before she was discharged from the hospital and even though she was on Heparin and even though she was on Coumadin, it showed that her blood was way too thick on March 7th. On March 8th and March 9th, it goes way up and then it is way too thin because they're giving her all of the blood thinners. When she's away from the hospital on the 9th, 11th, 14th and the 18th, she had her INR checked. The last three values, which were reported to Dr. Zopyros, show that her blood was thickening, even though she's on a blood thinner. That's a red flag because now you have a thrombocytopenia, a drop in platelets, you've got a DVT, and you've got blood that's too thick. Those are all red flags that you have a severe Heparin allergy. One thing I didn't mention to you, even though you stop the Heparin, the allergy continues. It sets off a process in your blood that continues. It doesn't just stop because you are stopping taking the Heparin. It can last for months after."

"So what happens after that? 14 days after her initial surgery, she goes back into the hospital with chest pains. She has to be rushed back to the hospital, Oak Mountain Hospital, the same place where she had the first surgery. And they immediately, without checking her for this Heparin allergy, start her on Coumadin and Lovenox. And I forgot to tell you that Heparin is Lovenox. Lovenox is the brand name, like Advil is for Ibuprofen. So they start her on the Heparin, and they start her on the Coumadin, even though she had all of the red flags of a Heparin allergy. They also performed a test on her to check to see what might be causing these chest pains. She's just had a triple bypass surgery, so it shouldn't be her bypass veins. But, what they found was, all three of the new veins that they had used to bypass her heart were completely clotted. That, the evidence will show is extremely rare. That is extremely abnormal. And what it shows is it that there is a clotting abnormality of the blood. There is really no other explanation as to why all three new grafts would occlude, or clot, except for a clotting abnormality. And so now what we have is, in her clinical picture, we have basically a situation where all of her bypass grafts have occluded, and the doctor is saying that the patient is essentially un-revascularized. Basically, it's just like she didn't have the first surgery. The heart is not getting the blood that it needs."

"So now we have a platelet count drop of 48 percent, we have an unusual and abnormal formation of blood clots in the left leg, we have unstable blood values during her discharge, and now we find out that she has a complete triple occlusion of the new grafts; something is wrong. What do they do? They kept giving her Heparin, kept giving her Coumadin. And they started doing some tests on her blood a couple of days later. But in the meantime, they begin consideration of another surgery, what's called a redo. They see that her vessels are completely clotted, and they say, look, we're going to have to redo the surgery. So, Dr. Zopyros decides that he's going to have to revascularize her; do another surgery. And that's very, very risky."

"You'll hear that redo surgeries, especially within a couple of weeks to a couple of months after a first surgery, are extremely dangerous and extremely risky because the body is still repairing itself. And it's not as easy to open up and operate and do all of the other things that you need to do. So he makes the decision, instead of testing her for Heparin allergy, instead of starting her on a reversal drug like Hirudin and waiting it out, he decides to go back in and do surgery. In the meantime, one of the doctors that were treating her states that she is clearly, clearly under-anticoagulated. All that means is that her blood is entirely too thick, even though she was on a blood thinner."

"Now, let's take a look at the March 24th box here, if you'll open that. Dr. Zopyros, on March 24th - and this is very important. On March 24th, when he decides and orders that she undergo another surgery, which was scheduled for the 28th, he also makes a note: 'Have recommended redo CABG,' which is cardiopulmonary bypass grafting. It's just an acronym or whatever you call those things, letter shortening for bypass surgery. Whenever you see 'CABG', that's what that means. But he says we need a workup of clotting. The reason why that's important is because that note shows that the same signs and symptoms that we've been going over and looking at, he finally recognized. He recognized! But the standard of care is when you recognize that there might be a Heparin allergy; you don't wait for the test results. You stop the Heparin, and you start the reversal drug, and you don't treat it with Coumadin. They kept treating her with Heparin. The blood can have several different causes for having an abnormal clotting, or a hyper coagulation. And there are a number of tests that you can run. There's one test called the protein C. One is called the Factor V Leiden. One is a protein S. They can look at all of these different things to see what might be causing the blood to be hyper clotting or hyper-coagulative. All of these tests were negative. They hadn't run a Heparin test yet."

"So finally, after all of these other tests are negative; they do decide to run the Heparin antibody test. The Heparin antibody test is not available at Oak Mountain. They don't even have the equipment to do a Heparin antibody test at that time. They do now. They didn't then. So they sent a blood sample to Magic City Hospital, and on the 27th - go ahead and click on that. On the 27th, the doctors finally have test proof that she has the Heparin allergy. That doesn't change anything, though, about all of the signs and symptoms that she had before. It's our claim that Dr. Zopyros should have recognized the obvious red flags, signs and symptoms of her Heparin allergy before now. But, if you remember, I told you that she was already scheduled for surgery. Now that they have confirmation and a lab test that shows that she has the Heparin allergy, they stop the Heparin. Instead of giving her the reversal drug and waiting, he decides to go ahead and do surgery anyway. You'll hear evidence that he should have waited. This was not an emergency surgery. He had scheduled it on the 24th for the 28th. It is not like he was rushing her to surgery on the 25th, the 26th, the 27th. He had scheduled it for the 28th, found out that she was Heparin positive, and decides to go ahead with the surgery."

"Now, here's what's important about that: He can't use Heparin. He can't use the blood thinner that he has always used. He has to use the substitute. Why is that a big deal? Well, the evidence will be that he had never ever done this type of surgery before. He had never used Hirudin. In fact, he didn't even really know what to use. He had to do some research on the 27th to even find out what substitute to use. He had never been trained on it in medical school. He had never gone and received training from other doctors on how to do it. He had never read an article on how to do it. He had never looked at a book on how to do it. He hadn't ever done anything that gave him any experience to do this type of surgery where you have to monitor and coagulate the blood with Hirudin."

"What the literature will show you, though, is that you have to monitor the blood with the ECT machine. And he didn't have it. And he decided to go ahead and do surgery anyway. The evidence will be that he didn't tell the family that he didn't have any experience in doing it. He did tell them, okay, we can't use Heparin. But he didn't tell them that he had never done it, never monitored the blood that way. So what he does is, he goes home on the 27th and, according to the testimony he gave in his deposition, he looked up on the Internet that night how to do the surgery.

During the surgery, they take her and they open her up, and they didn't do any pre-surgical blood testing on her blood, meaning that if you're going to do a surgery and if you're going to open her up and you're going to give her a new drug, a drug that you've never used before, they should have taken a vial of her blood and tested it to see what the baseline was, what the coagulation rate was. They didn't do that. They took her into surgery, they got new veins from her leg, and they started the bypass. While she was open, while the blood was going through the heart-lung machine, they injected it and gave her the Hirudin, which is meant to keep the heart-lung machine from clotting."

"They are supposed to be doing monitoring tests during this surgery every 15 minutes. They're supposed to check every 15 minutes to see how thick her blood is, to make sure the machine doesn't clot. While the surgery was going on, the machine completely clotted. They were not using the ECT machine, which you'll see is mandatory for the monitoring of Lipirudin, which is the Hirudin, during cardiopulmonary bypass surgery. So, in essence, what they were doing is, they were going into a surgery, they were thinning her blood with a certain drug, and they had no monitor that could accurately tell them how thick or thin the blood was. As you might expect, her blood completely clotted the machine, and when it clotted the machine, the blood flow stopped. They couldn't - they couldn't get a new machine up – although there was another machine in the room. They couldn't get it up and running in time to save her life, and she died."

"Now, we started investigating this case to try to find out what happened. And what you do is you order the medical records. Actually, before we ordered the medical records, Vicki went to the hospital and said, 'I want a copy of all of the medical records of my mom.' And they gave her some records, but it wasn't all of the records. They just gave her part of the records. We then later, after we got involved, ordered all of the records. And one of the things that we wanted to look at was the surgery records, the records of the monitoring of the surgery. And we wanted to see exactly what monitoring rates were going on during the surgery. And so we pulled up the records. And if you will blow up this part of the record right here (indicating). What this says - I - I can't see it. Try to get a little bit more of it. This is the perfusion record. As the surgery is going on, there is one person that's actually doing the blood monitoring and that kind of thing. And there's another person in there that's actually charting the values as they are recorded - I mean, as they are obtained. As you'll see here, there is a section that deals with Heparin management. They weren't using Heparin and the values represent Hirudin test results. The testimony will be from the doctor that they used two different tests to monitor the blood during the surgery. They're the same two tests that are most often used during a Heparin surgery, not Hirudin."

"In this area right here (indicating), you see ACT. We talked about that. That's the Activated Clotting Time test that is most often used for Heparin monitoring. Here's the column that records the values (indicating) -- and I'm sorry we don't have a better copy. There's a line here. And here are the times that they recorded the tests. These are the times that they actually monitored the blood. It says that initially, there was a test at 8:15. It says that they then did a test at 10:10, 10:28, 11:15, 11:41, 12:43 and 1:15. And they wrote the values down here. So I looked at that, and I was curious. I wanted to see what the backup tickets show because these tests - these machines have receipts that get printed out. So I got the tickets, and I looked at them. And let me show you what the record will reveal. Go on to the next one (exhibit). Go to the next one. We'll come back to that one. Actually - actually, wait a minute. Go back. I want to point this out now. After Ms. Carroll died and after the record was already complete and the top sheet was torn off, you'll see that this is a carbon copy of this document in the record. But the top sheet had already been torn off. And the surgical team went back in and added information after she died that was not on the original sheet. We'll go over that information in a little bit more detail in a minute."

"Here is an example of the tickets. There are 12 different tickets that they produced in order to show what the ACT test revealed during the time, during the surgery. I want you to take a look at the times that are on these tickets. 1631. 1631, that's military time. That means long after she died. The next test that they claim to have run during the surgery shows 1657. That's a long time after 2:08 PM. I forgot to tell you that. Her time of death was 2:08 P.M. 1631 would be 4:31 P.M. It would be after she died. Here's another ticket that they claim to have run during the surgery, test 1731 that would be 5:30 PM, after she died. What's the explanation? Well, the time is just wrong on the machine. Daylight savings time is what they said, although the evidence will be that daylight savings time wasn't until April 7th of 2002. This was March. So then I went ahead and compiled all of the tickets. Let's take a look at those."

"Keep going. Keep going. Keep going. Do you have the ACT chart? All right, see if you can blow that up a little bit. The defendants, when I asked them about the ticket time discrepancy, they said, hey, it was just that the time was off on the machine that we were using to test the blood during the surgery. But if that were true, let me show you what the evidence shows. Then the times on the chart - this is - remember I showed you 10:10, 10:28, 11:15, 11:41, and 12:43. There are going to be times that elapsed - elapsed in between the tests. Test 1 at 10:10, there's 18 minutes between that test and the next test being done. On the chart, they say it was 47 minutes before they did the next test. On the chart, they say its 26 minutes before they do the next test. Well, let's take a look at what the tickets show. The receipts that they gave me claiming to have monitored the blood during the surgery, first of all, there are three tickets from March 26th. Her surgery was on March 28th. Three tickets from a day that she didn't even have surgery. The evidence will be that there was absolutely no ACT blood testing or any other type of blood testing of her blood on the 26th; none. What do the other tickets show? They show that there is not a correlation in the same amount of time that has elapsed. In fact, there's not even the same amount of tickets. The first time lapse between the first test and the second test was 127 minutes instead of 18 minutes. From the second test to the third test, there's 29 minutes instead of 47 minutes. From the second test to the third test, there's 38 minutes. In fact, the values do not even correspond. Eight out of the nine tickets that they produced to show that the blood was being monitored come from a time that's stamped after she died. So I decided to look at the other tests."

"There was another test, the TEG test. Let's take a look at that. This is a graph that is printed out from what is known as the Thromboelastogram. Well, what you look at is the R value of the Thromboelastogram test. And they claim to have monitored her blood with the ACT machine and the TEG machine. So let's take a look at this. Her surgery began at 10:00 AM. So the testimony will be that they did an initial calibration of the TEG test. And if you'll notice the time, the time is right, 9:19. The actual printout was from 9:54. There is only one other TEG value receipt that's given to us in this medical chart. They claim to have been doing them during surgery. The testimony from them will be that, yes, we were monitoring the blood with the TEG test during surgery. I asked where the tickets are. Give me a ticket. Let's look at the only other ticket that was in the chart. She died at 2:08. This ticket was printed at 4:19, two hours and 11 minutes after her time of death. Let's look at the next one."

"The record will also reveal when we're looking to determine - and you, as the ladies and gentlemen of the jury, are looking to determine whether or not there was a violation of the standard of care. You'll be looking at the medical records. The medical records also have some additional problems in them. Vital problems, I'm just going to say they're facts. You will see in the record that the surgical team did not leave the operating room until 1522. She died at 2:08, which is 1408. You will see that all of the components and pieces of the chart are gathered together, in most all circumstances, the doctor dictates a discharge report or a discharge summary documenting what happened that same day; or the next day at the latest. The report is then put in the chart, and it's sent down to the medical records office, and then the chart is complete. Usually a chart will not be closed until a discharge summary is dictated and this discharge summary by Dr. Zopyros was dictated on April 15th. She died on March 28th – over two weeks later!"

"Now, there are going to be other things that we talk about. But, ladies and gentlemen of the jury, after you listen to all of the evidence in this case and after you listen to all of the testimony and all of the witnesses and the expert witnesses, we are confident that you will find that Dr. Zopyros failed to recognize the Heparin allergy in the first admission. He failed to recognize it as she was admitted on the second admission. He should not have gone forward to do surgery and that even after he made the decision to do surgery that he failed to do it the right way. And, ladies and gentlemen of the jury, we're confident that after this case is over, that you will find in favor of the family of Myrna Sue Carroll."

"Thank you for your time."

If a conspiracy theory could capture the jury's imagination, we were well on our way to a place where some doctors are not honorable and a place where the medical profession can be as corrupt as a Nixon Whitehouse. Modifying medical records, reckless medical decisions, all were part of a picture that had been painted of corruption – corruption at high levels of authority. All of this made me a bit uncomfortable. A part of me felt so naïve that I did not see any of this happening until after my mother's death. Another part of me was concerned as to how we can prove it in a manner the jury would accept. After all, I was accusing a trusted icon of committing mortal sins. I remained iconoclastic, irreverent, as one who sought to overthrow this traditional institution.

Defense's Opening Remarks by Mr. Goretti

Judge Kent gave permission for Mr. Goretti to begin his opening statement. As he stood and approached the jury box he removed his glasses and placed his thumb and index finger on either side nose as if to gather his thoughts. Pausing as if he were at a complete loss as to what to say, he then placed his eye glasses on its familiar perch and smiled. His mannerisms were less exaggerated than Mr. Laurence's. He moved slowly, but deliberately. He said a lot without uttering a word. Then he delivered his pitch:

"Thank you, Your Honor. May it please the Court, my name is Damian Goretti. Todd, my associate and I have the privilege of representing Andrew Zopyros in this case."

"His Honor, Judge Kent, told you this morning that this portion of the case, the opening statement, allows the lawyers to stand before you and tell you what we expect the evidence to be. Let me tell you something from the very beginning: the evidence that you get from this case over the next week or so is going to be, in many ways and in the most important way, very different than what was just outlined."

"Evidence like this comes from two sources: First, the witnesses who are called into the courtroom are put under oath by Judge Kent and testified to you; and, second, from the medical records, the story is going to be way different than what has just been proposed to you."

"The evidence in this case will demonstrate that Andrew Zopyros, in caring for Ms. Carroll, gave excellent care. The evidence is going to be that this death, tragic as it may be, was not his fault. You'll find that Andrew and others worked very hard to save her, but could not."

"Now, I want to mention two words to you - 'Them' and 'They'. I want you to think back over the last hour of talk. And every once in a while, you would hear Dr. Zopyros did this, or Dr. Zopyros did that. But how many times did we hear 'Them' and 'They'? Over and over, because the fact is, there are lots of people who were working with Dr. Zopyros. And I want to give you the whole picture."

"Before we go through the facts in detail, let's talk about how we got here. This case was filed about two years after Ms. Carroll passed away. And Mr. Laurence filed a piece of paper known as a complaint in the clerk's office. And in that complaint, certain allegations or charges were made against Dr. Andrew Zopyros, which remain pending today, very serious charges. He's charged with medical negligence, with professional misconduct. He's charged with acting wantonly in the treatment of Ms. Carroll. Wantonness means that they are claiming that Dr. Zopyros acted with conscious knowledge that what he would do would probably cause her death. They are charging that he acted with reckless indifference. And they ask that you punish him, that you punish him."

"In response to those charges, we filed a piece of paper that says this: Not guilty. Not guilty of the claim of medical malpractice or professional misconduct, certainly not guilty of the claim of wantonness, not due to be punished. But more importantly, the evidence that you hear from this stand over the next few days and from the medical records will prove he is not guilty."

"Now, the burden of proof is on Mr. Laurence. He must prove each of his claims, including a claim of a breach of failure to meet the standard of care. There's been a reference to that, but as we go through the case you're going to hear the term 'standard of care' several times, and it's important that you know what the definition is. At the end of the case, Judge Kent will tell you the definition of the standard of care is this, or words very similar to it."

Mr. Goretti stood directly in front of the juror's box and at times leaned over the railing to emphasize a point. The volume of his voice was not overbearing, in fact one had to listen closely to hear him. Each legal team had a staff member that sat on the first row of the visitor's section, upon request they would project images on the screen for viewing. At this point Mr. Goretti asked his associate, Rob, to present Number 1 which was the definition of the term 'standard of care'.

"Surgeons – in this case, CV surgeons – Cardiovascular surgeons - must use reasonable care, skill and diligence as ordinarily exercised in similar circumstances."

"Andrew must act reasonably."

"You will also find that in trying to prove these claims, Mr. Laurence must prove by what in the law is called substantial evidence. And it's important that you know what that means as well."

"Let's see number 2, Rob."

"The judge will tell you precisely this at the end of the case: That substantial evidence is that character of evidence that would convince an unprejudiced thinking mind of the truth of the fact to which the evidence is directed. So, the burden of proof is to convince you of what? That Dr. Zopyros, under these circumstances, acted unreasonably. Andrew acted very reasonably."

"Now, in just a minute, I want to go through the facts and show you some things you haven't seen before. But before I do that, I want to give you a response to some of the things you heard."

"First of all, the claim that Ms. Carroll had HIT."

"You're going to hear about platelet antibodies. You are also going to hear about H-I-T. You'll also hear about H-I-T-T. Both of these are pronounced hit."

"Now it is important that you understand the distinction. You'll see that at a later point in time it was discovered that Ms. Carroll had a platelet antibody. The doctors tell us, the literature tells us, that following cardiac surgery like Ms. Carroll had, 25 to 50 percent of the patients have a platelet antibody. So the presence of the platelet antibody, or if you want to call it an allergy, it is not evidence of either of these."

"Now, what is HIT? That is heparin-induced thrombocytopenia and thrombosis."

"Now, Mr. Laurence claims that Ms. Carroll had both HIT and HITT and you'll see, in fact, that's wrong. The medial course is simply inconsistent with that, and more importantly, the platelet counts, which we'll look at, are inconsistent with that claim. It's also important that you know that the surgery, the second surgery that was done on March 28 was an urgent surgery."

"Let's see number 1, Rob."

"This is very important; the standard of care under the circumstances."

"Under the circumstances of that time, surgery was absolutely mandatory. It was urgent. You're going to find that when Ms. Carroll came back to the hospital on March 21, she was unstable. And her condition, through nothing Dr. Zopyros did or didn't do steadily deteriorated, so that by the time the 27th and 28th came around, they had to do surgery. They couldn't wait."

"You'll find at that time, they had to do the surgery without Heparin. Dr. Zopyros and others researched the best way to do it; he discovered that everybody agreed using Hirudin was the best way. They also found some discussion about this ECT machine that you are going to hear about. I will tell you right now, the use of the ECT machine was not an option. It couldn't be done. You're going to find that they did the surgery appropriately, they monitored – I say 'They' – Dr. Zopyros and others monitored carefully and appropriately. And you're also going to find that Hirudin and monitoring of its use was not the cause of death."

"Now, let's turn to the facts in the case. You're going to find that on February 26th, 2002, Ms. Carroll was admitted through the emergency room at Oak Mountain by an internist by the name of Doug Kennedy. She had classic anginal heart attack pain in her chest radiating into the arms and jaw. It was very worrisome because it came on when she was not exercising, but at rest. Dr. Kennedy started her on Heparin; a form of Heparin called Lovenox."

"The next day, a cardiologist by the name of Dr. Pantheras – most call him Pan – did a catheterization where they inject dye into the vessels – the coronary vessels – or arteries of the heart."

"Let's see number 3, Rob." Mr. Goretti repeatedly displayed medical records as in this case the progress note documenting that Dr. Kennedy had prescribed Lovenox and that Dr. Pantheras had to perform the catheterization; this to build trust in the medical records."

"It says; admitted by Dr. Kennedy. Dr. Nicholas Pantheras did this left heart catheterization and found acute coronary syndrome and severe three-vessel coronary disease."

"In performing this catheterization, as is typical, he gave her a significant dose of Heparin, which nobody has any criticism."

"After that, Dr. Pantheras felt like surgery was probably necessary, Dr. Zopyros, Andrew, was consulted and asked to see Ms. Carroll."

"Let's see number 4, Rob." Displaying the progress note of Dr. Zopyros dated February 28.

"This is his note that day. He sees her on the 28th, February 28th. And he has planned this coronary artery bypass grafting, which a lot of times you'll see CABG or hear doctors say 'cabbage'. That's what it is. And he discussed the risk with the patient, five percent risk of death, risk of bleeding, infection, drug, and blood reactions. And they decided to proceed four days later."

"On the 4th, they do the surgery, and in all respects, it goes as planned. It's major surgery. The chest is opened, the heart is exposed, but everything seems to go well."

"Now, we come to the first post-operative day. Sometimes you'll see POD1 or something like that on the chart meaning Post-operative Day One. Very important day, especially important when you listen and think about what Mr. Laurence has said to you about 'they'."

"Let's see number 5, Rob." The progress note for post-op day 1 is displayed. Mr. Goretti points to a section of the note where certain lab results are recorded. The lab values placed around a geometric design so that the placement of the lab value – a numeric result – will indicate which test result is referenced.

"This is the note from the surgeon who saw Ms. Carroll the following day, post-op day 2. Now, here's what they wrote down about the labs. They use these little graphs to show different things. This was, for example the hematocrit, this is the hematology and what do we have here? That number, 163, that's shorthand for 163,000 platelets. Now, remember, Mr. Laurence says there were a massive drop in platelets, and that is a red flag – it is not a massive drop in platelets."

"Let's see, if you don't mind 1190, Rob." Mr. Goretti has displayed a page from a medical journal that list expected drops in platelet counts after surgery.

"Platelet counts fall. This is a study that has been performed for patients on the first day of post-operative surgery. These numbers are for patients that have undergone coronary bypass surgery. And if you look at these numbers, you'll find an average of 40 to 48 percent drop. All patients have this fall in platelets."

"Put number 5 back up, please, Rob." The progress note for post-op day 1 was displayed and further reinforced the 'Them' and 'They' defense by passing responsibility to Dr. Zopyros' colleague.

"And who was it, on the first postoperative day, which ignored this fall in platelets? It wasn't Andrew Zopyros. It was Dr. Houston, another board-certified cardiovascular surgeon who was in partnership with Andrew at the time and was covering for him that day, 'They' and 'Them'. Dr. Houston, by the way, is not sued in this case. Nobody made a claim against him."

"Well, that evening, on the 5th, the leg turns blue, and there is suspicion of DVT. And so we have heard this. Mr. Laurence kind of glossed over the fact that sometimes platelets fall, but hey, the next day, there was a DVT, a thrombosis; and, boy, what a red flag. Absolutely, at that point, HIT, Heparin allergy, whatever you want to call it, had to be suspected and diagnosed."

"Let's see number 6, Rob." The progress note that documents the deep vein thrombosis diagnosis was displayed to the jury. The note lists the doctors who discovered the DVT and those who continued Heparin therapy in the form of Lovenox.

"This is the next day. You've got a platelet count of 163,000. The doctor comes in and finds there's a DVT. And we hear the last thing you would want to do is what? Give Heparin. Well, this doctor gives Lovenox, gives Heparin. So we've got these red flags. We've got this horrible ignoring of the patient. But you know what? It wasn't Andrew Zopyros. It was Dr. Houston again, a board-certified cardiovascular surgeon. He knew about the platelets, saw the DVT, and ordered Heparin for the DVT."

"And up here (pointing to the displayed progress note), it says, 'Consult Dr. Micah.' Dr. Micah is a vascular surgeon. Keep in mind as we listen to this. The testimony is going to be undisputed that not just cardiovascular surgeons, but all kind of doctors give Heparin, treat patients who are on Heparin, and have to be familiar with the signs and symptoms, the red flags for Heparin-induced Thrombocytopenia or Heparin allergy, any one of the three."

"Well, Dr. Micah is a vascular surgeon; he's one of those doctors."

"Let's take a look at number 7, please."

"This is postoperative day 2. Dr. Micah sees Ms. Carroll, and he is seeing Ms. Carroll specifically to evaluate this DVT, this thrombosis in her leg. One thing he notes, he says, 'Diagnosed with left CFV.' What is CFV? It is Common Femoral Vein, DVT, which is deep vein thrombosis. What else does the note say? 'Assess, agree with bed rest and Heparin, Lovenox, signed, Dr. Micah.' So we're now two days after the operation, we've got all of these red flags that we've heard about that were ignored by 'Them' and 'They'. And the 'Them' and 'They' are not Andrew Zopyros. But, these folks aren't sued. These folks are not sued."

"The next day, on March 7th, which is postoperative day 3, Dr. Micah and Dr. Houston again see Ms. Carroll and continue the Heparin, the Lovenox. On March 8th – let's see number 8 – which is postoperative day 4, Dr. Zopyros sees her. Well, the platelets now are at 285,000, right back up to where they were, which is exactly what you would expect following cardiac surgery. What you would expect is the platelets to go down immediately afterwards and to come back in a few days."

"Let's see page 1138." Another medical journal is displayed for the jury to define the absence of a platelet count recovery is an indication of HIT.

"Reading from the journal, 'From a chronological point of view, the first abnormal PC (platelet count), platelet count evolution, which should lead to investigating patients for HIT after cardiac surgery is the absence of PC recovery within the first five days following cardiac surgery."

"Let's go back to number 8, Rob."

"Post-op day 4, we had recovery of the platelet count, exactly what is expected. On that day Dr. Zopyros' impression is that she was progressing. She had been started on Coumadin. The INR was about where they wanted it to be; maybe a touch high. He says DC

– discontinue – the Lovenox, not because he's suspecting antibodies or HIT or anything like that, but because he plans to send her home the next day. And, in fact, that's what happens on March 9th. Ms. Carroll goes home."

"Other than the DVT; which, by the way, every doctor will tell you is rarely caused by a platelet antibody, rarely caused by HIT - in all respects, the recovery during the hospitalization was expected and normal."

"The claim here is why in this first hospitalization didn't someone suspect HIT, test for Heparin antibodies? She never had HIT; she never had Thrombocytopenia."

"Let's see 8, Rob."

"This is the chart for platelets during this hospitalization. You'll find that – it's kind of odd – laboratories will vary as to what they define as normal. At Oak Mountain, the normal range for a platelet count is 130,000 to 400,000. She never had anything below 130,000. She never had Thrombocytopenia. And, in fact, she had the expected graph, if you will, of a drop immediately after surgery and a recovery within five days."

"Well, how else do we know that she didn't have HIT? The doctors will tell you that if somebody has HIT or HITT and you continue to give Heparin, what happens? The platelets stay way down."

"Well, the records show that on the 6th the platelet count was 163,000 and she is given Heparin. She is given Heparin on the 7th and 8th and her platelets, in spite of receiving Heparin, rises to normal, which is inconsistent with HIT or HITT."

"Now, we also know she didn't have HIT because of this. Let's see 8B, Rob. This kind of illustrates what I have been showing you."

"The date of operation was the 4th. These are the doctors that saw her on POD 1, 2, 3 and 4; Dr. Houston, Dr. Micah and Dr. Zopyros. Every one of these doctors was aware of the platelet counts. Every one of these doctors was aware, in treating the DVT, of the so-called red flags. And every one of them agreed that under these circumstances, following cardiac surgery, there was no reason to suspect Heparin antibodies, HIT or HITT. And of these three, Andrew is the one that's sued. Not the others."

"So she is sent home, and she's sent home on Coumadin, which is an oral blood thinner. Sometimes it is called warfarin. That's the generic name, I guess. And from the period of March 10th to March 20th she's at home. And she's taking Coumadin which you heard it's not at all unusual to require some time to calibrate Coumadin, especially when you are first starting. Lifestyles, diets, all affect Coumadin, even the weather. And so, patients are frequently tested, as she is, particularly in the first days on Coumadin because sometimes it will get too high, sometimes it will get too low, and they adjust the dosage. And that's what happened here. Nothing in the world unusual about that; and, in fact, you'll find nobody will take this stand and criticize anything Andrew Zopyros did between March 10th and March 20th, when she was out of the hospital."

"So that brings us to the next hospitalization. March 21st Ms. Carroll awakened from sleep with chest pain. This is an ominous sign. It shows that she is unstable in her situation. Appropriately, she is taken back to the hospital. And we hear of 'Them' and 'They' again. Please remember about 45 minutes ago, you heard this; she came back to the hospital, and what did 'they' do? With this history of the platelets, with this thrombosis problem, with the INR going up and down, 'they' put her back on Heparin. Do you remember that?"

"Well, they put her back on Heparin."

"Let's see number 9, Rob."

"These are the admitting orders when she came in. And here it is: Lovenox. They put her back on Heparin. 'They' was not Andrew Zopyros. Andrew Zopyros didn't even know she was back in the hospital that day. These are Dr. Kennedy's orders. He put her back on Heparin. He's not sued here either, by the way."

"All right, on March 22nd, the next day, they continued her on Heparin. In fact, the next day, another cardiologist, Dr. Pantheras' partner, Dr. John Iapetos, did another catheterization to find out what was going on. He found out unfortunately these three vessels were blocked that Andrew had replaced."

"Let's see number 10, Rob."

"During the course of the catheterization, Dr. Iapetos did what? He gave her Heparin. This is the same patient who's supposed to have all of these red flags. And at the end, he put her back on Lovenox, at the end of that catheterization. Dr. Zopyros had nothing to do with this."

"So now we're at the 22nd; still have all of those red flags we're talking about. And who has been treating her, ignoring the red flags? Dr. Pantheras, Dr. Iapetos, Dr. Kennedy, Dr. Houston, Dr. Micah, the 'They' we heard about, but never named earlier today."

"Let's see 053, Rob."

"And this becomes important. Dr. Iapetos, comments at the end of this report says, 'this patient's situation is extremely critical.'"

"Okay. Now, during this procedure, Dr Iapetos was able, with a catheter to do a stint. The hope at the time was that maybe we could go back in with another catheter in a day or two and back in with another catheter after that to revascularize the arteries."

"But then on the 23rd – let's see number 11, Rob – Dr. Pantheras comes back. He says to continue Lovenox; this is Saturday, by the way, March 23rd. He also has doubts at that time as to whether additional catheterizations can be performed to open up the arteries."

"Dr. Zopyros still has not seen Ms. Carroll."

"On Sunday, March 24th, Dr. Zopyros sees Ms. Carroll on his consultation. And this is his note; Andrew examines her and looks at all of the films, talks to others and says, 'The dilemma is how to proceed with further therapy. This presents a different issue from the point of view of prognosis.' That means the outcome. And he talks about the problems with various arteries."

"The doctor continued 'I have reviewed these films with Dr. Pantheras and informally with Dr. Livingston and both agree this presents a high risk angioplasty situation.' So, you've got two cardiologists who are saying we can't go back in with catheters and stints."

"On the 24th he says, 'I recommend repeat coronary bypass grafting. I discussed with patient and family in great detail. I quoted approximately a 10 percent operative risk because of repeat operation so soon after primary operation.'"

"At the end of that discussion, the family says and Ms. Carroll says we want to wait. We want to think about it. They talk about getting somebody from Magic City Hospital to look at her, and Dr. Zopyros' note says, sure, that's fine."

"Surgery was not scheduled that day. The situation is this on the 24th – let's see 18B."

"We had all of these doctors see her who has continued her on Heparin after supposedly all of these red flags are there: Zopyros, Houston, Micah, Kennedy, Pantheras, and Iapetos. And at this point, everybody is in agreement that, as Dr. Iapetos said in his note, she is in critical condition. We can't go back in with catheters and stints. And so the recommendation is surgery. But they're getting her on some medications, intensive medications. Lovenox is one of them."

"Well, the next day, on Monday the 25th, there's a change, and it's a very significant change. On that day there is a change that is part of a series of events that require that they do surgery on the 28th, a few days later."

"Let's see number 15, please."

She starts having angina at rest: angina in the hospital on all of these medications. She's had another heart attack; this Dr. Pantheras' notes."

"She is not a candidate for PCI (stinting). Redo CABG surgery is the most reasonable option."

"She's got to have surgery. That's what her cardiologist is telling us. Dr. Pantheras, by the way, called Dr. Ocean's office at Magic City Hospital to request a second opinion and he was out of town for a week, or so, so he talked to the family, and they decided to stay for redo surgery."

"Let's see number 16."

"This is the 25th. Dr. Pantheras says; let's check for Heparin-induced antibodies, which is fine. That same day Dr. Zopyros' note says, 'Chest pain relived by intensive medication. Patient has been on Plavix and is off now. Plan to redo CABG on the 28th."

"So, here's our situation. We're on the 25th. She's had another heart attack. Every doctor has said you've got to have surgery. And this new heart attack means we're going to have to get on with it. So, on the 25th it is planned for the 28th, three days later. Here's why, 'She has been on Plavix and is off now.' They took her off Plavix. Plavix is an antiplatelet medication. It has to wear off. Usually, the doctors like for it to wear off for four or five days; a minimum would be three days."

"Significantly, Dr. Pantheras says, let's check for a Heparin antibody, but he put in the chart that same day what? Continue Lovenox, continue Heparin. Nobody is suspecting HIT or HITT. So things have gotten dramatically worse on Monday, the 25th, with the heart attack."

"And then on Tuesday, March 26th there is another significant development."

"Let's see number 17, please."

"These are Dr. Pantheras' notes. He does an echo which reveals severe mitral regurgitation, a new development and an ominous development."

"Dr. Zopyros will explain it to you and he'll do a better job of it than I can. But here's is what I'm going to tell you: What mitral valve regurgitation means is that the mitral valve within the heart is being pulled apart. It's not working efficiently. It affects the effectiveness of the heart, and it's being caused by decreased blood flow to the heart muscle. It complicates the situation significantly."

"Because of the need to repair the mitral valve, which would add significant risks, Dr. Pantheras says, 'I've discussed with the patient and Dr. Zopyros'."

"So, now on the 26th, we have this: we have her coming in, being seen by Dr. Iapetos. The situation is critical on the 22nd. On the 25th, she has a heart attack, and they plan the surgery. On the 26th, mitral valve regurgitation is discovered or develops. Things are getting progressively more significant. We are now, as I said, on the 26th, and Dr. Pantheras continues the Heparin. They continue the Heparin."

"Then on Wednesday, March 27th, we have another complicating factor. The Heparin antibody test that Dr. Pantheras had ordered on the 25th comes back and it comes back positive. So what we have is this: We have a situation where Ms. Carroll is found to be one of the 25 to 50 percent to have positive platelet antibodies."

"Now, does that mean she has HIT or HITT? In fact, they don't think she does because they've been treating her with Lovenox all of these days."

"But it means this: It means they've got to be concerned about this developing, so they appropriately stop the Lovenox."

"Now, Ms. Carroll, at this point, is a patient who has been just getting by. The doctors – several doctors – have told her she's got to have surgery. You can't use a stint. She's had a heart attack on the 21st and another heart attack with maximum medical therapy in the hospital on the 25th. She's developed mitral regurgitation on the 26th. And then on the 27th, they have to stop one of the medications important in getting her by, the Lovenox."

"Surgery is planned for the next day. Under these circumstances, they had to do it. They absolutely had to go forward with that surgery. So what did Andrew do at this point? He did exactly what you'd want him to do. Very few surgeons have experience with Hirudin. But he does his research to find out what's the best alternative. We've got to go forward with the surgery. We've got to do it tomorrow. They stay late working on that."

"Well, they discovered that, first of all, the best alternative under these circumstances is a drug called Hirudin. But it has drawbacks. One of the drawbacks is this: There is no antidote. What does that mean? In surgery, cardiac surgery, you give a patient Heparin, you anti-coagulate him or her while you're exposing the heart, while you're attaching the grafts, while the cross-clamp is on. And then about the time the cross-clamp comes off and you want to start closing the patient, you give a drug called Protamine, which reverses the anticoagulant, which is what is desired."

"With Hirudin, there's no antidote, no Protamine-like drug. When you give the Hirudin, you just stop it, and then you have to wait for it to wear off. That's a problem."

"The other problem is, you've heard a lot about monitoring Hirudin. The fact is you'll find there's really no good way to monitor it. But that was – and everyone agreed – the choice for this surgery. So then they do some research to find a way to monitor the drug. They discover some people recommend an ECT machine. Well, that is a problem, there was no ECT machine. They didn't have one at Oak Mountain. There are very few in the country. They were in the experimental stage. They don't even make them anymore. And most importantly, they determined they could not get one in the next day."

"Mr. Laurence says it takes three to five days to get the machine. You will discover that it takes five days to get one. They couldn't wait. She was at risk of sudden death. They had to go forward."

"So what they did is, Mr. Swindle, who is a Perfusionist, called an expert, a nationally-known profusion authority in Minnesota who has been president of the National Perfusionist Association. He called him because he knew this fellow, his name is Aaron Ridge, and he had some experience with Hirudin. They talked about it, and Dr. Ridge recommended monitoring with the ACT and TEG. And that's exactly what they did, what they were told."

"And that brings us to the surgery itself. Let me pause and talk about this type of surgery. This was a redo CABG."

"The first time a chest is opened, a virgin chest, if you will, the heart is fairly easy to locate by folks like Andrew. It's in what is called a pericardial sac, which can be opened, divided easily. When you have a redo surgery, though, things are different inside. You'll see internal trauma, adhesions. Adhesions are internal scar tissue."

"Surgeons will tell you that in a redo CABG, when you go back in, the pericardial sac is not there, no neatly packaged heart. It's like trying to locate the heart in a bunch of crazy glue. And you've got to find the aorta, to find the vessels that are to be bypassed. That's a typical redo."

"This was not a typical redo. You see, most redo surgeries are done months, or years later. This is what is called a fresh redo, within the first month or two. And every doctor will tell you that is the most difficult time. The adhesions are still forming and are still bloody. They are called wet adhesions. That takes the degree of difficulty to the next level. This is what Andrew faced."

"And that's illustrated by the records, I'll spare you the details at this time, the surgery began at 8:20. At 10:03, which is an hour and forty three minutes into the surgery, the Hirudin was given. That means it took that long to locate and access the heart; a time that usually take fifteen to twenty minutes. It then took another thirty seven minutes to expose the aorta so the cross-clamp could be positioned. It took fifty seven minutes to place two bypasses, which usually takes twenty minutes, or so. All of this because of wet adhesions."

"Now, in doing so, numerous holes called second adhesions opened; numerous holes in the heart and lung, where the two organs were stuck together. Nobody criticizes Andrew for that. That is the stuff that happens in a surgery like this."

"But what resulted is this: It took another hour and twenty minutes as Andrew attempted to repair the heart and the lung. And there was a lot of bleeding. There was massive bleeding."

"Let's see number 20, Rob."

"Andrew describes in his note dictated the same day, 'There was active bleeding on multiple sites of the lung. In addition, there was a large degree of bleeding medial to the left anterior descending which represented a small right ventricular tear.' That's a tear in one of the heart's chambers."

"Multiple sutures with bovine pericardial', which is the type of graft, 'were placed to secure this closure, which was very difficult. There also were lateral adhesions to the ventricle because of the lung, which was adhered to the lateral wall from prior internal mammary harvesting. This resulted in a large area of bleeding lateral to the left anterior descending in the distribution of the high lateral wall.'"

"Andrew will demonstrate all of this later."

"Multiple sutures were used to secure homeostasis', that's trying to stop the bleeding, 'but this continued to bleed, requiring placement of felt strips."

"And during this hour and twenty minutes, unfortunately, time ran out. And then the bypass machine clotted, which is terribly unusual, but it happened. It is very rare and extremely significant. Because you see, Andrew was able, when the machine clotted off, to immediately refill the heart with blood and do all of the things doctors do to restart the heart."

"But his op note, again dictated that same day – let's see number 21."

"It says, 'In spite of the inability to sustain contractility on the patient, because of the patient's inability to sustain contractility, in spite of Inotropes and manual massage, the patient died at 2:20.'"

"What is that saying? He was able to separate Ms. Carroll from the machine, fill the heart with blood, and do the things like manual massage and Inotropes to try to start up the heart. But the heart had lost contractility after four hours of bypass, after an hour and a half of manipulating the heart to repair the holes, and as unfortunately it sometimes happens, this heart couldn't contract on its own. It had lost contractility."

"This was off the bypass. The unfortunate truth is, had the machine not clotted, he could have kept working, but the contractility to the heart was already lost."

"So the evidence is that everything was done absolutely and appropriately by Andrew. Despite his best efforts and the efforts by 'Them' and 'They', Ms. Carroll could not be saved."

"Now, before I go to some other remarks that I had prepared to make, let me address one thing I heard today that I think is interesting. You heard talk about records that 'They' produced. 'They' is the hospital. The hospital produced most of the records. Some of the other records were produced by PUG, which is the Perfusionist group, a separate entity. We're going to talk about those records, and there's a lot of innuendo made by Mr. Laurence. Let's make this clear. The record you saw up there, Andrew Zopyros had nothing to do with any of them."

"First of all, they're accurate. Mr. Laurence is wrong about their inaccuracy. They're accurate. But secondly, those aren't Dr. Zopyros' records. On those pages you saw, he didn't make a single mark. They were made by the anesthesiologist or the perfusionist."

"Let's see 077 again, please."

"Again, there's some innuendo we heard. The note states that the patient is pronounced – that means dead – at 1408. At 1522, Mr. Laurence says the OR team leaves the operating room. Well, this is actually the scrub tech; her initials are on the record. As if there was something sinister going on. Do you know what was going on for that hour and twenty minutes, or so? They were closing the surgery, cleaning the patient, cleaning the operating room. That means it took an hour and a half to close the room down entirely, get it cleaned for the next surgery."

"Now, what that has to do with this case, I don't know."

"Well, then, why are we here, if everything Andrew did was appropriate? You're here because you are going to hear from one person and one person only who is going to have any criticism of Dr. Zopyros. The only person who will take that witness stand and have any criticism whatsoever: His name is, Benjamin Arnold. He's from Red Canyon, Colorado. He's been hired by Mr. Laurence to testify against Andrew."

"Now, you will need to decide the credibility and believability of the witnesses. I want you to keep that in mind when you hear from Benjamin Arnold, who we expect to take the stand tomorrow. Listen carefully to his professional experience because there are some questions there, particularly his experience over the past seven years."

"One thing there's no question about is this: He is a hired professional witness. He charges handsomely for his testimony. He admits to making over $80,000 a year. For every hour he is on the stand talking, he is going to charge $1,000. You're going to find this about him, he's smooth, he's polished, and he's glib; because he is a pro at it. And what does he say? Well, he says, first of all, that Andrew should have diagnosed HITT. We've already talked about that. She never had HIT or HITT. She didn't have thrombocytopenia."

"What will Benjamin Arnold say that Dr. Zopyros should have done? Incredibly, he says in his deposition that Andrew should have postponed the surgery from three weeks to three months."

"Couldn't do it, couldn't do it; couldn't wait five days. They had to do surgery. But that's what the fellow who's been hired to come in here will tell you."

"On the other hand, we've asked some folks to testify, to look at the case, a couple of cardiovascular surgeons, one in Decatur and one in Tuscaloosa. Most importantly, Dr. Player from Tuscaloosa is uniquely qualified for two reasons: One, he has special training in performing redo surgeries. Two, he's one of the few surgeons who has used Hirudin. And we will tell you that everything that Dr. Zopyros did was appropriate. He did everything he could."

"And finally and most importantly, you're going to hear from Andrew Zopyros. I've spoken longer than you wanted me to. I know that. I apologize, but I had to cover this and I haven't said much about Andrew, so let me end with a few words about him."

"Andrew is originally from Detroit, from the south side of Detroit. Grew up there, went to the University of Detroit, graduated in 1971 with honors, was accepted into medical school and finished there in 1975. He was then accepted for surgery training at Stanford University in California."

"In 1981 he came to Birmingham, along with Grace. They've lived here since with a daughter and four sons. He's board certified in thoracic surgery. He is one of the most experienced surgeons you will find. He is an outstanding surgeon, He is a careful surgeon."

"Mr. Laurence said that he was indifferent to his patient. The evidence is going to be that he was nothing but indifferent. He and others, the 'Theys' did everything they could do. The evidence is going to be that this was an unfortunate death. It's also a sequence of rare circumstances which forced him to operate; that everything that Andrew Zopyros was appropriate, was reasonable, and within the standard of care."

"And at the end of this case, you'll find that a verdict is due to be rendered on his behalf."

"Thank you, Your Honor."

I had just witnessed a tale of two patients – it was the best of care, it was the worst of care. The tale of Mr. Laurence was the saga that I knew - the story of missed diagnosis, breaching of the standard of care, lack of informed consent and the death of my mother. Mr. Goretti's tale was that of a desperately sick woman who was fortunate to have the good doctor's care. And that several other doctors – referred to as 'them' and 'they' - had missed opportunities to make her well.

The claims of both attorneys mystified me. I found merit in both arguments and this troubled me. To have any measure of doubt at this time, after years of pursuing accountability, is blasphemous. Could I be that easily swayed from that which I know so well? I had experienced the attitudes of the doctors; quick decisions, no decisions, no sense of urgency until it was too late and then knee-jerk reactions. And I had observed the strength of my mother, intrepid in facing the unknown and game-faced to spare me added anguish. The two were very much different. My mother demonstrated more patience and respect for the practice of medicine than did the doctors collectively. Even though Mr. Goretti had presented a performance worthy of an Oscar, he would not create any doubt in my mind as to what happened and who was responsible. Propaganda, half-truths, party-lines, however one may describe this song and dance, I was not budging from what I have discovered to be reality. Unable to cast off the effects of Mr. Goretti's discourse from my immediate focus, I did not initially hear my name called as the next witness. It was now my opportunity to tell my mother's story; from her perspective and that is why I am here – this *is* in my control.

CHAPTER 3

A Daughter's Tale

Never grow a wishbone, daughter, where your backbone ought to be
Clementine Paddleford

The opening statements had consumed much of the morning. The jury was already divided; one group who watched things happen and another group who wondered what had happened; and neither were capable of making anything happen. Each side presented their cases to the jurors with great prejudice. Each attorney spoke for over an hour with a fifteen minute break separating the opponents, this to allow the jury time to absorb the information and regroup; and go to seek relief.

I took the stand at 11:00 AM. The view from this perspective was quite different from my seat behind the plaintiff's desk. On the stand, all eyes would be focused on me. I then began to think of the coaching the doctor most likely had received and the lack of instruction I had been given. As I thought about it more, I realized that, nervousness notwithstanding, genuineness and sincerity certainly has its place; and my faith in doing the right thing was strong. I awaited my turn under the microscope and the emotions that would certainly surface.

The moment I had waited for had arrived. Two thousand days of nervous anticipation each of which built on the previous; a snowballing effect that prevented any diminishment in my enthusiasm or resolve. I wanted to tell the epic of my mother's experience at the hands of a medical system where communication is supposedly encouraged and mandated but responsibility is shed like loose-fitting clothing. The tale of where doctors walk the halls of a high-tech hospital as if they were high priest of a medieval cloister, untouchable by the common man; unscathed by criticism. The tale of lost innocence when questioning the edicts of a doctor becomes heresy; and a waste of time. I wanted to make an impassioned plea on one hand and I felt the pressure to not make a mistake on the other. Rehearsed confidence abandoned me like a distant memory – there one moment and gone the next – within my grasp only to fade away - I felt very alone on the stand.

Testimony of Vicki Anderson

Mr. Laurence did not rehearse or script my testimony. He told me to follow his lead and tell what I know. With that I took the stand and was sworn in and focused my attention on the jury. Mr. Laurence began the questioning by asking me to tell the jury about myself.

I began by telling the court of my birth at Bessemer General Hospital, Bessemer, Alabama on October 16, 1959 to a woman who was eighteen years of age; my mother was a young adult by the most liberal of definitions. And it was in that area that I spent my childhood and adolescent years. Attending McNeil Elementary, Raimund Elementary and McAdory Jr. and Sr. High schools graduating in 1978, my years as a student were fulfilling. Mother made sure that opportunities to participate in activities like band, choir and academic clubs were available; her personal sacrifice for my participation was freely given and never mentioned. My undergraduate degree from the University of Alabama and continuing education studies at Milsaps College and Rice University afforded me with many opportunities and those opportunities came without student debt. My dad and my mother worked so that my beginnings in the professional world were much better than their own.

My career as a Petroleum Engineer began with an off-shore assignment with Gulf Oil Company. Mother drove me to a site at the southernmost tip of Louisiana; Venice was literally the last outpost, an end-of-the-road community and what lay beyond was the Gulf of Mexico. She watched as her daughter commuted to work aboard a helicopter; a far cry from her days as a waitress at the Ponderosa – I sensed her pride and that motivated me to excel. After several years had passed I accepted a position with Western Oil Company. Assignments with Western included long-term projects in Siberia, Venezuela, Ecuador, California, Kansas, Louisiana and Texas. Mother's claim to the women's liberation movement was vicarious; she enabled me to make her statements for her and I spoke with clarity. She adhered to what I now know as the Texan's philosophy of self-worth; mother was all cattle and little hat – she valued substance over show and that is what I personified to her. No need to protest; just live the life. I was also employed by the State of Alabama Oil and Gas Board; at which time I co-authored a best-selling technical book; mother bought a dozen copies.

I am currently married and live in Kingwood, Texas. And from there I pursue my passions; family, work and mother's case.

I felt ill at ease discussing myself; what I do and where I do it. Observing the opening statements, I realized that it is not as much what is real as opposed to what is heartfelt. This is the process to humanize me; interesting as that can be. With that Mr. Laurence ask me to tell the court about my mother's experience.

I was on assignment at a drilling site near Liberal, Kansas. My brother had tried to contact me several times on the evening of February 26, 2002 and was unable to do so. I had not informed him where I was staying; both he and I are likely to be anywhere as we are required to travel extensively in our respective jobs. So he searched the Internet for a listing of all of the hotels in the area. He called each until he found where I was registered. He did not leave a message for fear of overly alarming me. He instead continued to call until he reached me at approximately 2:00 AM. It is not uncommon for me to work extended hours; I can't leave a site until the required testing has been performed. He gave me the details regarding mother's condition and he assured me that she was not in immediate danger. I packed and checked out of the hotel and drove three hours to Amarillo, Texas to fly home to Houston. There I repacked my luggage and booked a flight to Birmingham arriving on the evening of February 28.

When I arrived at the hospital I learned that my mother had suffered a heart attack. The heart attack occurred on the afternoon of the 26[th.] I learned that Mother had spent the morning jogging her usual three miles and had performed her daily routine of cleaning and cooking when she experienced pain in her chest. She was taken by ambulance to the emergency room. I was told that she had been given care that anyone suspected of having a heart attack would have received. She was stabilized and an arteriogram was performed prior to my arrival. The procedure indicated that three arteries were seventy to eighty percent blocked and could not be stinted. I do not understand to this day why stinting was not an option; I trusted their opinion and had blind faith in their assessment and ethics. Dr. Pantheras performed the procedure and rendered his medical opinion; an opinion that bypass surgery was needed. He said that a surgeon would come to the room and discuss the operation; that was Thursday evening. Dr. Zopyros did not visit until Sunday evening which was three days later. I didn't know whether to feel that there was not a sense of urgency regarding mother's condition, or if the doctor was irresponsible. During the interim nothing noteworthy happened.

Mr. Laurence then asked about the details of the conversation with Dr. Zopyros Sunday evening, March 3rd.

The Doctor told us that he had consulted with Dr. Pantheras and he agreed that bypass surgery was necessary and that she was scheduled to be the first into the operating room the next morning – Monday, March 4th – at around 6:00AM. I asked the doctor if he anticipated any abnormalities based on what he knew about my mother's situation. His explanation was brief and reduced to a level closely akin to a reply one might give to a child; short and ambiguous. After answering a question his body language suggested a quick exit only to have that interrupted by another question; I was obviously an annoyance to him. He was not detailed when explaining the surgery to the lay person. I was not sure what to ask and he was not forthcoming with any words of comfort. In fact, he was a bit distant. He closed the door of conversation when he abruptly said, "If there is nothing else…" With that he left the room. I then began to talk about other things to divert my mother's attention to more pleasant thoughts.

I stayed with mother and sleep was difficult for her; even with the assistance of medication. Automated blood pressure checks that were performed each hour, oxygen saturation sensors that would beep if not properly positioned on the index finger, and interruptions by nurses to inquire 'how's it going', made for a night of multiple naps. The next morning the nurses began to prep her for surgery around 5:00 AM; at least this interruption made sense as the surgical team readied her for the procedure. Family and friends had gathered to wish her well and the pastor whispered a prayer and she was removed from the room around 6:00 AM. The family followed her to the doors leading to the operating area. At that point I leaned and told her that I will see her in the recovery room. The nurse then showed us where to wait and that she would be out of surgery by midmorning. Mother was in good spirits and wanted to move on to recovery and then home.

Waiting was most difficult. My level of comfort was tempered by my understanding of her condition; and I was not comfortable because I was not prepared. Dr. Zopyros had begrudgingly shed some light on the procedure and Dr. Pantheras had filled in some of the gaps. My emotions vacillated between faith in the doctors and fear of the unknown; I waited for the nurse – good news from the nurse.

At 10:30 AM we were notified that the surgery was completed and she was doing well and we could see her in a short time. I was thrilled to hear that the surgery was a success and I was enthused when I saw her; although, it was disconcerting to see the tube from the respirator in her mouth. My sympathy for mother and her ordeal overwhelmed me and my empathy for the current state affected me physically; I became ill thinking of the life support interventions. Family members rotated sitting with her; CICU has specific rules for who can visit and when. She was moved out of post-op into a private room the next morning, Tuesday, March 5th at 10:00 AM. She was awake and in good spirits.

Mother was obviously weak from the surgery and the effects of the anesthesia contributed to her drowsiness. Between naps she felt the need to have discussions that were short in duration but weighty in substance. I got the feeling that the seriousness of the surgery had set in and that there were things she needed to say. She recalled the birth of her grandson, my nephew and how that brought back so many memories of my brother and me. And how there were so many times that she did not know how to do something but she never had any doubt as to what was the right thing to do.

I was told to get her out of bed and take short walks. Later that evening on the 5th; that was Tuesday, she wanted to go to the bathroom. A distance of about eight feet and a few steps into the trip she complained that her left leg hurt badly. At the time, I thought it was uneventful, perhaps fatigue from surgery, maybe it hurt because of the vein harvesting. Returning her to the bed, I looked more closely at the leg. It was extremely blue in color from the knee to the foot and swollen; swollen twice the size of her other leg. It was the left leg; no veins were harvested from the left leg. I called the nurse and she in turn contacted the doctor. We were told to have mother stay in bed until an assessment could be performed.

The next morning, Wednesday, March 6th a Doppler scan confirmed that blood clots in the femoral area had caused the pain, swelling and discoloration. Dr. Micah, the vascular specialist diagnosed the condition as a deep vein thrombosis. Earlier that morning a nurse awakened my mother to perform a blood test and return a few minutes later to get another. The needles were painful and it aggravated me that she had to experience needless pain for an unnecessary test. So, I asked why another test when one has been taken and she said that something was 'out of whack.'

With that Mr. Laurence presented an exhibit on the projection screen of the blood platelet count results and the entry for March 6th was blank. He then asked me is this the day the nurse collected two samples? I responded that it was. Laurence paused, with a staged look of confusion. He then turned and made a comment that it is interesting that no lab values were recorded for the two samples. His point was to demonstrate sloppy record keeping or a possible cover-up of critical information; the 'out of whack' statement concerned us both.

He then asked why you suppose the nurse took two samples and did not record any results, any lab values. And did I think that the 'out-of-whack' statement had anything to do with the missing data. I struggled with my response, not knowing what to say. The platelet count was obviously missing and I simply did not know, or remember what could have contributed to this scenario. Laurence transitioned by saying, 'interesting!' He then asked me to continue.

The pain continued daily and it was my understanding that adjusting medications was a key in correcting the condition. Heparin had been used from the time of admission to thin the blood and continued until the date of her discharge on Saturday, March 9th. After the discharge Coumadin was prescribed as a continued medication to regulate the blood clotting levels.

She complained daily of pain; this from a woman who did not succumb to verbalizing any discomfort or displeasure – to do so would be a waste of energy and integrity. The pain began when she attempted her first walk to the bathroom and continued well after discharge. This troubled me the most. I remembered Dr. Pantheras saying that she would feel the effects of the bypass surgery immediately; I thought it would be for the better.

I was concerned about the inability to stabilize the INR values – the clotting level of the blood and when Dr. Zopyros discharged her on the 9th I asked if another Doppler should be performed – he suggested we could revisit that test in six months. In other words, I got the feeling to mind my business and this was not it; I did not have a high level of comfort with his cavalier response, but I remained silent. With that, we went home with instructions to have regular visits at her local medical clinic to monitor the INR values. The site of home improved her spirits. She and her husband had purchased the small home and had methodically improved and enlarged it until it was what she wanted. Pay-as-you-go was not only a financial principle it was a standard of faith; the verse she would quote remains with me to this day, 'the borrower is the slave to the lender'. She gave a lot of herself to family, friends and church, but was not indebted to do so.

I took a family leave option from work to stay with mother for two weeks. She was unable to drive and her husband was disabled and was restricted from driving. My role was that of chauffeur; go-for, maid and cook; all of which I was happy to perform. Visits to the family clinic to monitor the INR levels were the most important clinical events. These occurred on Monday, March 11th, Thursday, March 14th and Monday, March 18th. The levels were important because the values represented the state of the blood regarding its thickness; its propensity to clot, or not. And the values were not stable and the value on March 18th was extremely low. The values for the three tests were; 5.2, 1.2 and 1.1 – lower the value means the blood clots too easily. Although I didn't understand all that I knew about the importance of the values, I did know that stabilizing them was a key in her getting well; and she was not getting well.

She was scheduled for another monitoring visit on the 21st but early that morning at approximately 2:00 AM she had another heart attack. An ambulance was called and she was taken to the emergency room where the staff made the presumption that she had experienced another heart attack. Medical intervention was performed including the use of Heparin. She remained stable and another arteriogram was performed.

I could not understand why this happened. Even I knew that the presence of blood thinners in her body should have prevented a heart attack. And if a heart attack had occurred with medication that would seem unusual. How it could have happened puzzled me, even more. How could additional arteries become blocked so quickly? Could the arteriogram have missed additional blockage? My trepidation at discharge had been validated by the second admission.

On Friday, March 22nd an arteriogram was perform by Dr. Iapetos and the test indicated that all of bypass grafts had occluded – clotted. A stint was inserted into one of the grafts to provide some relieve but that was not an option on the remaining two. Dr. Iapetos did not have an explanation as to why the grafts clotted.

At this time, my blind faith in the abilities of the doctors had been replaced with a demand for an accounting of how this could happen. I was careful not to question the doctors in the presence of my mother for fear of alarming her. I did not lack the courage to confront the doctors; I lacked the knowledge to ask the right questions. Mother sensed something was unusual and that I was stressed. She mentored me by encouraging me to be patient and persuasive in my dealings with the staff. And that they will resolve the problem.

The next day, Saturday, March 23rd, several doctors visited with comments concerning the occluded grafts. Dr. Pantheras did not have an explanation except to say that the surgeon must have made a mistake. Dr. Allen did not have a clue and, finally, Dr. Zopyros commented that mother probably had some kind of blood disorder.

At this point, I knew that the doctors were not working in concert. The progress notes and the chart became the medium of communication. Sentence fragments and chicken scratching replaced the time tested principles of practicing medicine. That is, record data from the patient's perspective, which is a subjective opinion. Verify the data using independent means, which is from an objective standpoint. Assess the data to identify the problem. And create a plan of treatment. Most practitioners use this format and use this acronym SOAP as its name; Subjective, Objective, Assessment and Plan. The charts certainly did not show that kind of detail.

Sunday, March 24th Dr. Zopyros said that a Re-do of surgery was necessary. We requested a second opinion. No additional details or information was volunteered.

The doctor consulted with us regarding the need for an additional surgery. He did not elaborate on the complexity of a redo surgery.

Wet adhesions, the absence of the pericardial sac, the additional time required to perform a redo; were not topics of discussion. My uneasiness with what had happened thus far created a sense of caution within me. Even though I did not know all of the details, I still wanted a second opinion. I formally made that request to Dr. Zopyros.

Monday, March 25 Dr. Pantheras attempted to secure a second opinion from Dr. Ocean and he was out of town. Later that morning around 10:00 AM mother had another heart attack and that was confirmed by an EKG. At this point I had reached my breaking point; no one was researching the cause of her condition – everyone was reacting instead of acting – waiting on the next doctor to have an epiphany.

Mother remained calm. The source of her composure was in large part due to her faith in God and to a much lesser degree her trust in the doctors. She, as did her friends and neighbors, had an unusually high level of confidence in this facility and its staff. I think that had to do with the local employer's contractual relationship with the hospital; a self-funded insurance plan that was not accepted at other facilities.

The question was asked during my deposition as to why we did not get a second opinion. I had requested one and with the turn of events – the heart attack on the morning of the 25th – I shifted my attention to what could be causing the clotting and subsequent heart attacks. In retrospect it was a mistake to not pursue a second opinion, but the emotions of the moment overwhelmed me and I acquiesced.

On Tuesday, March 26 Dr. Pantheras introduced a new diagnosis regarding a mitral valve leakage. Dr. Pantheras told me that the valve problem was not a critical condition and that if it were convenient to repair the condition during the redo surgery, it would be done. Otherwise she could live with it and correct it later.

Dr. Pantheras told us of the new condition and what it meant to her health. He said that it was something she could live with and its effect would lessen with drug interventions. Pantheras did explain things in greater detail than did the others. He in effect said the valve was not closing completely and blood was leaking, or backwashing, in to the lungs. At worst it would cause shortness of breath.

Dr. Pantheras informed us that he had ordered a Heparin antibody test on Monday the 25th and the results were returned on the Wednesday, March 27th. The results were positive which meant that the surgery could not be performed using Heparin. Dr. Zopyros consulted us and said that an alternative to Heparin would be used and he had selected Hiridun; which would work just fine. In his conversation he made reference to Duke University and his experience with that institution when referring to alternatives to Heparin. I was led to believe that he had been trained at Duke University in the use of Heparin alternatives. I trusted he knew what he was doing.

Mother spent the day engaging in conversation, reading and working crossword puzzles. She sat next to window for most of the day and would take an occasional nap. She was confident in the decisions she had made; and she did not make any medical decisions without my input. She felt as though I had a higher level of understanding because of my professional standing; although that may be true in some respects, she was nonetheless a very good judge of character.

On the other hand, I focused on the obvious; had the Heparin allergy been discovered too late. Dr. Pantheras said that mother probably did not feel any effect of the first bypass surgery – her bypass grafts most likely clotted that night her leg began to hurt. So, for 21 days she was at best no better than she was when she was admitted on February 26. And in many ways, the treatments had made her worse with the introduction of Heparin into her system. Compound the allergy and the wasted time with the doctor's failure to recognize the condition and it became a recipe for a tragedy.

At 6:00 AM on March 28th the surgical team took mother to surgery. And at 2:15 another surgeon, Dr. Hines, informed us that there were complications with surgery regarding holes in the lining of the heart. At 2:30 we were informed she had died – the bypass pump had clotted.

At the time, I could not understand how clotting the bypass machine could have happened. This was not discussed as a remote possibility. Is this the sort of thing that happens with any degree of regularity? Our family was lead to a private sitting area where the surgeon and the hospital chaplain made the formal declaration. The chaplain uttered a few words in prayer and I can't remember what she said. Mother's husband, Pop, did not have a complete understanding of his surroundings and did not realize the gravity of the meeting until the prayer had ended. He then asked when can mother go home and at that time it was further explained and made real to him.

Two days later mother's body was buried. The service was performed on a cold and rainy March afternoon - the final act of a desperate struggle that covered thirty one days of decisions and second-guessing. The funeral director made a comment to me that the deceased had gone through a great ordeal as evidenced by the body.

After the funeral I could not accept that how things went downhill so quickly. I wanted answers. I went to the hospital and requested all of the medical records. I reviewed the documents, taught myself medical terminology, and sought advice from others, subscribed to medical websites and read books and articles. It did not take me long to see a pattern among the doctors of lack of communication with colleagues and the patient and an unfamiliarity with Hirudin and its effects. And an apparent recklessness displayed by the doctors. I needed a deeper understanding of what happened and an acceptance by those entrusted with my mother's care of accountability.

Cross Examination of Vicki Anderson by Mr. Goretti

Mr. Goretti had a mannerism that frightened me. Physically he was frail - a bit scrawny except for his height. His sunken eyes were framed by dark circles that reminded me of the grim reaper. His gait was exaggerated as if his legs were reaching forward to pull his body along; this made him appear to glide across the floor. Nonetheless as he walked toward the witness stand I became sick – my stomach hurt.

He chose the areas to discredit me carefully. It would not be in his best interest to attack the daughter of the deceased. Little did I know that the power of forgiveness far outweighs the wit of arrogance. He knew that an over-the-top exploitation of key elements of my testimony could be neutralized with an apology and an explanation to the court. After all, he has established himself as the protector of that which is good.

The first assault was orchestrated to re-establish the doctor's bedside manner. I had testified that we had waited three days for an audience with the doctor and when it did occur it was underwhelming. Mr. Goretti would not allow me the opportunity to elaborate on my assessment of the meeting. He asked closed-ended questions that required a simple yes or no response.

"Did Dr. Zopyros answer all of your questions?"

"Did Dr. Zopyros present himself in a professional manner?"

"Did Dr. Zopyros explain, at that time, the surgical details to your satisfaction?"

Every attempt on my part to answer, 'Yes, but...' was met with, 'that will be all.' I became frustrated and my emotions got the better of me and my eyes began to tear. The burden I had carried for five years suddenly overwhelmed me. I began to slide down a track from which it was extremely difficult to recover. Goretti did not miss the opportunity. Instead of pouring it on – pouncing on my vulnerability - he came to my rescue. He handed me a box of tissues and asked if I needed a recess. The jurors celebrated his humanity; this sympathetic act from man that had shown a propensity to rip one a new one. This display of diplomacy was a clever act of contrition; a seedy exploit of accommodation.

The target of his attack was my testimony that voiced my frustration regarding multiple venipunctures. The morning of March 6, the nurse collected two vials of blood on separate sticks. Her reason for doing so was the need to re-test because the numbers were 'out of whack.' Mr. Laurence had asked me at that time if the medical records that were displayed listed a blood platelet count. My response was no and the innuendo was made that the values were not recorded because they were inconsistent with a normal recovery. As it turns out, the tests were not regarding the platelet count at all. And Goretti suggested to the court that Laurence and I were conspiring to deceive the court.

The last sortie he delivered regarded medical records. Mr. Laurence stated in his opening remarks that in my attempt to understand what caused my mother's death I had asked for and received copies of the medical records. The suggestion was made that the records I had in my possession differed from those that were subpoenaed. And to add fuel to the fire I testified that what I had received was a complete file regarding the case.

Mr. Goretti then began an onslaught questioning my knowledge and experience regarding best practices of medicine. He asked me to differentiate between a nurse's note and a progress note; between a discharge summary and an op-note. He asked if I could audit a chart and identify missing pieces. Also, he asked if I knew when documents are expected to be submitted as timely. Of course, I knew little about the workings of the hospital in that regard and he made a point to expose my gaps of understanding.

All in all, his attempt to discredit my evaluation of the doctor's bedside manner was at best a draw. His attempt to accuse me of conspiring with my attorney to hoodwink the jury was simply farfetched. And his attempt to expose my lack of understanding regarding the infrastructure of the hospital had merit. He had done his job. To simply ignore my testimony without cross examination may have constituted negligence on his part. He had run the bases and I was excused.

What a hollow feeling. Empty. I could have said more, I had planned to do so. Mr. Goretti accusing me of orchestrating a fraud with Mr. Laurence angered me. I can't believe I was led down that rabbit hole. The potassium and magnesium lab tests that were ordered on the 6th were not the issue in my mind – why didn't the doctor order a platelet count - that was my reasoning. I should have been better prepared; after all he crossed me with my own notes. I should have expected it and played more the part of a victim. Victim: That is counter to my nature. I wanted to take the battle to him – not turn and run. The morning session had adjourned for the lunch break. What was I having for lunch? Crow, it seemed!

———

That evening I could not rest. There were lose-ends that I felt needed attention. One that troubled me was the Potassium / Magnesium tests that required two sticks; and was that the source of the 'out-of-whack' statement. Even though the tests had nothing to do with platelet count it did have something to do with Heparin. I began to review my medical journals and checked on-line subscriptions to medical websites to learn why the nurse would have made the out-of-whack comment. The findings revealed that Heparin will elevate potassium levels – if there is an increase in the amount of heparin that is given to the patient there is a resulting increase in the potassium levels – it becomes out-of-whack! In retrospect, this may have been a small red flag that something was unusual; I emailed my discovery to Mr. Laurence. I have to make a contribution.

Reliving my past is a demon that haunts me. Second-guessing, instant replays, flashbacks; reliving decisions and consequences have become a form of time travel. I find myself in an ethereal theater performing the same scenarios time and again. Whether it is an accomplishment at work or a failed relationship, I am transported to that venue. Since my mother's death, I have relived each moment of her final days in a surreal setting. A setting where I make different decisions, persuade policy makers, make demands of the dishonest, push the unmotivated and encourage the brave. There must be closure to the quest, or I may never close the curtain on the all-too-real drama.

CHAPTER 4

Between a Rock and a Hard Place

AEneas had been cautioned by Helenus to avoid the strait guarded by the monsters Scylla and Charybdis. There Ulysses, the reader will remember, had lost six of his men, seized by Scylla while the navigators were wholly intent upon avoiding Charybdis. AEneas, following the advice of Helenus, shunned the dangerous pass and coasted along the island of Sicily.
ADVENTURES OF AENEAS
THE HARPIES – DIDO - PALINURIUS.

Mr. Goretti always arrived early and stayed late for each session. He carried an old leather briefcase; an accessory that could either be described as an old friend or a good luck charm. His lanky gait and over sized suit made for an awkward appearance; it was a paradox when considering his reputation in the legal community. Striking a pose as if he were a Flamingo; he would shift his weight to a single leg while placing the temple tip of his eye glasses in his mouth. Motionless, except for his eyes, he watched everything that moved. He would at times follow Ms. Santiago to her office for coffee. From that vantage he would lean inside the doorway to watch the members of the jury. One sensed a deep vein of patience, still waters that run deep. There was, however, an uneasy prospect that he could erupt and become unmanageable.

Mr. Laurence on the other hand always arrived under the wire. His sprint to beat the clock added to my level of anxiety; actually it made me ill. Upon his arrival, his paralegal and associate attorney would flutter about him as moths around a flame. Careful to keep their distance – to prevent having their wings seared – yet close enough to hear and respond to his directives, they were willing and able. If I didn't know otherwise, I would have had to presume him to be disorganized and confused. He was quite the contrary, however. Sharp and precise would describe his delivery, cold and calculating would best depict his constitution. I could imagine him as a riverboat gambler, a statesman, a salesman or a history professor. He presented a multifaceted persona, talented and articulate. I most wanted to hear his interpretation of the trial; I longed to talk shop. Maybe that's why he orchestrated his arrival as he did.

There is a strange similarity in the anxiousness I feel here and the nervousness I felt at the hospital - an ominous feeling; a fear that things could slip away. Nevertheless, I have a need to know. The raison d'être, my reason for being, has always been a need to know. And that is what has led me to this place. I have carried the dust of this journey for a long, long time. And I have been unable to shake away its effects on me. It has become a part of me as if I have breathed it every day. In many respects I feel like I am yesterday's answers; something of the past. Worn by time's currents to the shape I now possess. As one often hears as an explanation for something that can't be changed; it is what it is. That is my mental state; I am what I am; unable to provide anymore enlightenment. In many respects I am emotionally spent, and intellectually bankrupt. Perhaps some new answers to old questions would be in the offing as I heard Mr. Laurence call Dr. Zopyros to the stand.

Dr. Zopyros' stature exceeded that of Mr. Goretti; tall, with droopy shoulders; poor posture. His facial features resembled an actor, an actor whose name was on the tip of my tongue, but, yet, not too well known, a supporting-cast type. He wore a gray suit and a conservative tie; he had the look of Middle America. He sat at the defendant's table with his legs uncrossed, hands on his lap and with a concerned and staged countenance. His appearance was not without orchestration. Mr. Goretti's law firm has facilities that are outfitted with a courtroom. A court chamber that would resemble a Hollywood sound stage equipped with cameras and staff to prepare the defendant for every probable scenario; rehearsed improvisation. It is obvious to me that all of his mannerisms are out of character, mechanical in nature. Careful not to exhibit anything that may cause a juror to doubt his sincerity - rigid as to not appear over confident to alienate another.

Glancing toward the visitor's section I saw his wife. She, too, is tall and is dressed as if she were attending an interment. No brightly colored clothing, no jewelry except for a wedding band and a well placed tissue as a theatrical prop in her hand. Her makeup was understated. And with no application of lipstick she looked haggard; visibly worn from worry. She, too, was well coached. The daughter sat next to her mother and held her hand. Her appearance erred on the side of modesty. Neither gave a hint that they were of a higher social standing than anyone on the jury. The exception was the Louis Vuitton that was carefully hidden under the bench, behind her legs. Mr. Goretti did not miss any detail. The defendant had the look of a victim; I felt as though I was on trial.

As the Doctor took the stand, he adjusted the microphone. It fell apart in his hands. It was a scene that would have been best scripted for Chevy Chase; it was an act that further humanized him to the jury. He clumsily recovered, placed the microphone closer to mouth, and adjusted his seat. Positioning the chair so that he could face the jury, Mr. Laurence began his direct examination. I had hoped for a public flogging. Judge Kent conducted the swearing in protocol and all eyes were focused on the doctor.

Direct Examination of Dr. Zopyros by Mr. Laurence

Mr. Laurence began his direct examination by asking the doctor to state his name for the record. Dr. Zopyros was obviously nervous and extremely uncomfortable. His answers were preceded by a roll of the eyes. This left one to wonder if this were an unconscious physical manifestation as he gathered his thoughts, or if it was a rehearsed gesture. Regardless of the source, he looked ridiculous.

When asked, as a judicial formality, his medical specialty and where he practices medicine, his response was inaudible; no one could hear or understand his response. Mr. Laurence asked that he lean closer to the microphone and speak louder. This annoyed the doctor, the request disrupted his nesting, interrupted his comfort zone. Would the actor forget his lines?

Cutting to the chase, Mr. Laurence asked the doctor if he had performed surgery on Ms. Carroll on March 28th, 2002. And did the heart-lung machine clot during surgery and did the patient die? Dr. Zopyros nodded and without emotion answered yes to the questions. Although it had been over five years since my mother's death, hearing it discussed with callousness was unsettling; damn disrespectful. If it were not for the fact that I wanted, needed, answers and closure, I would put an end to this circus. And it was for that reason I compromised and restrained my emotions. Mr. Laurence then asked if the clotting of the heart-lung machine caused Ms. Carroll's death. He responded, "That's incorrect, sir, she bled to death".

Mr. Laurence approached the witness stand with both arms extended. Taken aback by the answer, he asked, "Your testimony is that she died because she could not stop bleeding?" I sat there in disbelief recalling the doctor's comments the day my mother died. He told me the heart-lung machine had clotted and that caused her death. I could not help but to glare at him, this made me angry. I have little patience for someone who confuses correctness with convenience. And this is what the doctor is doing, conveniently changing the conditions to benefit his defense. He never made eye contact with me. His focus was on the jury and his attorney. I waited for his explanation. The doctor's response was that he was unable to control the bleeding and that was the cause of death. This approach was contrary to all of the medical records and depositional testimony that was produced by either side. How was he going to sell this to the jury?

Mr. Laurence accepted for the moment the doctor's statement as to the cause of death. Then he asked the doctor to respond to a letter that he had sent to a colleague. The colleague was the admitting physician for the first hospitalization on February 26th.

The letter was sent the day after the surgery and stated the patient had died on the operating table. The death was due to a massive generalized thrombosis – a complete clotting of her blood. The doctor's testimony and the letter were inconsistent. The prospect of having to explain this conflict made the doctor uncomfortable. Searching for the words, he looked away from the jury and toward his attorney. The action was clearly a plea for help. Mr. Goretti did not make any exaggerated movements, he did however slowly take his right hand and place it on the table and tap it three times. Mr. Goretti's every move was scripted; calculated to provide a return on his investment of time and effort. I interpreted this as a sign to calm down, to take it easy. Schemes to have his client focus on previous instructions, directives to stay the course. After all, the defense will have the opportunity to make the necessary adjustments during cross examination. Dr. Zopyros saw the tapping and nodded. Gathering himself he responded to the question that exposed this contradiction by stating the letter is accurate, but incomplete.

Mr. Laurence was quick to remind the doctor that in his sworn deposition he stated that the clotting of the heart-lung machine was a significant factor in the cause of death. The doctor made several attempts to squelch the contradiction. He emphasized that the re-do-surgery created many challenges. And the raw surface of the heart caused adhesions that were oozing blood. And it was that bleeding that could not be controlled. His defense strategy at this time resembled more of a political debate than a legal discourse. Each time the clotting question arose, he answered with the 'uncontrolled bleeding' response. He told us what he wanted us to hear. He did not tell us what really happened. The defense's rationale is that if you say the same thing over and over again, it will become fact. The difference: Testimony being truly stated contrasted with testimony as a statement of truth. My fear as I watched the jurors is the paradox of clotting versus uncontrolled bleeding. Could the jury comprehend the difference? My confidence was low regarding their ability to discern fact from fabrication. Would they understand a statement of truth is reality and a remark truly stated is suspicious?

The doctor described the patient's final moments by stating that as the pump clotted, he abandoned efforts to continue repairing the wet adhesions and that even though a second heart-lung machine was available, he chose not to use it. An attempt was made to fill the heart with blood and to begin manual massage. But the contractility, the squeezing action of the heart, was lost due to the time the heart had spent on the aorta-clamp; not pumping on its own. In his opinion, the heart muscle was essentially dead. He stated that the loss of contractility meant the heart would not pump on its own. He said the situation was beyond his control at this point. And to repeat what was previously done would achieve the same results. Nothing more could be done.

Documents in the chart were not in agreement with subpoenaed evidence and depositional testimony; making sense of the information was confusing and contradictory. The plaintiff's strategy, in part, was to demonstrate these inconsistencies as a pattern of ineptness and abuse. The question was then presented by Mr. Laurence, which document is correct, which one describes what happened. Was it the letter sent to the admitting physician, Dr. Allen, which stated that the heart-lung machine and the arteries in the patient's body had clotted? Or was it the op-note that described uncontrolled bleeding and oozing adhesions? The doctor responded by asking what is inconsistent with the op-note?

I understood the records better than anyone; I had built the case from scratch. When I initially contacted Mr. Laurence to represent me in this effort, he refused. His reason centered on the difficulty in proving and winning a malpractice case. I then conducted more research and re-presented the evidence that is now being heard. He was then sold on the credibility of the facts; would the jury buy the story? Would the inconsistencies of the two documents make it difficult for the doctor to retain credibility with the jury? Would the jury see this as a problem in believing anything he says? And if the letter is incomplete, as the doctor admitted what else did he not fully document; what else is missing? Did he misrepresent the facts to a colleague? This was the beginning of the evidence to legitimize a tale of corruption and cover-up in high places.

Mr. Laurence continued to hammer the documentation standards of the doctor; inconsistent information to colleagues is one thing; modifying medical records is another. The next line of questioning focused on the op-note for the surgery for March 28th. The op-note is a detailed report, a chronicle, of the actions and interventions of the medical staff, including the doctor. The significant question the attorney asked of the doctor is how many op-notes are typically dictated for a surgery and his response was, "One, always one". A question was then asked of the doctor, if a surgeon were to purposely alter or modify medical records for personal gain or to hide mistakes, or to commit fraud, should he be punished? His response was, "Yes, absolutely." He was then asked if it would be improper to do the aforementioned actions. His response was without hesitation, "It would be unethical; one should be punished for doing so".

The op-note for the surgery was presented on the projection screen for the jury's examination. The doctor was asked if this were the op-note that he dictated regarding the surgery on the 28th. He took some time and agreed that it was. He was encouraged by Mr. Laurence to take additional time and make sure; is it complete, is it accurate, is it your document? He became annoyed by the questioning; the doctor confirmed it again with a clearly audible tone and volume. He responded by saying, "It is, sir, and how many times am I required to say yes?" Mr. Laurence smiled and said, "OK, let's move on." Then the attorney asked to have the projection screen display two additional op-notes regarding the same surgery. Three op-notes were now displayed that were dictated by the same surgeon, for the same surgery on the 28th and with many irregularities. The defendant leaned forward, pushing the microphone away, to get a closer look at the documents.

The three op-notes were quite different. The first op-note had evenly spaced wording and paragraphs, had the appropriate headers and footers and had the look and feel of an original. The second op-note displayed a paragraph the first op-note did not have. The paragraph did not have the same spacing as the remaining document and had a border as if a narrative had been typed, printed and then cut and taped to the original. This piece-milled construction then copied to be presented as an original. The inserted paragraph did not align with the document and the font did not match. This seemed to be a very poor attempt to create a record to make it appear as the original. The third document did not have a header or footer and did not have the questionable paragraph. All have been signed by the doctor and all were in the chart. Each report had a different Job Number indicating that each was prepared by a different transcriptionist. To make the situation even more clandestine, the original chart that had been subpoenaed from the hospital for the trial was lost; conveniently missing. The information regarding the missing chart was not allowed as evidence because of a pre-trial motion made by Mr. Goretti to exclude this detail. His reasoning was that it would cause undue prejudice against the defendant. And, after all he didn't take the chart; it wasn't the doctor's fault it was missing. I wondered!

If it were not bad enough that three post-op notes for the same surgery were in the file, the questionable paragraph that had been added was constructed to make reference that Heparin was not used during surgery. In a paragraph that consisted of five sentences, Heparin was mentioned four times. Second to the listing of Heparin, was the frequency of the word, Hirudin. This was an obvious attempt to insert into the op-note that Heparin was not used during surgery. And that Hirudin was used in its place as an anticoagulant. The style of the inserted narrative was inconsistent with the host document. The preceding paragraphs flowed with technical and medical terminology and required a dictionary to understand. The questionable paragraph looked as if a subordinate was tasked with its construction, or the amendment was produced in haste. There was a noticeable lack of technical jargon and multiple grammatical mistakes. The quality of the fraud was poor, I felt embarrassed for its creator, whoever it may be.

Mr. Laurence repeated his previous question adding the condition, "Which report is complete?" "Which report is accurate?" "Which report is your dictation?" The attorney positioned himself between the defendant and Mr. Goretti in an attempt to block any coaching. Mr. Goretti rose to his feet and stood in front of the projection screen to make himself visible to the defendant. Mr. Laurence asked if he had an objection to any of the questions. Mr. Goretti's response was no. Mr. Laurence then asked him to get out of the way; he was blocking the jury's view. The request for Mr. Goretti to move drew a frown from the judge and a chuckle, or two, from the jury. The judge reminded the doctor that a question had been asked. Dr. Zopyros then responded with a weak voice, "All of the documents are my dictation."

Mr. Laurence then made a sweeping path, circling the Plaintiff's desk to position himself next to the jury. He then asked the doctor, "How many op-notes are dictated for a surgery?" The doctor responded with the answer of one. Following up with, "Why are there three op-notes for the same surgery in the chart?" He did not respond. The attorney asked that the record indicate the defendant did not answer the question. And finally asking, "Why are the op-notes different, did you change the notes, did you authorize someone to modify the record?" The doctor did not lift his head to answer, he responded with a muted no. Mr. Laurence turned toward the jury and shrugged his shoulders.

The doctor did not have an explanation as to why three notes existed; he admitted the three notes were his dictation but with different detail. Why would someone orchestrate a fraud and leave the original. Was someone asked to insert the amended document and remove the other op-notes and did not. Was the doctor set up? Was the weaver caught in his own web? I wondered where this may lead. Exposing medical records fraud to erode a doctor's credibility is one thing, but why did the doctor feel the need to modify the record? What was yet undisclosed? What did I not know?

The answer to my question was soon discovered as the attorney asked to have the discharge summary displayed. This document created great concern because of its content. The doctor, under direct questioning, described this document as a synopsis of a patient's experience while hospitalized. This document could serve as an overview of a previous condition if a patient were to be re-admitted, the function to aid the hospital staff in assessing the patient. Or, if death occurs, it documents the final medical interventions for the patient. Nonetheless, this form of documentation is required of the discharging physician. The doctor when hard-pressed by the attorney said that all discharge summaries are dictated the same day and represents, at least symbolically, the final entry of a chart.

The patient died on March 28th and the discharge summary was dictated on April 15th; 18 days later. The note was signed by the doctor, although he had always assigned this task to his physician's assistant. This break in protocol alarmed me. To change one's policy and procedure at this point indicates an exceptional circumstance, one in which the doctor had great concerns. Why would the doctor volunteer this information; first, that he does not dictate the discharge summaries. And, second, the break in protocol to wait several days to have it dictated. The delay in dictating the discharge summary, the doctor dictating the narrative instead of the physician's assistant, was inconsistent with the past. Add to that the doctor's unsupervised possession of the medical records file. There were too many opportunities for someone to commit or authorize an act of fraud. The patient's chart, the medical records, had been in the doctor's possession until the summary was dictated. The question was then posed to the doctor that caused an outward display of rage; did he alter any documents during the 18 days the records were in his possession? His eyes glared at the attorney. His stiff posture broke from its rehearsed positioning. He seemed to lift from his chair, ready to engage Mr. Laurence as he denied modifying any records. Why were the records in his possession? Did the attorney strike a nerve?

The final component of the discharge summary that raised eyebrows of those that were listening was the reference to the cause of death. The final sentence of the discharge summary described that cause: 'Unfortunately, she did proceed to plat (clot) her venous line as well as the pump in the operating room and was unable to be taken off cardiopulmonary bypass and was pronounced dead at 2:08 PM." The only sentence in the discharge summary that references the patient's death describes the cause of death as clotting or platting the venous line and the heart-lung machine; uncontrolled bleeding was not mentioned. Dr. Zopyros admitted signing the discharge summary.

I remember Dr. Hines telling me at 2:15 on the 28th that mother had a fifty percent chance of surviving the surgery. As I learned later in my research, she was already dead at that time; the recorded time of death was 2:08 PM. I vividly recall Dr. Zopyros telling me the heart-lung machine clotted and death was the result.

Once again, Mr. Laurence asked the doctor which one of the following documents accurately describes the cause of death: The discharge summary, the letter to the admitting physician, or any of the three op-notes. Not expecting an answer that would have any substance, Mr. Laurence opted for theatrics and turned to the jury and continued his direct examination of the defendant.

Mr. Laurence summarized this part of his questioning by asking the doctor if all of his medical case records were this sloppy. This drew an objection from the defense attorney which was sustained by the judge. Rephrasing his question he asked if three op-notes which are categorically different a common place occurrence in his medical charts. He asked if the discharge summary is inaccurate as to the cause of death. And before the doctor could answer, Mr. Laurence directed a comment toward the jury. Just above a whisper he said, "Maybe he forgot what really happened... It took forever to dictate the discharge summary... Or is the real story lost in lies." Hopefully, he is creating some doubt in the jury's mind as to the integrity of the doctor. Mr. Laurence then began to create doubt as to the doctor's medical savvy.

Mr. Laurence prefaced his next section of questioning by introducing a unique allergy. Heparin-induced Thrombocytopenia (HIT) is a diagnosis for a condition that exists when a patient has an allergy to Heparin, and when clotting and a low blood platelet count is present. Heparin-induced Thrombocytopenia is a broad term used to describe that generalized Heparin allergy. The standard of care for patients with a Heparin allergy is cessation of the use of Heparin and the introduction of a thrombin inhibitor; a clot prevention therapy. Each factor of the definition of HIT was presented on the screen for the jury's viewing. The medical records proved the patient met all conditions for the diagnosis. The doctor would not agree with proof sources provided by the attorney to define HIT. And he was extremely evasive relating that information to the patient's circumstance. A proof source was displayed that was authored by an expert regarding HIT. And when asked if the doctor agreed with his findings, he stated that the author may be an authority regarding HIT as he is a hematologist, but he is not a heart surgeon. The doctor did not suffer from a lack of self admiration. Another source was displayed from a periodical, the *Annals of Cardio-Thoracic Surgery* that the doctor admitted reading each month. And when asked if he agreed with that definition of HIT he said the publication was not always trustworthy and at times was notorious. The journal's description and the expert's definition of HIT is the presence of a thrombosis (clot) and a positive heparin allergy test. The doctor categorically refused to give any credence to either as he rolled his eyes.

Mr. Laurence presented the medical record documenting the deep vein thrombosis (clot) of the left leg that was diagnosed on March 6th. He also presented the record of the arteriogram that was performed on March 22 indicating the clotting of the three bypass grafts that were attached on March 4th. The two thrombotic events coupled with the positive Heparin antibody (allergy) test result on March 27th proved a unique condition. This condition by definition is Heparin-induced Thrombocytopenia; the doctor remained firm in his denial of the existence of HIT.

The attorney continued to press the issue by restating the hematologist's definition of HIT as the presence of Thrombocytopenia or Thrombosis and a positive result of a Heparin allergy test. The doctor refused to admit the patient met the criteria for this diagnosis claiming that the existence of Thrombocytopenia, a type of anemia, had to also be present. The attorney continued to press until the doctor agreed that either could be a condition. Conceding this part of the argument did not surrender his assertion that the patient did not have HIT. He held to the contention that an absolute blood platelet value must also be present. His definition for this diagnosis is an unexplained drop in the blood platelet count; a value of 100,000 or less.

The discussion continued regarding platelet count. This topic proved to be a key indicator of the doctor's inexperience with this phenomenon. He was either professionally inept to discuss this condition or strategically adept in avoiding being coerced into a conversation in which he did not want to a party. The doctor agreed that an unexplained drop in the blood platelet count could be a sign of HIT; an emphasis was placed on unexplained. Mr. Laurence reading from the hematologist's article stated that a drop in the platelet count would occur five to fourteen days after an exposure to Heparin if an allergy is present. The doctor responded by stating there was not a significant drop in the platelet count after the first surgery when Heparin was used on March 4[th.] And the small drop after surgery is characteristic of bypass surgery.

He then leaned back in his chair. Confident as if to signal to all who were present that he had delivered a knock-out blow. He felt secure he has caught the attorney in his own web. Mr. Laurence turned and winked at me; what would be his counter punch? My fear is that the details were nothing more than numbers, data that has no meaning to the lay person. Will the jury understand the importance of the platelet count?

The medical records were projected onto the screen that listed the medications that were ordered by the admitting physician and given to the patient. Lovenox, the commercial name for Heparin was ordered and given daily. The admission date was February 26th. Listed on the record for that date was the platelet count of 311,000. The progress note for March 6th, two days after surgery was displayed and the blood platelet count listed was 163,000; a significant drop; a 48 percent drop. This statistic would in itself flag a knowledgeable provider that the patient's condition may be untenable. The doctor, however, asserted that there is a characteristic drop in the count after open-heart surgery. And this in itself is not noteworthy; a post operative drop in platelet count is to be expected.

Once again the doctor leaned back in his chair with an air of confidence. He looked toward the jury and smiled. He made a small hand gesture to his wife. He waited for the attorney to climb off the mat. Mr. Laurence understood the importance of a pause; a delay not only to gather his own thoughts, but to allow the doctor to display premature elation. A climax at this point is premature. My experience in the court room was emotions can shift on a dime. So, I waited for the hammer to fall. The response that was returned was one the doctor had not expected.

The characteristic drop in platelet count the doctor referred to is for bypass surgery that is performed utilizing a heart-lung machine; an on-pump procedure. The heart-lung machine churns the blood as it oxygenates and recycles it through the body. The process damages the blood in some respects, shearing the platelets. This accounts for loss of a small percentage of the platelets. There is also a dilation factor that accompanies an on-pump surgery. Blood is added to the bypass pump reservoir to compensate for bleeding and to assure adequate quantities exist to fill the machine. The blood that is used to prime the pump does not have platelets. The dilution of the patients whole blood with the platelet-poor blood used to prime the pump significantly reduces the overall platelet count. This is the justification for a substantial drop in blood platelet count following bypass surgery. The combined effects of the dilation factor and the shearing effect are noteworthy. It is, however, characteristic of surgeries performed with a heart-lung machine. What happens if an off-pump surgery is performed?

The medical record documenting the surgery performed on March 4th was projected on the screen. This surgery was in fact performed off-pump. This off-pump surgery is a procedure where the heart is repaired as it continues to beat, functioning on its own without use of a heart-lung machine. Significant drops in platelet counts are not characteristic for this type of surgery and can't support the doctor's testimony. The blood is not damaged, no shearing of the platelets. The dilation factor for on-pump surgery is non-existent. There are no large quantities of blood without platelets needed to prime the pump. No substantial quantities of platelet poor blood is introduced into the body by transfusion. So what is the cause of the drop in the platelet count? Mr. Laurence framed his pitch beautifully. It is now time to address the true cause for this condition.

There is what is called the 'five to fourteen day rule' for a drop in platelet counts due to a Heparin allergy. How does this fit into the patient's timeline? The medical record was once again projected onto the screen displaying the medications given to the patient. On February 26th – seven days prior to the March 6th platelet count of 163,000 – Lovenox, which is Heparin, was given, given each day until discharging the patient on March 9th. The significance is that a major drop in the platelet count occurred within a specified time; the seventh day of the 'five to fourteen day rule'. Coupling that with a surgical procedure and a noteworthy drop could not be ignored. The doctor agreed to accept for discussion sake the five to fourteen day rule that is used to diagnose HIT. The doctor's explanation that the drop in the platelet count did not occur within the definition stated by Mr. Laurence was a risky response. He offered his defense based on the rationale that he was responsible for his actions. And he should not be responsible for the actions of others. How could a cardiologist or a vascular surgeon understand the intricacies of a heart surgeon? The attempt to segregate his surgery from the actions of the other doctors was too provincial. How effective could he be in convincing the jury that 'it was not his job' to go the extra mile? Passing the buck had become an art form and he was instantly becoming a master. He quickly added that the drop occurred within two days, not five to fourteen days, of the cardiac bypass surgery. The dates of March 4th and 6th, respectively; a point he continued to emphasize as a predictable occurrence. The doctor smiled as he made the statement and waited to watch Mr. Laurence struggle with that realization.

Mr. Laurence had two hands to play. Both were equally accurate. One was obviously not anticipated by the defense. To bait the doctor into a web of disclosure, to admit key aspects of the chart, the attorney repeated previous evidence and medical records. Displayed on the screen were the progress notes for February 26th, the date of admission, and March 6th two days after the first bypass surgery. Two items were highlighted and emphasized: Lovenox – Heparin - was prescribed and given to the patient; the platelet count was 311,000 on the 26th and 163,000 on the 6th. The introduction of Heparin, a significant drop in the platelet count and a thrombosis, a clot, met all of the conditions for a diagnosis of HIT. The doctor refuted the suggestion and inserted the caveat that he is a surgeon and the surgical event does not fit within the timeline presented. That is, the massive dose of Heparin that is normally given in bypass surgery was within two days of the platelet drop; not five to fourteen days. Mr. Laurence feigned a setback and asked the judge for a moment to gather his thoughts. His body language was that of a scolded child. He played the part expertly. He then flipped through a file and wrote a note to his assistant asking where they were going for lunch; theatrically wasting time. I saw the note. He saw that I saw the note and, once again, winked as he prolonged the play of his second hand. The judge asked the attorney to continue. With that request, Mr. Laurence turned and took a position next to the defendant.

Displaying the progress note for March 6th, highlighting the deep vein thrombosis and the platelet count, he then displayed along side of that note the admission records for March 21st; the second admission. Couple that with that an existing Thrombosis. And a recently administered large dosage of Heparin as a part of bypass surgery; HIT should have been diagnosed. The events of an exposure to Heparin, the development of a thrombosis, and a drop in platelet count all occurring within fourteen days; was a significant flag. The timeline was presented and the question asked of the doctor should HIT be suspected at this time. His response was there were not enough reasons to follow that line of logic. He was also asked as a precautionary action, should a Heparin antibody test have been ordered. His response was once again that there was no reason to suspect that condition. At times in an attempt to promote his defense, he came across as absolutely incompetent; both comical and tragic.

Mr. Laurence asked if a cause had been identified as to why the DVT developed. Were there any tests ordered to determine the root cause of the DVT? What caused the thrombosis? Why didn't you, or 'Them' and 'They' do something? The doctor sat quietly and stared at the floor. He then mustered a response.

The doctor used the word 'constellation' to describe the number of possibilities that could cause any condition; this condition. Breaking into a diatribe of medical detail and terminology to impress the jury, he chased many rabbits. Losing jurors in many rabbit holes before

Mr. Laurence could corral him. The question was then asked if a Heparin allergy was not suspected, what was. What lab tests were ordered to narrow the list of causes; the number of stars, if you will. The doctor's response was no additional tests were ordered other than the standard series of labs. No additional tests except for an ultrasound that was ordered by Dr. Micah to diagnosis the DVT. This test did nothing more than confirm the existence of a clot and did not provide a reason why the clot had developed. Mr. Laurence displaying his own brand of theatrics placed his hands on either side his head, running his fingers through his hair, asked what it would have taken for you to have done your job. Mr. Goretti bolted from his chair to object and the judge agreed. The point was made!

Mr. Laurence shifted his focus and questioning to cover the time span from the discharge on March 9th through the second admission on March 21st. Dr. Zopyros discharged the patient. He prescribed Coumadin which is an oral drug to thin the blood; it is an anticoagulant. His instructions were to have her primary care provider monitor the effectiveness of this drug and communicate the results to his office. This oral blood thinner is monitored utilizing a specific test that is valued in INRs – International Normalized Ratio.

INR values monitor the effectiveness of Coumadin as a blood thinner. A normal INR range is 2.5 to 3.5. Higher values indicate thinner blood – fewer coagulants and a propensity to bleed. Lower values indicate thicker blood – more coagulants and a propensity to clot. On March 9th the INR value of 4.12 indicated the patient platelet count was low; thinner blood. Additional INR tests were performed on March 11, with a value of 5.2; on March 14th, with a value of 1.3; and on March 18th, with a value of 1.1. The INR values drop significantly from 5.2 to 1.1 which indicates the blood is becoming thicker, more apt to clot. The unstable values concerned the primary care provider. This prompted his nurse to caution the patient to be careful of injury when the INR value was 5.2, for fear of uncontrolled bleeding. The nurse also cautioned the patient when the INR value was 1.1, in fear of increased clotting and blockage in the arteries. I remembered how the inability to stabilize the INR values made me crazy. And the unstable INR values paled in significance to the doctors' inability or unwillingness to treat the condition. The doctor confirmed that his office had been receiving the test results and did not have reason to suspect any abnormalities. Mr. Laurence then began his questioning of the second admission.

The patient was re-admitted on March 21st with chest pains. And on March 22nd a cardio catheterization was performed. The results of that procedure verified the three grafts had occluded – clotted. Mr. Laurence asked the doctor if this is a rare occurrence. His reply confirmed the question; extremely rare. The doctor was then asked why this might occur. He listed several reasons that could have caused this occurrence: One was that the conduit material was not good; bad veins and arteries harvested from the right leg and chest. Two was irregularities inside the grafts that would inhibit blood flow. Three was abnormalities in clotting. Four was graft spasms – intermittent vascular constriction of blood flow. Five was the presence of relaxing chemical agents of the blood that would cause the blood to not flow well in the grafts. Mr. Laurence listed each of the doctor's possibilities on a whiteboard. His next set of questions painted the doctor into a corner.

He then asked the doctor if he noted in the chart that the conduit material was bad. The doctor answered, "No."

He then asked the doctor if he noticed any changes in the grafts that would have caused the occlusions. The doctor answered "No."

He then asked if spasms were observed that would inhibit blood flow. The doctor answered, "No."

He then asked the doctor if he had any reason to suspect any relaxing chemical agents of the blood. The doctor answered, "No."

With each answer, Mr. Laurence marked off a possibility as unlikely. This visual representation of the doctor's thought process was revealing. Sitting in the witness box, reviewing a medical case that occurred five years earlier, the doctor displayed logical thinking. Did he follow the same logical steps without the aid of an attorney prior to surgery?

So, there's only one option left and it concerned clotting abnormalities. The doctor was trapped in a corner that he had painted. Listing all of the possibilities that could cause the condition, the doctor said he did not think she had a problem with clotting. He remained defiant, stubborn in his rhetoric. Mr. Laurence then asked what then could have caused the clotting. The doctor could not suggest any additional reasons. His constellation of possibilities faded to become a single point of light. That prompted the attorney to ask angrily, "Are you now convinced that a Heparin allergy test should have been ordered?" Mr. Goretti objected and Mr. Laurence ignored him, and without breaking his rhythm, continued his questioning.

Mr. Laurence presented the doctor's progress notes dated March 24th. He pointed to the section of the note that stated a re-do-CABG (bypass graft) was needed. Asking the doctor how he had arrived at this conclusion the doctor responded by saying he had read the cardio catheterization report. This report was prepared by Dr. Iapetos, a cardiologist and an associate of Dr. Pantheras. Mr. Laurence then displayed Dr. Iapetos' report. Pointing to the section that indicates this report was produced on May 19th. This report was created six weeks after the patient's death. How could a document have been read prior to it being constructed? Dr. Zopyros struggled for a response and recanted having read the report. He then said he had possibly watched the film of the procedure and had made his decision from the viewing. The doctor struggled, not only with the correct answers, but also with his voice. It broke when he was pushed and the volume diminished when he was confused. He clearly did not have a gambler's mental toughness outside of the operating room. Here he had to account for his actions. He had to answer questions. Mr. Laurence asked the doctor if he were making this up as he goes. He then asked if the doctor had instructed Dr. Iapetos to create the report. Had he coached him as to the contents? The doctor responded with a loud no; no to all of the questions. No!

Piling on the inconsistencies, Mr. Laurence questioned another part of the progress note. This section referenced an order to perform a clotting workup. The attorney's statement posed the question to the doctor and those in attendance, why is a clotting workup ordered if no one suspects a clotting problem. Why then wouldn't the workup include a Heparin allergy test? The doctor stated that he did not suspect any clotting disorders and that Dr. Allen had ordered the tests. The attorney responded by asking the doctor if he had an ethical responsibility to read the orders of other doctors in making medical decisions? The doctor's response was that Dr. Allen is not a heart surgeon. Mr. Laurence then reminded the doctor that he is not a hematologist. Mr. Goretti objected with no response from the bench. Mr. Laurence reiterated the standard of care regarding cessation of the drug if it is contraindicated, harmful to the patient. Why was Heparin not discontinued when the clotting workup was ordered?

A concept was then introduced by Mr. Laurence, the concept of Team - the idea that the surgical staff is a team. And that the team leader is the surgeon. One important responsibility of the team leader is to coordinate pre-surgical planning. In this case, a critical component of the pre-surgical planning was to research, coordinate and implement a surgical strategy to use an alternative to Heparin. Heparin is a blood thinner, an anticoagulant that permits the use of blood in surgery in a controlled state. An allergy to Heparin had been diagnosed and surgery with Heparin was not possible. And surgery could not be performed without an anticoagulant.

One member of the surgical team is the perfusionist. The perfusionist is the team member that operates the heart-lung machine during surgery. The heart-lung machine oxygenates and circulates the blood when the heart is clamped and not beating. The perfusionist also monitor's the effect of anticoagulants during surgery; recording clotting levels and adjusting the dosage of the drug. In this case, the perfusionist was tasked with using an alternative to heparin. The alternate that was chosen was Hirudin. Hirudin is an anticoagulant that is derived from leach saliva.

The perfusionist that was present at the surgery on the 28th was Mark Swindle. The doctor was asked by Mr. Laurence if he had a conversation with Mr. Swindle on Friday, March 22nd regarding use of an alternative to Heparin; which was six days prior to surgery. The knowledge of this conversation was discovered when Mr. Swindle was deposed prior to trial. The doctor confirmed the conversation and the date, much to the surprise of those in attendance. The doctor had just testified that on Sunday, March 24 that he did not suspect an allergy to Heparin. Then to admit having a conversation to use an alternative to Heparin two days earlier was a contradiction. I am not surprised by the doctor's inconsistencies. He errs on the sides of telling everything or telling nothing. Telling what he thinks one should hear. And not telling what should be disclosed. Ethically, he is profoundly confused.

The attorney sought clarification and asked the doctor again if he and Mr. Swindle had discussed using an alternative to Heparin on the 22nd for Ms. Carroll. His response was one that angered me greatly. He had admitted never using an alternative to Heparin and did not know of a surgeon who had. And had never had a case where all of the bypass grafts occluded. He then said that his conversation with the perfusionist was a casual conversation. The discussion wasn't about a particular patient, just talking shop, if you will. The doctor suggested that Mr. Swindle may have conducted his own research regarding an alternative. Maybe he had heard about Ms. Carroll. Maybe it was a coincidence.

Mr. Laurence asked the doctor when he began his research into the use of alternatives to Heparin. His response was when he was informed of the positive antibody test results on the 27th. At that time he testified that he spent several hours researching the proper use of Hirudin, research related to dosages and reactions. His source for information was the Internet and when asked if he had saved or printed the documents, he replied no. There is no documentation to support his research.

What wasn't told to the court was that on the 27th when he consulted with patient and family he comforted us with the assurance that he had experience with alternatives to Heparin. He also stated that he had experience with Hiridun at Duke University. His comments precluded the need for additional questions. Experience with the use of alternatives at a prestigious university closed the conversation regarding the discussion of options. In fact, the doctor did not list any options, good or bad. At the time, this elevated my level of confidence.

The doctor was asked to define Informed Consent. His response was that generalities were discussed with the patient such as the things can happen as a consequence of surgery and the major risks of going into the operating room. This is his routine activity prior to surgery. The attorney then asked several specific questions regarding the conversation with the patient and family prior to the surgery. Did you discuss your conversation with Mr. Swindle that occurred on Friday, March 22 regarding researching an alternative to Heparin? He responded by saying, "I don't recall one way or the other". Did you discuss with the family that you had never performed surgery without Heparin? His response, "I don't recall one way or the other". Did you tell them that you had never performed surgery with Hirudin? "I don't recall one way or the other". Do you recall telling them that the perfusion team did not have any experience with Hirudin? "I don't recall one way or the other, sir". Did you tell them that in your research you discovered that a specific machine is required to perform the surgery, an ECT machine to monitor the use of Hirudin? "I don't recall one way or the other, sir". In retrospect this makes me sick. I didn't know to ask these questions. The doctor's comment that he had experience at Duke University seemed adequate at the time. If I could relive the moment, I would have taken the risk of driving my mother to another facility, to another set of doctors, to a fighting chance. As it were, playing the lottery had better odds.

Mr. Laurence asked specifically regarding informed consent and if the family had a right to know that he planned to use an alternative to Heparin and that he did not have experience with that protocol. His reply, "I don't believe that was necessary, sir". Again the attorney pressed by asking did the family have a right to know this was your first surgery using Hirudin. Did they have the right to know that this was your first re-do surgery following a clotting phenomenon? Should they have been informed that this was your first surgery monitoring an alternative to Heparin? Did you did think it was important to tell the family these things prior to surgery? "I don't believe that was necessary, sir"

Monitoring of Hirudin, or the commercial name Refludin, requires a specific machine to assess clotting levels of the blood. The

ECT, Ecarin Clotting Time, machine is designed to monitor the levels of Hirudin. Machines that are used to monitor Heparin, the ACT, Activated Clotting Time, and the TEG, Thromboelastograph, are not designed to monitor Hirudin and are unreliable.

Hirudin is a direct thrombin inhibitor; an anticoagulant. Unlike Heparin whose effects can be reversed with another drug, Hirudin metabolizes through the liver; it has to wear off. It is administered by a direct IV drop. It has a half-life of eighty minutes. Which means its effectiveness would diminish by fifty percent in eighty minutes. So, a continuous drip is required until the surgery is completed.

The attorney asked why an ECT machine was not used for the surgery. The doctor responded that the literature he read was equally divided as to the need for special equipment, the ECT machine or the use of the ACT machine. He admitted that documentation existed that an ECT machine is required for monitoring Hirudin during surgery; but he then discredited the literature's worthiness. He rationalized his contempt for the data by insisting that it was relatively new and lacked clinical trials. And that no one was an expert regarding the monitoring of Hirudin with any machine at that time. The attorney then asked if the hospital did not have the necessary equipment, was an attempt made to locate the machine. His response stunned me. I could not help but to wonder what the jury thought of this casual attitude of the surgeon. He stated that he presumed the perfusionist had made an attempt to find an ECT machine. He presumed that efforts had been exhausted in the search. But they had decided they could get by on what was available; using the ACT and TEG alternatives. Getting by was not discussed with me regarding the surgery, my mother was already getting by. I thought the goal was to make her better.

Mr. Laurence presented a book for the doctor's review. This publication is authored by the premier expert regarding HIT and the book's content is exclusively related to Heparin-induced Thrombocytopenia. The doctor was asked to comment on a section that was presented. The last sentence of a key paragraph stated, "The use of Lipirudin (Hirudin) in cardiac bypass surgery is currently restricted to patients with HIT". If the doctor did not suspect

HIT why would he use Hirudin? He disagreed with the expert's restrictions and asserted that the so called expert is a hematologist and not a surgeon, and how could he have the same experience and knowledge; the same intuitiveness and skills set. Agreement with the text would have perjured his testimony, admitting the patient had HIT.

Questioning continued with a focus on the management of Hirudin. The literature presented by Mr. Laurence listed a protocol that mandates the monitoring of the drug at fifteen minute intervals. The defense's expert witness that was hired to support the doctor's case testified in his deposition that testing should be performed at fifteen minute intervals. The general consensus is frequent monitoring intervals are required. The attorney spent a great deal of time quoting proof sources on the need to have a protocol. A protocol that would test more frequently than Heparin the clotting levels for Hirudin. The doctor has consistently disagreed with standards suggested by experts and documentation. Mr. Laurence turned once again to the medical records.

The attorney read the medical record that listed the start of surgery at 8:00 AM. Then he pointed to the record that listed the initial dosage of Hirudin at 10:03 AM. Both times were confirmed by the doctor. The first ACT test was performed at 10:10 AM and the next test at10:28 AM; eighteen minutes later. The remaining tests were taken at 11:15 AM, 11:41 AM and 12:43 PM; all times were documented in the chart. The doctor confirmed that the documentation of the entries were accurate and represented a standard policy and procedure.

The tests that were listed in the medical record were performed on the ACT machine. Each time a test is performed a report, a ticket, is generated listing the clotting values, a range of normal values and the date and time of the report. The tickets were subpoenaed and were presented for review.

Eight of the nine tickets that were displayed had a time stamp that was after the patient's death. Further review indicated that three of the tickets were dated on the 26th, two days prior to the surgery. The doctor was asked if he, or anyone to his knowledge, had ordered an ACT test prior to the surgery. He response was no. Mr. Laurence then asked how do you explain the incorrect dates and times. The doctor did not respond. The attorney requested an audible answer. He received an awkward no and an elaboration that the time on the machine may be incorrect.

The first ACT ticket has a time stamp of 1:17 PM. The patient died at 2:08 PM. The remaining tickets have time stamps after the time of death. The doctor was asked if he still believed the medical record to be accurate and responded yes. The values of the tickets were handwritten in the chart with an associated time. A spreadsheet was projected onto the screen that listed all of the ACT tickets, their value and the date and time. This presentation was prepared by the attorney to place the values in an easy to read format. The spreadsheet also listed the intervals of the test; the time between each testing.

Conceding for the moment that the machine's clock may have not been set properly, Mr. Laurence then asked if the time interval from the tickets should match the chart. That is, regardless of the actual time stamped on the ticket the time lapse between the tickets should represent an absolute value. And that value should match the chart. He agreed and the attorney quickly pointed to a discrepancy. The times written in the chart representing the ACT tests were: 10:10 AM, 10.28 AM, 11:41 AM and 12:43 PM. The interval between the first and second testing was eighteen minutes. Reviewing the first and second tickets the times of 1:17 PM and 3:24 PM were stamped. This is a one hundred and twenty seven minute interval. If the medical records are to be trusted how could there be such a discrepancy? Why would the handwritten values entered in the chart represent different times and intervals than that of the tickets.

Mr. Laurence asked the doctor if he had an explanation as to why your perfusionist, your team member, logged an eighteen minute interval between the first and second ACT test, and the actual tickets showed a one hundred and twenty seven minute delay. Mr. Goretti stood and objected. Objected because the perfusionist miss-charted the entry, and there was an ACT test at 8:15. Mr. Goretti was suggesting that an ACT test to establish a baseline for clotting was incorrectly referenced in the interval calculations. In other words, which test time is used as the first? Mr. Laurence responded by saying that contradicts the doctor's testimony. The question that was asked of the defendant was specific to the test results after the introduction of Hirudin into the body. Both attorneys exchanged a heated volley of innuendo when the judge called a bench conference. Mr. Goretti objected to the chart because it is inaccurate. Mr. Laurence stated it accurately chronicled the activities of the perfusionist. The defense wanted it both ways. Either the chart is correct as the doctor testifies, or it is inaccurate as the defense attorney contends. Convenience is a river that follows the path of least resistance thus making it crooked. And the testimonies, the stories, have been anything but straight!

Mr. Laurence moved to the next set of tests that were used to monitor the blood during surgery. The Thromboelastograph measures the clotting time of the blood. The protocol for this test requires frequent monitoring, the defendant's expert witness suggest ten minute intervals. The first test was taken prior to the introduction of Hirudin at 10:03 AM. The time of this TEG test was 9:50 AM. A report in the form of a graph was generated from the TEG machine and logged in the chart. The next TEG test was logged 3:16 PM, one hour and eight minutes after the death of the patient. The doctor had previously testified that several tests, both ACT and TEG, were taken during the surgery. His previous testimony to justify the use of the ACT and TEG tests in lieu of the preferred ECT machine was emphatic; that timely testing is the key when using the ACT/TEG option. His testimony stated that he and the perfusionist were comfortable using these test provided continuous monitoring was performed.

Gathering himself, the doctor attempted to clarify the lack of TEG reports in the chart. He remembered that it is not a standard protocol to save the reports. They are shredded after the chart is logged with the values. On the surface this seemed to explain the occurrence to a point. Then, Mr. Laurence asked why a TEG test report would be generated long after the death of Ms. Carroll, and to break from protocol to have it placed in the chart. The doctor responded that the appearance of the report in the chart is a mystery but the timing of the report can be explained by a faulty clock. A faulty clock; that excuse has been used to explain the inconsistencies for both the ACT and TEG reporting. The attorney asked with an exaggerated look, was the clock wrong for the first test prior to surgery. The defendant answered, "No." The attorney then asked why the clock would be reset with the incorrect time before the last test. There was no response. The attorney continued his questions regarding the TEG testing. Why there were only two TEG values recorded when the protocol suggests multiple tests were required? The first TEG result logged at 9:50 AM and the last logged at 3:16 PM. The doctor did not respond. The attorney asked that the record show the defendant did not respond.

The next document that was presented caused some rumblings in the courtroom; whispered conversations, a couple of wows and a sole expletive. The image on the screen was the medical bill for the second hospitalization. The bill listed goods and services provided by the hospital and by professional staff members. Mr. Laurence began his explanation of the document by starting on March 25. Pointing toward a line that listed Lovenox – Heparin – that was indicated as billed and dispensed. The same was done for March 26. And on March 27, Lovenox was not listed as dispensed, that was the day the result of the positive Heparin allergy test was returned. Then Mr. Laurence displayed March 28; the day of the surgery. On this date, Lovenox was listed as billed and dispensed. Was this contraindicated drug given to the patient?

Mr. Laurence asked the doctor if Heparin was given to the patient during surgery. His response was an adamant no. The attorney then asked if it were given, would it be a breach in the standard of care. The doctor said that it would be a breach; but asserted that it was not given. Laurence then asked the doctor, "Have you not, up to this point, supported the medical records as an accurate detailing of the medical interventions for the patient? And, wouldn't you agree that the bill is a financial summary of those records?" The doctor responded, "I guess that is so."

After a long pause, one that was interrupted by the judge, Mr. Laurence turned to the defendant and directed a line of questioning and comments aimed at the heart of the direct examination. The attorney stood in front of the stand, pointing his finger at the doctor, he said you never anticipated that anyone would investigate the tests reports and tickets. You didn't think anybody would see the backup for the chart entries. You ordered the tests after she died to construct a story. You coached the perfusionist in what to say and how to document the story. Sloppy records and malfunctioning clocks, you don't expect the ladies and gentlemen of the jury to buy any of this, do you? The doctor denied all of the allegations. Mr. Laurence then asked if that would be unethical and improper for one to do those things. The defendant responded with a barely understandable answer of yes.

Relentlessly, Mr. Laurence pushed the doctor by summarizing his testimony. You have tried to explain the cause of death as uncontrolled bleeding. This is inconsistent with the three op-notes, the discharge summary and a letter to a colleague. You have denied the existence of a blood coagulation problem until it was too late. You refused, even to this day, to admit the patient had HIT. You accuse the doctors that assisted with Ms. Carroll's care as being responsible for not identifying a problem with Heparin. You did not think it was necessary to discuss your lack of experience performing re-do surgery using Hirudin. You did not inform the family that special equipment to monitor the anticoagulants during surgery was crucial. You are responsible for the surgical team; clocks, equipment, charting and staffing. So, I ask you at this time do you feel as though you did anything wrong? The doctor's response was, "No." Would you, having the opportunity, do anything different? The defendants answered, "No." You would not change one thing about the care you gave her? Dr. Zopyros said, "I would not"!

Mr. Laurence made a statement with his mannerism as he allowed his shoulder's to droop and his head to fall slightly backwards. It was a message of absolute frustration. I was exhausted, having hung on every word. The defendant was noticeably fatigued. His wife was wiping tears from her eyes. Members of the jury were energized as they sensed a break in the action. The attorney announced to the court, "That's all I have at this time, Your Honor."

The judge instructed the jury to not discuss the trial with anyone and adjourned until 8:30 am the following day. We rose as the judge exited through the door behind the bench. We then waited until the jury made their exit and moved our conversation to the rear of the court room. Each member of the legal team had a slight smile on their face and I was anxious to hear their thoughts. For the most part the topic was the admission by the doctor that if someone is guilty of the acts discussed today, punishment would be expected. Mr. Laurence was encouraged by the direct examination but tempered our enthusiasm by reminding us the jury has the ultimate control. And that tomorrow is another day as the defense has their day in court, so to speak.

I made my way across 21st street. The day started with sunshine and was ending with rain. And so often is the case, I did not have an umbrella. Sitting in the car, soaked from the deluge, I tried to make sense of the day. As a habit, whether it is work, play, reading a book, learning something new, or in this situation; I reduce complexities to a simple statement or concept. A cocktail party explanation of what happened. I searched for the meaning and the words that would define the moment. My mother died because of a medical condition that was not recognized; was not diagnosed. Those who treated her were either blind to the symptoms or indifferent to the cause. A 'win a few, lose a few' attitude was all too prevalent. So, what am I to make of the day's happenings?

Was the doctor truthful with me the day prior to surgery? Did he truly comprehend the technical components of the re-do surgery? For some reason the words integrity and knowledge comes to mind. Integrity defined as who you are. And knowledge defined as what you know. Integrity without knowledge produces good intentions without desirable results. Knowledge without integrity produces unexpected outcomes. What does lack of both produce? It is what has happened to me, the loss of my mother.

CHAPTER 5

The Oath

He that imposes an oath makes it, not he that for convenience takes it;
then how can any man be said to break an oath he never made?
Samuel Butler (1612–1680)

Heavy traffic delayed my arrival at the courthouse. Crossing 21st Street, dodging traffic, bypassing the assistance of the crossing attendant, I rushed to the entrance of the courthouse where a line had formed to pass through security. Everyone emptied their pockets, removed their belts and placed their bags and brief cases onto the conveyor to x-ray the contents. Each person that moved through the security portal set off the alarm. This forced the guard to inconvenience himself to further scrutinize each visitor. Expecting a pat-down search for contraband, I was shocked at the lackadaisical approach of the guard. The additional inspection required exposing the ankles of each security risk by lifting one's pants leg. What a waste of time! It was clearly the unification of civil service mentality and a naïve honor-system; a passive don't ask and don't tell Homeland Security ritual. More theatrics – this being more of an exercise to make people feel safer than one of actual security.

Dr. Zopyros was scheduled to take the stand. The re-direct of his testimony would be an attempt to right the wrongs from his previous experience with Mr. Laurence. The episode had weighed heavily on him and he had the look of the vanquished; a state one would not wish upon any decent being. His testimony had exposed inconsistencies in his reasoning and his presence on the stand was less than stellar. The lack of credible answers and a weak-chinned deportment created a guise that made the defendant appear to be shifty and self-serving. All in all, he had a lot of ground to recover.

With everyone in place Ms. Santiago asked, "Defense ready"? "Plaintiff ready"? "Alright then, I'll get the Judge".

Judge Kent entered the court and took his seat behind the bench. He welcomed the jury and directed the defendant to take the stand and reminded him he was still under oath. As the doctor gathered himself and slowly made his way to the stand I couldn't help but mull over the phrase 'Under Oath'. What did that really mean? An oath is a vow, a promise, a pledge to do and say the right thing. How would situational ethics affect his guarantee to be truthful? Did anyone really expect the doctor to respond to questioning in a manner that would compromise his defense? Did anyone really think that he would admit to any wrong doing? I had been on the witness stand. And as nervous as I was, I felt that I had nothing to hide. I knew the facts and when weighed in a balance the doctor was found wanting. So, what a waste of time – like visitors passing through a security gate that provided no security, we are asking the accused to play fair and take the blame for his actions – lift his pants legs and expose his ankles. Hopefully, this would not be another union of civil service policy and human naïveté; a lackadaisical merger of good intent and gullibility. Realistically, the only way to pull justice from this facade was to lead him into an oversight and hope the jurors catch it!

Cross Examination of Dr. Zopyros by Mr. Goretti

Mr. Goretti ambled toward the witness stand, shaking his head and smiling. His gait was more appropriate for a stroll in the park than this judicial setting. Positioning himself alongside the defendant he placed his right hand on the doctor's shoulder. Pausing as if posing for a portrait, he then placed the index finger of his left hand on his chin. Slowly tapping his finger and with a puzzled expression he asked the doctor. "Are you as dishonest as Mr. Laurence suggested?" The doctor was taken aback by the question and before the defendant could respond, he asked another question, "Would you think it would be wrong to be dishonest in front of the jury if you were a lawyer like Mr. Laurence?" For a moment time stood still. The Judge had assumed his usual reclined position, staring at the ceiling. The legal aids for both teams were busy organizing their work areas. Laurence had placed his writing pad in his lap and had leaned back in his chair to record items to re-direct. And with Mr. Goretti's inflammatory question, time moved at flank speed. The judge snapped his attention toward the attorney, the aids stopped in mid-task to await the fallout and Mr. Laurence provided an equal and opposite reaction. The confrontational question drew an impassioned objection. Laurence jumped from his seat and hurled his writing pad across the desk. Before Judge Kent could respond to the protest, Mr. Goretti made an aggressive posture toward Laurence and pressed the question by asking, "I want to know, the court wants to know!" Mr. Laurence raced to the bench repeating his objection. The judge sustained. Mr. Goretti stood nose to nose with Mr. Laurence waiting for a response. Neither of the adversaries flinched; no outward signs of vulnerability were displayed. Moments passed and finally Judge Kent asked the defense to continue. Mr. Goretti then smiled, never losing his focus on his counterpart and responded, "Yes, Your Honor. It will be my pleasure". Mr. Goretti with the curtains pulled, on center stage and under the spotlight had entered the theater with bravado; it was his moment in time. His fifteen minutes of fame. He had set the tone and the pace for the next six hours of testimony.

Mr. Goretti hurriedly moved toward the projection screen. Taking his place as if he were a circus ringmaster, he instructed his team to begin the performance. "Rob, page number 8", he barked. This exhibit was produced. It was a complete listing of services, drugs and supplies that were billed for the hospitalization. Each item had a description, a charge amount and a dispense date; an official inventory of provisions and interventions. Mr. Laurence had previously presented this document as an inventory of surgical supplies. His intent was to create a sense of doubt in the juror's mind that the medical records are inconsistent. And to astonish the court that a mistake had been made in the doling out of an unauthorized drug. A particular medicine that was determined to be harmful if used, contraindicated, a deliberate act of malpractice.

In the course of the direct examination of the doctor an item with a dispense date of March 28th was singled out. The item was a medicine. Heparin was listed as billed; dispensed and charged to a patient's account on the day of surgery. The patient's allergy to Heparin and the doctor's use of Heparin would be a wanton act by the defendant; an incontestable deed of malpractice. Mr. Laurence had previously hammered the doctor regarding his supervision of the surgical team and his responsibility for the use of the forbidden drug; a relentless torrent of questions and accusations. The defendant admitted his ownership of the process and participants. He did not, however, offer a response at that time to this line of questioning. How the use of a banned drug could have occurred. He did not at the time deny the use of Heparin.

Mr. Goretti pointed to the bill and indeed it listed Heparin with a dispense date of March 28. Then with a titter he asked to see the next page of the bill. His mannerisms were obviously prepared as if he were performing in a community theater; correct lines and timing with hyperbole. This portion of the record listed items that were credited. That is, items that were billed as if they were used and then 'taken off' – removed - because they were not. On this page Heparin was listed as a credit; a drug that was not used. Mr. Goretti then began a personal attack on Mr. Laurence. He suggested that Laurence had attempted to mislead the jury many times. And this was the most shameful attempt; one that makes him reckless in his practice of law. This drew an objection from Mr. Laurence and was sustained by the judge.

Goretti continued by saying, "If your attempt to mislead the jury is not true, why did you stand in front of the projection screen to cast a shadow to block the Heparin credit from the jury's view." Mr. Goretti then mocked Mr. Laurence's body language. This ad-libbing was intended to demonstrate Mr. Laurence's intention to hoodwink the jury. Twisting his angular frame while bending to cast a shadow, his actions drew open laughter from the doctor's wife and an objection from Laurence. The objection was interrupted by Mr. Goretti when he turned to Laurence and said. "Don't do it! Don't you, dare do it!" And following that with, "Object to what, you are a little late, Mr. Laurence, you introduced the bill. You started it with this trick you tried to pull".

Judge Kent then admonished the attorneys to stop squabbling and address the court. This volley in turn caught the attention of the jurors, awaking some and amusing others. The judge, holding back a smile, sustained the objection regarding Mr. Goretti's exaggerated body language. The Judge then denied the presumed objection regarding the bill stating, "Mr. Laurence, it was your idea to introduce the bill as evidence; you have to roll with the punches". This shifted the momentum of the trial. The emphasis was refocused from the disingenuous doctor to the unscrupulous attorney. Legal maneuvering made for dirty business and muddied the waters of reason; reputations and egos being the most susceptible to staining. Although this may have been an even trade with regard to magnitude; with each side scoring style points. All things being equal, however, the doctor wins.

Mr. Goretti then asked, "Would it be a fair and honest thing to represent to the jury that this credit indicates that you gave her Heparin that day?" The doctor responded by saying, "No, it would not." Mr. Goretti would not relinquish the emotional control of the courtroom. Taking another stab at Laurence's integrity, his intention was to dehumanize him and discredit the merits of the lawsuit. He then followed up by asking, "But that is what he, Mr. Laurence, tried to do, isn't it?" The doctor replied, "Yes, sir". Mr. Laurence objected and the judge sustained. It was too late; at this point jurors were smiling.

One could sense that Goretti was on a roll. The lay of the land was familiar, his footing firm. With the accusation of inappropriately dispensing Heparin put to rest, he moved to the next allegation. Barking his request for Rob to display Number 1388, the aggressive strategy continued. The ACT test results were displayed. After that he requested Rob to display Number 1393. The two documents cataloged relevant information. Document Number 1388 was a constructed spreadsheet listing time and values of the testing in an easy to read format. And document 1393 was the actual medical record. The documents compared and contrasted the time of testing and the resulting values for ACTs.

The projected image was a hodgepodge of numbers and times; confusing and repetitive. The argument presented by Mr. Laurence centered on the inconsistencies of the intervals; the times between testing. Distrust in the intervals, recorded times and values would create a question in the jury's mind that the doctor was not in control of the surgical team. And that proper testing with respect to standard of care had not been followed. Laurence asserted that there was an eighteen minute interval between the first and second tests as documented in the chart. Additionally, he proclaimed there was a one hundred a twenty minute interval between the second and third tests. The one hundred and twenty seven minute interval would be a violation in established protocol; ACTs were to be taken at every fifteen minutes. The test documentation was handwritten from tickets generated by the ACT machine. And the dates and times on the tickets did not match the dates and times recorded in the chart.

Mr. Goretti contended that the eighteen minute interval was between the second and third tests. And the one hundred and twenty seven minute interval represented the baseline test performed at 8:15 AM, prior to surgery, and the first test performed after the introduction of Hirudin at 10:28 AM. The argument began a debate on where to start the comparison; what test result represents the first test. Resolution to the dispute was impossible. Dates and times did not correlate. The dispute had become too difficult for the jury to follow. Mr. Goretti sensed the jury's boredom and instead of expending a vast amount of energy to win a battle he decided to quit that engagement and win the war. He quickly shifted gears moving from the deliberation of the details, to becoming a salesperson.

Mr. Laurence had spent a great deal of energy exposing time and date anomalies; an exhaustive barrage of detail and conjecture.

Credibility of the reports teetered on the explanation of these anomalies; could the data be trusted as an accurate accounting of what really happened. Mr. Goretti made the more convincing argument without the support of evidence. Turning toward the jury and positioning himself to block the plaintiff's attorney from the jury's view, he pointed toward the courtroom clock. He then asked the doctor, "Can clocks be wrong as the one in this courtroom?" The doctor concurred with the example. He added, "Clocks can be wrong, they are often incorrect. Does anyone really know what time it is?" The courtroom clock had not been changed from daylight savings time. Then Mr. Goretti asked the doctor if he was responsible for the time settings on the ACT machine; and if he is responsible for printing the reports. The defendant responded with, "No". Then the doctor was asked if he had ever set the time or printed a report. The defendant once again answered, "No". And regarding the tickets that had an incorrect date, he asked, "How did these tickets get into the chart?" The doctor responded with, "I don't know." Mr. Goretti then suggested that the tickets were left on the machine from a surgery performed two days prior to the 28th. And the tickets were simply torn from the ACT machine and placed in the patient's chart by mistake. To further validate his hypothesis, he presented a surgery log that indicated no surgeries were performed on the 27th. As for the incorrect time on the tickets, well, clocks are often wrong. Before moving to the next line of questioning, Goretti placed an exclamation point to the time and interval question by asking the judge if he is responsible for setting the courtroom clock. Before His Honor could scold Goretti, he apologized for the question. End of discussion.

The defense had at this point discredited the bill; the document that listed surgical supplies and interventions. The bill suggested Heparin was administered during surgery as it was charged to the patient's account and had been credited as an item not used. The defense had explained the discrepancies regarding inconsistent time intervals for the ACT tests. Mr. Goretti had even convinced the jury that no clocks can be trusted as evidenced by the timepiece in the courtroom. By anyone's assessment, the defense had shot down the first two allegations. The next targets in his sights were the three op-notes.

I could not image how Mr. Goretti was going to contend with the facts to manipulate the jury's perception of the differences in the op-notes. His gesticulation as he prepared himself for the next barrage of information did not show any trepidation. He turned from his desk with a legal pad. From my vantage the note pad had three large Roman numerals. Each numeral had one word written beside it. I stretched to decipher the data and could not. Mr. Goretti then asked Rob to present pages 54 and 57; two of the op-notes that had been questioned by Mr. Laurence.

Mr. Goretti then asked the doctor how many op-notes are typically dictated for a surgery. His answer, as it was under direct examination was, "One, only one". The defendant was then asked if the op-notes were his dictation. As with previous testimony, he answered yes, to both documents. The attorney then pointed toward the header which identified the document as an Operative Note and the footer which listed the page number and the dictation software vendor's name. Unlike his nervous demeanor under direct examination, the doctor was calm and confident. And when he was asked the next question he presented himself as a software expert; a shift from being technology-challenged physician to being a savvy computer specialist.

Mr. Goretti asked the doctor to explain the difference in the op-notes. The first op-note had even spacing and fluidity and the second had the added paragraph with different fonts and irregular spacing. The doctor shifted his focus from the screen to the jury; turning in his chair to engage the listeners. This in turn redirected the juror's focus from the screen to the defendant. The animation of his hands and facial expression as he explained how this scenario could happen were noticeably rehearsed. His explanation described how a document sent to a specific printer could generate a document that is clean and orderly as Page Number 54. The printer that produced the clean document is one that is configured to accept print jobs from the hospital's software; an authorized, networked device. The document on Page Number 57 was probably printed on a non-approved printer that has been connected to a PC; an unauthorized, slaved device. So, the same op-note containing the same information will print differently depending on the printer that is selected. The defendant concluded by saying, "This sort of thing happens all of the time." Declaring that print jobs vary from printer to printer gave the jury a tangible explanation for the variance in the op-notes. If they were looking for a reason to trust the doctor, he had given them cause. Plausibility did not matter, his explanation was a technical essay based on improbability. Completing the explanation he lowered his hands and turned toward the attorney to await his next queue.

The attorney then focused the doctor's attention on the suspicious paragraph. Each point in the section was addressed. First, the 'wet adhesions' reference was shown to exist in other medical records. Second, the avoidance of Heparin mentioned in the paragraph was also listed as a drug not utilized in the perfusionist record. And, third, the use of Hirudin as an anticoagulant was referred to in other records as a drug that was dispensed. Mr. Goretti's point was to beg the question as to why would the doctor go to the trouble to add a paragraph for self-serving reasons when the same information was already listed elsewhere. That is, the doctor would have had to modify more than the op-notes to cover his tracks. Hopefully the jury realized the attorney's skill in spinning a story is much greater than the doctor's talents in scheming; clumsiness should not be a defense.

Mr. Goretti's next question was bold and risky. He effectively placed every juror in the doctor's shoes and asked, "Now, let's you and I think about something. If you were going to go into an operative note; and let's assume you have the ability to do the cutting and pasting that was suggested by Mr. Laurence. And you did that, you changed it. Would you then leave the first operative note that you supposedly changed in the chart and sign it?" The defendant's response was, "Of course not".

The defense's attempt to sidestep the multiple op-note matter was not completely successful. The explanation of the added paragraph as a network printer glitch may have been above the juror's level of understanding. Of course this concerned me that they may discard the testimony completely; or else disregard it as unimportant. Or, that they may accept what they did not completely understand as a statement of truth; either option requires a high level of faith and a good set of blinders. And the introduction of the notion of the doctor as a clumsy falsifier of documents; an impotent mole if he were to leave the original op-note in the file was absurd! This had a comedic effect on the jury; no one could believe the doctor to be that dim-witted. This was a crack in the armor of the defense; defense by smoke and mirrors is no defense. This could be an opportunity for the plaintiff to exploit.

This concern did not escape Mr. Goretti. He is smart enough to not fight a battle he cannot win; his strategy to avoid the subject completely was a sound legal maneuver. And any attempt to dwell on the issue would make it more of a concern to the jurors; and lend credibility to Mr. Laurence's conspiracy campaign. Shifting gears to focus the court on a more positive note, Mr. Goretti asked the doctor to go back to the beginning, "Tell the ladies and gentlemen of the jury a little about yourself". It is time to re-establish the balance of the clumsy doctor.

The doctor is the son of immigrants; parents struggling to make ends meet in a community located in Detroit. Attending a public high school and earning an undergraduate degree from the University of Detroit in Medicine in 1971 he was a middle class student. His achievements in college presented him the opportunity to attend Stanford University in California. There he trained in cardiothoracic surgery completing the requisites in 1982. At that time he moved to Birmingham and entered into a professional arrangement with Vulcan Clinic. Since moving to Birmingham the doctor has had published works in several books and periodicals. He conducts eight to ten teaching seminars a year. Added to that, he is the point-person for research projects; one of which involves the re-engineering of the heart for improved blood flow for heart attack patients. For this achievement he holds a patent. The attorney asked the doctor, "How many years have you practiced medicine in Birmingham?" His reply was twenty five years. The attorney then asked, "Is practicing medicine all that you do?" His reply was, "Yes except for the time I am in the courtroom."

This retreat from the details of the hospitalization gave the jury an opportunity to see the doctor as a person who had worked his way up the ladder. He appeared to be much more relaxed and controlled as he discussed his saga. An average person from humble beginnings; who was now victimized by the legal system. The doctor made reference to the time he spends practicing medicine as full time, except for the time spent in court. This was an attempt to show the jury how unexpected the suit was and how out of place the doctor was in the court room. The truth is; this is not his first visit to a court room as a defendant. He was recently sued for a Heparin related case where a patient's foot was amputated because of a misdiagnosed condition related to Heparin. This medically related fact is inadmissible as unrelated to this case. With the recoil to more pleasant topics completed, the testimony returned to the accused. The coming to America success story returned to the medical history.

Mr. Goretti returned to the details of the first admission and the doctor's involvement with that hospitalization. Medical records were displayed that diagnosed the patient as having unstable angina. That is, she had a heart attack while at rest, a condition that is considered more serious than a heart attack that occurs as a result of physical stress. The notes indicated the doctor was consulted on February 29th after an arteriogram was performed. The attorney then asked the doctor to step down from the witness stand and take a model of the heart to explain how an arteriogram works.

As the doctor took his position, each juror leaned forward as the demonstration began. The defendant described how a catheter is inserted into the femoral artery and how it is guided to the heart; snaking its way through the body. And when reaching the heart he described why dye is released and how a movie is made as the colorant makes its way through the arteries. He then explained that if a blockage is present the dye will stop, pooling in the affected area, indicating the source of the angina.

This worked perfectly for the defense. Long forgotten are the irregularities of the op-notes and fresh in the minds of the jurors is the doctor, the educator. This is what the jurors wanted to see, confirmation that a chosen member of the clan still has his anointing. The doctor continued his lesson by comparing the size of the model heart with that of his own. He passed the model to the attorney and then fashioned his hands to represent the size and shape of his heart. Locking his fingers and twisting his hands to improve his view, the necessary adjustments were made. This process took more time than it would seem. He then placed his clasped hands on his chest; this placing of the hands on his chest to indicate where the heart is located in the body. More than that, the body language looked to be more of a plea for leniency than an anatomy tutorial; an act of contrition. He paused in a prayerful pose, his position frozen so that all could make the reference. After what seemed to be an uncomfortable period of silence, he retrieved the model from the attorney and continued to explain the workings of the heart. Some workings more subtle than others, I feared.

The doctor pointed to the mitral valve. A mitral valve condition had been diagnosed on March 26th. At that time, Dr. Pantheras suggested that this condition could be resolved in the future and did not present an imminent danger. The doctor, however, did not mention the cardiologist's opinion and took advantage of the opportunity to paint a gloomier picture, a more ominous prognosis. He explained that there is a minimum systolic pressure that is required to make the valve work properly; to close completely. The complete closing of the valve would prevent blood from backwashing into the lungs, "The blood was not going in the direction God had intended", he said. And as he stated the patient's condition had worsened and her blood pressure could not support the valve's function. The attorney asked what does this mean in layman's terms and the doctor responded, "She was drowning in her own fluids."

The juror's reaction to the statement was mixed. Some looked aghast. Some looked sickened and others were emotionless. Having the doctor get up close and personal with the jury was genius. Having him explain in graphic detail a patient so close to death was dramatic. Painting a picture that she was literally going under for the third time and he, her lifeguard, jumping into harm's way in an attempt to save her was heart wrenching. Even though we all enjoy a tale of intrigue and corruption what we don't want to believe is that our doctors are less than saints; people placed here by a higher calling to serve our intimate medical needs. And to believe otherwise would upend a balance, a precarious equilibrium needed to accept without question their interventions in our lives. I saw this on each of the jurors' faces; a countenance one might witness at a revival meeting. The only thing missing was the sound of an occasional hallelujah.

On a roll, the doctor continued his in-service. The attorney asked a simple question, a very direct question, "What causes a heart attack?" The query once again raised the interest level of the jury. It seemed that they could relate to the subject, everyone knew someone that had experienced this condition. And everyone will eventually face heart failure. The doctor pointing to a chart of a heart placed on a tripod in front of the juror's box gave a twofold answer. One type of heart attack is caused when plaque dislodges from the artery wall and blocks the flow of blood; creating a damming effect. Another type occurs when the heart works harder and requires more fuel, more blood. And a narrowed artery due to plaque inhibits that flow of required blood to the heart muscle. Without the necessary blood flow, the heart muscle dies; this is myocardial infarction. The patient suffered from the narrowing of three arteries. The doctor pointed to each artery that needed bypassing and demonstrated the connection points of the grafts. A remarkably simple concept wrought with potential complications.

The attorney then asked the doctor to use the charts on the tripod to describe the first bypass surgery. Flipping to a page that displays a full image of a body, the doctor described the vein harvesting process. The first harvest is not a vein at all. It is the mammary artery located behind and slightly to the left of the sternum. It is a reliable conduit, a predictably effective channel for the blood to flow because it is so large. The remaining grafts are harvested from the right leg. This graft material can be a bit more challenging. Varicose veins, or diseased veins, cannot be used. The grafts are then attached on one end to a reliable source of oxygenated blood. The other end is attached to the diseased artery beyond the blocked or affected area.

The process of revascularization takes about two and one half hours to complete. The doctor then turned toward the attorney and shrugged his shoulders and smiled. This mannerism signaled to the jury that this is an extremely routine procedure; an everyday occurrence; a walk in the park for a miracle worker. The attorney asked the question to make sure no one had any doubt, "Anything happen during this surgery that was out of the ordinary, anything to flag you as being an unusual risk?" He raised his hands and said, "Nothing, nothing at all." All seemed right with the world as the jurors leaned back into their seats. The doctor returned to the witness stand. All in all, the past thirty minutes had been a windfall for his case; knowledgeable, engaging, accommodating; all of the qualities one would want from a medical provider. He finally displayed a caring bedside manner; a characteristic not experienced by his patient.

Mr. Goretti returned to the nuts and bolts of the evidence. He asked Rob to display page 288, the platelet counts for the first hospitalization. The doctor was first asked to explain in layman terms why the platelets are important. The defendant described platelets, or thrombocytes, as the cells circulating in the blood that are involved in the cellular mechanisms of primary homeostasis leading to the formation of blood clots; the body's way of repairing wounds. A low level of platelets predisposes a person to bleeding, while high levels may increase the risk of thrombosis, or clotting. Platelet values were then displayed for dates prior to and after the surgery. The doctor was asked to comment on the values, were they within normal ranges or not. According to the doctor, all of the values were within normal range. And when he was asked to comment on the value recorded the day after surgery, he admitted there was a significant drop, although an expected drop. All of the values in his opinion were standard.

Mr. Goretti asked why a drop in platelet counts occurs after surgery. The doctor's response was quite interesting. Even though he had lost the jury's attention with the technical terminology, he said that during surgery there is a loss of blood. When the bone is cut, fat bleeds, fluid is lost; that is an expected consequence of surgery. Lost blood is replaced with what is called packed red blood cells. This type of blood transfusion lacks platelets and the patient received four bags of the packed red blood cells the night of her surgery. When testing platelet counts the introduction of this type of transfusion will cause hemodilution. Hemodilution is the mixing of whole blood with blood that does not have platelets. The doctor used as an example, salt water. Adding fresh water to saltwater reduces it salinity until the point, if enough fresh water is added, the saltwater will no longer taste salty. And if salinity is platelet count, the blood becomes platelet poor. I could only imagine the sleeping juror's thoughts of what does saltwater have to do with anything!

The point had been made. The platelet count may have been affected by hemodilution. This may offset the argument that off-pump bypass surgeries do not contribute significantly to a drop in platelet count. With each detail, Mr. Goretti provides an answer – a rebuttal to each accusation.

The reason for the extreme effort to coach the jury on platelet count trending, when and why there are fluctuations in the count became apparent. Mr. Goretti asked that Page 1219 be displayed for the court. The displayed document presented a page from a book authored by an expert on Thrombocytopenia. The text was read by Mr. Goretti, "Most often HIT presents as an unexpected platelet count drop five to ten days after surgery." Displaying exhibit 298, the medical record documented a platelet count of 163,000 on March 6th. The doctor was asked if this were an unexpected fall; his was response was no. Then he was asked if the lower platelet count of 163,000 occurred within five to ten days after surgery; he responded it happened the next morning, less than five days. Then he asked the doctor the root meaning of the word Thrombocytopenia. Its root meaning is low platelet count. Mr. Goretti asked the doctor what blood platelet value is considered low where you perform surgery. He answered, "100,000." The attorney then said that some sources list a value of less than 150,000 as low, did the patient fall below that mark. He answered, "No." And finally, he asked did the patient have Thrombocytopenia. The defendant said, "Absolutely not!"

Mr. Goretti walked toward the jury rubbing his temples with each index finger. He paused as if to sort through the information. He then summarized the testimony for the jurors. "The patient has surgery; bleeding and loss of fluids occur. The patient is given a transfusion to replace the fluids. The transfusion blood is packed red blood cells without platelets; does not have any. A test is performed a day or so after surgery and the platelet count is low. The cause of the low platelet count is hemodilution. The mixing of the blood without platelets with the patient's blood causes a reduction in the overall platelet count. So, by the time the patient is discharged, the count is back to baseline; which is what is expected. Then, let's look at the material to see what happens next."

He read a passage from the expert author's test. "From a chronological point of view, the first abnormal platelet count evolution which would lead to investigating patients with HIT after cardiac surgery is the absence of platelet count recovery within the first five days following surgery." The count dropped to 163,000 the day after surgery and then rose to 285,000 the day of discharge; which was five days after cardiac surgery. The doctor confirmed this increase as a defined recovery; a recovery within guidelines of the expert's text. The attorney also inserted that a thrombosis, a clot, did not occur within the five to fourteen days after surgery, a secondary condition for HIT. The doctor confirmed that a clot did not occur after discharge.

Mr. Goretti once again positioned himself in front of the jury. Focusing his attention on the jurors he said, "Let's get back to the real world". Requesting that Page Number 246 be displayed, he directed his questions to the doctor. While not surrendering eye contact with the jury, he asked "This is the Progress Note for the day representing the platelet count of 163,000, correct?" The doctor confirmed his statement. The attorney then asked, "Who was the doctor that saw her?" The doctor answered, "Dr. Houston". Smiling he asked the defendant, "You are not Dr. Houston, are you?" Before the doctor could respond he said, "Of course you are not." The attorney had been successful in clouding the waters as to the definition of HIT and now he is distancing his client from responsibility.

The attorney continued this approach by requesting the presentation of Page Number 254. This progress note documented a low platelet count and an Ultrasound test that was ordered by Dr. Micah. The Ultrasound confirmed a thrombotic event; clots near the femoral area. Dr. Micah, as did Dr. Houston the previous day, continued the prescription of Heparin. Once again, the attorney further distanced his client from accountability by stating the obvious; his client was not treating the patient the days when HIT may be suspected. This theme continued for each day until the patient was discharged. And at discharge the platelet count had risen substantially. At that time the blood thinning drug was changed from Lovenox, which is Heparin, to Coumadin. Coumadin is an orally prescribed blood thinner.

The defense had accomplished several objectives to this point. One significant achievement was shattering the allegation regarding the dispensing of Heparin during surgery. The billing of Heparin and the crediting of the drug proved to be a pivotal event; one that cast aspersion on Mr. Laurence and doubt on the veracity of the case. Another was Mr. Goretti's contempt of time and the distrust in clocks. This defused the 'who did what and when' bomb that could have given the conspiracy theory legitimacy. The single open item that was not fully addressed was the op-note. This issue was glazed over by the defense as an act of a careless forger; a tongue-in-cheek rationalization to dismiss the aberration as farfetched fantasy of the plaintiff. No explanation was provided and the multiple op-notes were not given a second thought. Add to that the distancing of the doctor from the patient's care on significant days regarding key conditions. He feigned ignorance regarding the decisions made by others between the surgery and the discharge date; an avoidance to second-guess a colleague. With the tone of the trial in tuned to his predilection, Mr. Goretti moved to the events of the second hospitalization.

Mr. Goretti continued his strategy of distancing the defendant from direct medical intervention for the patient. From the time of the initial discharge on March 9th to his awareness of the second hospitalization on the March 22nd, he absolved the doctor of any responsibility. Although the defendant was responsible for the monitoring of the Coumadin, testing was performed by another doctor and the results of the testing sent to Dr. Zopyros. The INR, International Normalized Ratio, values, test results for the effectiveness of this drug, were unstable and migrating toward a level that would indicate a thicker, more clotting susceptible blood chemistry. The values ranged from a high of 5.2 on the day of discharge to 1.1 nine days later. An INR value of 1.1 meant that blood viscosity was well below the normal range of 2.5 to 3.5; a red flag that something was wrong. The doctor said he reviewed the results and concluded there was no reason to expect any abnormalities. The patient was readmitted on March 21 with chest pains.

Mr. Goretti asked the doctor to summarize from the medical records the justification to perform a second surgery. The doctor leaned forward in his chair to view the monitor that displayed the patient's chart. Adjusting his glasses to improve his vision, he began by stating that the patient was re-admitted on the 21st with angina; chest pains that occurred while sleeping. A blood test was performed that indicated that the enzymes, Protonin, were elevated. The attorney interrupted and asked the significance of this finding. The doctor went on to explain that when heart muscle dies, myocardial necrosis occurs and a specific chemical is released. The chemical is unique to the heart muscle and the presence of this enzyme in the blood indicates loss of blood supply to that organ. Continuing, he said an arteriogram was performed by Dr. Iapetos which indicated the grafts had clotted. Dr. Iapetos inserted a stent into a graft to provide temporary relieve. Once again, the attorney interrupted and asked the doctor to describe a stent. The defendant responded, stating that a stent is a collapsed wire cage that is positioned in the affected area of the artery. When positioned correctly it is re-shaped; expanded to increase the opening of the artery for improved blood flow. The attorney then asked why the remaining grafts were not stinted. The doctor then read from the record. It was the cardiologist's opinion the grafts were tortuous; too crooked to safely navigate the stent into place. There was a fear of puncturing an arterial wall and that prevented the cardiologist from attempting this procedure.

Pausing for a moment to read ahead before speaking, he then continued the rationalization. The record documents a discussion to utilize other treatment options. The options centered on pharmaceutical solutions. All were dismissed as potentially ineffective; a waste of time and effort. And at that point, when additional stinting was unviable and alternate options unavailable, the decision to move forward with the surgery was made. The defendant shrugged his shoulders as if to communicate his frustration with having to explain his actions.

Mr. Goretti's tactical approach in defending his client was more than mere coincidence. The previous testimony had painted the picture of a serious condition; one that included an unexplained and unanticipated clotting of three bypass grafts. Pulling away from the medical details, he asked the doctor a question that would legitimize his qualifications for proceeding with another surgery. Much like the deviation from the medical details taken earlier to have the doctor relive his life's history, he now would be given an opportunity to brag a bit regarding his experience. The attorney positioned himself in front of the jury making eye contact with each; he then asked the defendant, "How many CABGs, coronary bypass grafting procedures have you performed in your career?" The defendant actually looked surprised by the question. He paused as if to use his fingers to calculate the total and then replied, "Thousands; seven to eight thousand." The doctor was then asked how many of those were re-do surgeries. He replied, "Approximately ten percent." And in addition to CABGs, do you perform other surgeries such as valve replacements? The doctor responded, "Yes, several of times". The jurors affirmed their kudos of the doctor's testimony with a symbolic glance toward their cohorts and a nodding of the head. With the doctor's experience solidified in the juror's mind, the attorney went to the next step; preparation for surgery.

Mr. Goretti then asked what significant event happened next. The doctor continued reading from the chart. On Monday, March 25 the patient had chest pains while at rest in the hospital. An electrocardiogram was ordered and the results indicated ongoing ischemia; blood loss to the heart. Heavy medication was ordered to reduce the pain and effects of the dysfunction. The attorney asked the defendant if a patient has had two heart attacks and clotted bypass grafts, generally what are the options. The doctor responded, "Surgery, surgery, surgery." If the patient cannot have angioplasty, then an operation is required. Treating the patient with medicine runs the risk of sudden death.

The doctor continued his translation of the chart indicating Dr. Pantheras had ordered a Heparin Allergy test on the 25th. The attorney then asked if that suggested that the patient had Thrombocytopenia, he answered, "Absolutely not!" The doctor went on to say that many patients develop an allergy to Heparin after surgery. The attorney then distanced his client from responsibility by asking, "If Heparin antibodies are suspected, should this medicine be discontinued?" The doctor answered, "Yes." The attorney continued, "Did you order the allergy test?" The doctor responded, "No." "Did you suspect Heparin antibodies?" Once again, the doctor answered, "No." Mr. Goretti turned toward the jury and asked, "Them and they may have suspected a problem, not you. Is that correct?" The defendant answered, "Yes, them and they."

The attorney then asked the doctor to continue his reading of the chart. Alternate medical interventions involving angioplasty and pharmaceutical options were dismissed as unviable. Moving forward with plans for another surgery, a more pressing problem moves to the top of the list. Readying the patient for a re-do surgery. Weaning the patient from certain medications that would compromise the surgery also increased immediate medical concerns. The patient was taking Plavix, a drug that causes the blood cells to become less sticky, resistant to clotting. This medication provided some relief and protection from additional angina. But, it also creates an unstable surgical environment; uncontrolled bleeding. The doctor responded to a question from the attorney regarding an appropriate weaning time. He responded, "Five days is optimal; three days at least."

Mr. Goretti asked what significant events occurred on Tuesday, March 26. The defendant continued reading from the chart regarding a procedure that was performed. An echo indicated that the mitral valve was dysfunctional. The patient did not have chest pain but did have mild dyspnea. Which means Ms. Carroll was getting short of breath. The cause of the shortness of breath is the result of inefficient blood flow. The atypical holosystolic murmur means that the leakage can be heard with a stethoscope. The magnitude of the mitral regurgitation was severe. The valve itself was normal but the heart muscle supporting the valve has been compromised due to decreased blood flow. The muscle had become weakened, or had died; myocardial necrosis. The lack of muscle support caused the valve to remain partially open and blood flow reversed. This condition did not permit the blood to become fully oxygenated and made the patient short of breath.

Mr. Goretti realized the danger in assuming the jury could make sense of the testimony. Recapping a segment of testimony as a means of maintaining focus is one thing, telling the jury what to think is another. At this point the attorney turned toward the jury and said, "Let me get this straight. The patient had suffered a heart attack on Monday, March 25th and Doctor Pantheras ordered a Heparin allergy test. And on Tuesday, March 26th, a procedure indicated another problem, a serious condition. The patient was diagnosed as having Mitral Valve regurgitation; a critical dysfunction of the heart that affected the patient's ability to breath".

Mr. Goretti asked the doctor to go on. The doctor read from the medical chart for Wednesday, March 27th. The result of the Heparin Allergy test was returned from Magic City Medical Center. The test was positive for antibodies; an allergy to Heparin. The attorney interrupted the doctor and asked, "Who ordered the Heparin Allergy test on the 25th?" The doctor responded, "Dr. Pantheras." "Who continued the prescription of Heparin on the 25th and 26th?" The defendant responded, "Dr Pantheras." The attorney then asked, "What happened when Dr. Pantheras reviewed the results?" The doctor responded reading from the medical records that Heparin was discontinued.

The attorney in a dramatic gesture sat on the edge of the defendant's desk. Looking down with his shoulders slumped; he looked the part of an exhausted combatant; emotionally spent. He had worked those in attendance that had paid attention into an impassioned state. On one hand he had painted the picture of a desperately ill patient with a deteriorating condition and limited medical options, and on the other, a heroic doctor's attempt to save her. His mannerism was unmistakable. He remained motionless and with an eerie intuitiveness, just as the judge raised his hand to admonish the attorney to continue, he rose and walked to the defendant and placed his hand on the doctor's shoulder. He asked, "With Heparin no longer an option, how did you proceed with the patient's care?"

The doctor followed suit, shaking his head as if reliving the moment, he continued his account of the final day. An anticoagulant is required to perform surgery. With Heparin no longer an option, an alternative was selected; an alternative that has significant limitations. Hirudin was chosen as the most desirable choice. The major drawback in using Hirudin is that there is no drug that will reverse its effect; no antidote. The drug has to wear off, if you will. There was some discussion regarding the need for an Ecarin Clotting Time – ECT - a machine to monitor the effects of the drug; an instrument to manage the coagulation of the blood. The hospital did not have an ECT machine; some literature suggested its necessity. The perfusionist and his staff attempted to locate the apparatus and was unsuccessful, none to be found. Additional research indicated that the surgery could be performed using existing equipment; the Activated Clotting Time (ACT) and the Thromboelastograph (TEG). Mr. Goretti read from a publication regarding the use of Hirudin in CABG surgeries. The document endorsed by several thoracic surgeons stated that monitoring Hirudin surgeries with a TEG is consistent and reliable. The attorney asked the doctor, "Under the circumstances in Ms. Carroll's case, was the use of the ACT and TEG appropriate in keeping with the standard of care?" The doctor responded, "It was." Mr. Goretti asked, "Was it reasonable to do?" The defendant replied, "It was very reasonable to do."

The defense had to this point discredited anomalies regarding medical record keeping as incidental. They had distanced the defendant from direct responsibility for misdiagnosing medical conditions. They had dissociated the doctor from his colleagues regarding the prescribing of harmful drugs. They had described the doctor as a blue collar individual who had worked his way up the ladder. They had portrayed him as a good kid, conscientious student, a gifted surgeon and a family man. And now, the final face the doctor will wear is that of an interventionalist whose actions were reasonable and one whose actions displayed sound logic. The last hurdle was to address the charge made against the doctor, the charge of acting wantonly; reckless endangerment.

The doctor compared and contrasted the condition of the heart for each of the two surgeries. The first surgery found the heart encased in a pericardial sac, neatly packed and easily located in the chest. The heart of the second surgery was difficult to locate and was covered with wet adhesions that resembled a spider web; a network of tenuous conduits. The second-surgery heart with its wet adhesions was stuck to everything around it; similar to properties of wet plastic wrap. Re-do surgeries within the first year will find the heart to have a web of swollen blood vessels, wet adhesions, which have the consistency of cotton candy. The swollen vessels that envelope the heart oozes blood when touched. Suturing the surface area is like stitching a mailing stamp to Jell-O. The doctor had framed the pitch of a surgical intervention that had little chance of success.

The re-do surgery began at 8:20 AM on Thursday, March 28th. Hirudin was introduced into the patient's body at 10:03 AM. The interval represents one hour and forty three minutes. The doctor spent that time opening the chest, dissecting the wet adhesions and locating the heart; a time that normally takes fifteen minutes. After the tubes were attached to the aorta and the atrium to circulate the blood through the bypass machine, potassium was injected into the heart to stop the pumping action. At that time the cross-clamp was positioned to secure the heart; this took an additional thirty seven minutes.

The heart was cross-clamped for one hour and fifty three minutes, roughly two hours. During that time, the affected areas of the heart were located and cleaned of wet adhesions to connect the bypass grafts. This cross-clamp process took thirty minutes for the first surgery. During this two hour segment of the surgery, the struggle was to separate the wet adhesions of the heart from the lungs. Separating the two caused tears in the heart and repair work using glues and patches were necessary. The effects of the Hirudin wore off and the blood began to thicken. The perfusionist alerted the surgical team the heart-lung machine clotted. The cross-clamp was removed and the heart filled with blood. The heart had been idle for over two hours. Inotropes were introduced to stimulate the heart muscle to contract; to pump on its own. Manual massage was used to assist the chemical stimulation. The wet adhesions continued to bleed. The contractility of the heart was lost; it would not function on its own ability. Hirudin was stopped at 12:34 PM and the patient was pronounced dead at 2:08 PM.

The doctor contended the anticoagulant, Hirudin, did its job. It had effectively thinned the blood and had provided enough time to perform the surgery. The cause of death was not the clotting of the heart-lung machine. The uncontrolled bleeding caused by the wet adhesions required too much time to repair; time that proved to be a detriment to the heart muscle. And the time the heart spent cross-clamped, not beating on its own capability, affected its ability to restart. Contractility was lost. And without contractility, the clotting and bleeding were inconsequential.

Mr. Goretti asked a couple of final questions, "I've asked you questions about this before, but to be absolutely clear and for legal reasons, I'll ask you again: Are you familiar with that degree of reasonable care, skill and diligence normally had and exercised by cardiovascular surgeons today and in 2002? And are you familiar with the standard of care?

The doctor responded, "Yes, I am."

"In the first hospitalization, Ms. Carroll was discharged on the 9th of March. Was your care reasonable and appropriate in keeping with the standard of care?"

The doctor replied, "Yes, it was."

"In the second hospitalization from the 21st of March through the 28th of March, were your decisions reasonable and appropriate in keeping with the standard of care?"

The doctor responded, "I believe they were."

"Did you do the best you knew how to do?"
The doctor answered, "I did my best."
Mr. Goretti retired and the court recessed.

The morning began when Judge Kent asked the defendant to take the stand. He reminded the doctor that he was still under oath. As a result of my recent exposure to the legal process, the concept of making an oath made me suspicious of its veracity. My concern centered on the definition of oath that one would tell the truth even if it were to his detriment. Once a nonbeliever, I'm now converted; I see the light. I am now convinced that the promise to 'tell the truth so help you God' is not that difficult uphold. It is a matter of perspective; where one sits in the stadium affects how one sees the game. After all, what was Mother's cause of death? Was it the lack of the heart's contractility, wet adhesions and uncontrolled bleeding, clotting the heart-lung machine, undiagnosed HIT or a system where a surgeon looks the other way to pass the buck? After all, is it the fall or the sudden stop at the end that causes the problem? To me all things are sequential and relevant; an order of events that produces a result. So, at what point does an event take on a new meaning; when is an event defined as a sudden stop. The defense did not recognize any stops; obviously the doctor asserted she simply fell through the cracks; and continued to fall. It is easy to lose focus and begin to doubt that which you know so well. Harder still to forget is one's beginnings and with me it that starts with my Mother.

I did not leave my chair during the recess. I opted to observe the goings-on of the jury and the defense. The jurors were a mixed bag of personalities. It was very difficult to assess their partiality. My only hope was that they stay awake and pay attention to the happenings in the court room. Before this experience, if I were pressed to define testimony I would have stated it to be a truthful recollection of events. And if that were true then those jurors that sat with their eyes closed would be acceptable trustees of the process. However, there is far more to it than mere words. Mannerisms; nervous tics, shifty eyes, stammering responses, coaching signals, cadence, all were components that affect the meaning and intent of testimony. To be a responsible juror requires complete sensory application; an ability to hear beyond the spoken word.

The defendant had exited the witness stand after Mr. Goretti's cross examination with a smile on his face and a spring in his step. The defense had leveled the playing field and in some respects tilted it toward their liking. The doctor had been knowledgeable and engaging. The defense attorney was successful in steering clear of pitfalls that would compromise the defendant's credibility. All in all, if the trial were to end at this point, without any doubt the jury would find in favor of the doctor. The trial was not over, however, and Mr. Laurence would have an opportunity to re-direct the witness; to expose the pitfalls that were cleverly navigated.

The defendant returned to the stand and was reminded by the judge he was still under oath. The relaxed and confident countenance that he displayed while being guided by his attorney was long gone. In its place was a furrowed brow and a slightly opened mouth; a look more in line with an exhausted distance runner than that of a gifted surgeon. What would happen next? What would Mr. Laurence spring on him? The pressure was on the doctor to maintain consistency; to stay the course. His story was believable and it was his game to lose. Mr. Laurence positioned himself in front of the defendant to address the inconsistencies; to bait the doctor to wander off course.

Re-direct of Dr. Zopyros by Mr. Laurence

Mr. Laurence exposed the most obvious inconsistency by first asking the doctor if he swore to tell the truth. And by swearing to tell the truth, had he been honest in his testimony. And by being honest in his testimony had he mislead the jury. And by misleading the jury would that not be breaking his oath to tell the truth. The doctor's response was expected; his style was not. In answering the questions, his tone and condescending demeanor was in stark contrast to his previous mannerisms of politeness, humility and accommodation. The words he chose were slanted toward a hateful, defensive deportment. Each response was tagged with 'Sir'; clearly a stab at Mr. Laurence. He was clearly a different man under rigorous scrutiny.

The attorney displayed the letter sent to Dr. Allen dated March 29, 2002. The letter stated that the patient had died on the table of a massive generalized thrombosis; an extreme clotting event. The doctor had previously testified that the cause of death was uncontrolled bleeding. And as a consequence, trying to manage the bleeding the heart lost contractility; the ability to pump on its own. This inconsistency was the most flagrant desecration of his testimony. Laurence pressured the defendant to explain why one document, the letter to a colleague, would list a cause of death that was different from the op-notes. The doctor had admitted in previous testimony that the letter was at the very least incomplete. And that the op-notes were to be trusted as accurate. The goal of the attorney was not to argue the validity of one over the other; the aim was to create a suspicion in the juror's mind that the doctor was self-serving. How could a trusted doctor of medicine construct a letter to a colleague hours after the pronouncement of death; then become an unscrupulous counterfeiter in 'doctoring' the op-notes six weeks later to cover his mistakes? Irrelevant to the case, the notion was put forth to the jury as to how many times this sort of thing happens? Expecting to hear a response of never, the doctor replied, "I am sure it happens from time to time."

Mr. Laurence turned and smiled at Ms. Hartselle. He had clearly delivered a severe blow to the doctor's credibility. What had not been clear to me until now was why the doctor ran the risk of alienating the jury by acting with such hostility. Suddenly it dawned on me as I glanced toward a juror. She saw Mr. Laurence smile at his colleague and that seemed to disgust her. I conducted a quick appraisal and saw many more with a similar reaction. Mr. Goretti had played this beautifully. Sending his client to the stand to take the punishment that the plaintiff doled out and reacting with such humanity made him one with the jury. Fighting to save one's reputation is expected. Assisting one in that protection is honorable; and that was the jury's inclination. The defense had orchestrated a scenario where the doctor was the victim, the jury was the savior and the plaintiff was the criminal. How abruptly the tide had turned.

Continuing the theme of creating suspicion in the jury's mind, Mr. Laurence introduced the 'when did you know what you know' line of questioning. The doctor had testified that he was informed of the test results on March 27th indicating the presence of Heparin antibodies; an allergy to Heparin. His testimony also revealed that he and his staff began to research alternatives to Heparin that same day; the day before surgery. Laurence then introduced depositional testimony of Mr. Swindle, the doctor's perfusionist. The defendant had instructed him to research alternatives to Heparin on Friday, March 22nd; six days prior to surgery. The discussion centered on the need for an alternative anticoagulant because of a patient's allergy to Heparin. The doctor did not deny the discussion and simply stated it was a general conversation, shop-talk, and did not pertain to any specific patient. Laurence asked the doctor how many patients he had treated that had the severe clotting anomalies as did Ms. Carroll. The doctor was consistent with his answer and said, "None." The attorney raising his arms above his head in bewilderment could not believe that a random conversation, out of the blue, would have taken place as a matter of coincidence.

The doctor's knowledge, or suspicion, of an allergy to Heparin six days prior to the surgery was significant. His testimony conducted by Mr. Goretti implied that the need for special equipment to monitor and manage the use of Hirudin was not available. And that it would have taken four to five days to have the special equipment, an ECT machine, delivered. His testimony, under oath, put forward the need to act immediately on March 27th to perform the surgery following day with the existing equipment. Mr. Laurence turned to the jury and presented an observation to consider; how much of the urgency to perform surgery was created by the surgeon's failure to act on March 22nd; a day that he and his colleague discussed the suspected Heparin allergy. March 22nd represented a pivotal day in the patient's life, three days prior to the third heart attack, four days prior to the Mitral Valve diagnosis and five days prior to the confirmation of the Heparin allergy and six days prior to death. The delay wasted time; time that could have been utilized to secure the appropriate equipment. And time to wean the patient from Plavix. And time to train the staff in the proper protocol using Hirudin. Time that he said was not available the day before surgery.

The participants in the civil action are required to disclose a list of evidence and witnesses that may be utilized during the course of the trial. The defense had listed a surgeon that had experience performing surgeries similar to this case. This expert witness published a protocol for his staff for several scenarios including the use of Hirudin as an anticoagulant for CABGs. The document listed a local company that could supply the necessary monitoring equipment, an ECT machine, and guaranteed delivery in three to five days. The protocol lists the utilization of ECT, ACT and TEG machines for maximum effectiveness. The hospital furnished the ACT and TEG equipment. The set of rules further defined the frequency of monitoring for each test. The policy required Activated Clotting Time (ACT) testing to be performed at fifteen minute intervals. The doctor was asked if the frequency of testing complied with this standard. His facial expression was that of one caught in a mistake; a weaver caught in the web that he wove. Medical records documented four ACT tests performed for a six hour surgery; one test prior to the procedure to establish a baseline. Conventional protocol mandated testing to be performed at fifteen minute intervals. The defendant listed this surgeon as a colleague to support his decisions regarding the care of the deceased. Under scrutiny, not one key item on the protocol had been followed. In fact, the defendant was not aware the protocol existed prior to the discovery phase of the legal proceedings.

The heart of the case centered on the doctor's monitoring and interpretation of the platelet count. There would not have been a second and third heart attack, uncontrolled clotting and a failed second surgery if certain warning signs had been observed. The doctor denied the patient had Thrombocytopenia until the very end of the trial. And did not recognize its possible existence until it was too late. Mr. Laurence concluded his re-direct by exposing this fiasco. The attorney retrieved a book from his case and held it before the defendant. Posed as if he were an evangelist at a tent revival, he glared at the doctor and stated that he and Mr. Goretti began the cross examination using information from this book. And you said that Ms. Carroll never had HIT. The contention all along was in the numbers. What platelet count value defined HIT? The doctor asserted that HIT requires a value less than 100,000. The hospital declared a benchmark of 130,000. The book authored by a renowned expert placed the value at a fluctuation from baseline of fifty percent; not a fixed value. The patient's platelet count dropped by forty eight percent seven days after the initial exposure to Heparin. The defendant held tightly to his rule that regardless of other conditions that existed, the count never reached the level to cause him concern. Other conditions were in fact an important caveat. The numbers alone were enough to alert a savvy physician that the patient's health was veering off course. Combine that with a major thrombotic event and an attentive surgeon would have recognized the problem; the sound of the alarm would have been deafening.

Mr. Laurence asked the doctor to read aloud from the text that stated the drop in platelet count value of fifty percent coupled with thrombosis is defined as Thrombocytopenia. The doctor continued to read at the request of the attorney, "Heparin-induced Thrombocytopenia should also be suspected whenever a patient develops thrombosis while receiving Heparin." The doctor agreed with the statement but made an interesting comment. He said, "The patient was not receiving Heparin when the clot developed." The attorney spun around and displayed a genuine look of disbelief. The clot had developed in the femoral area of the left leg the day following the first surgery. The patient was admitted seven days prior. Heparin had been given each day of the hospitalization with a massive dose the day of surgery. The day the clot developed, Heparin was not dispensed. When the diagnosis of DVT, deep vein thrombosis, was made the second day after surgery Heparin was again prescribed and given to the patient.

The attorney shifted the focus from the first surgery to the second admission. The question asked of the doctor regarded a type of HIT called sub acute Heparin-induced Thrombocytopenia. Basically, a patient who had exhibited symptoms of HIT that remains unresolved. Once again the attorney presented text from the book that describes the standard of care for a patient with sub acute HIT to postpone cardiac surgery. And when surgery is performed an Ecarin Clotting Time, ECT, machine is required to monitor the coagulation tendency of the blood. The doctor made exaggerated motions; shaking his head in disagreement that HIT was never a viable diagnosis. He displayed exasperation when the requirement for the ECT was mention. Completely in denial that the patient had a problem except for the fact she was dying.

The attorney asked, "What caused Ms. Carroll's clotting?"

The doctor responded, "I don't know."

The doctor had listed a number of possible causes for the clotting in his previous testimony. All of the causes were eliminated except for clotting abnormalities. The doctor qualified his testimony and said the list was not an exhaustive index. The attorney asked if an allergy to Heparin could cause a clotting abnormality. The doctor agreed. Laurence then asked, "Is it still your testimony to the ladies and gentlemen of the jury that even though the Protein C, the Factor V Leiden, and all of the other clotting abnormality tests except for the Heparin antibody test were negative, it is still your testimony that you don't believe she had a clotting abnormality as a result of Heparin antibodies?

The defendant answered, "That's correct."

CHAPTER 6

Rent-A-Doc

Character is like a tree and reputation like its shadow. The shadow is what we think of it; the tree is the real thing.
Abraham Lincoln (1809–1865)

———————

The hallway that leads to the court room is long and not well-lit; the building that encloses it is well over one hundred years old. Plastered walls, tile flooring and a more recent addition of a dropped-ceiling made this portal cavernous. A wooden bench placed near the door of Judge Kent's courtroom served as the waiting area for the next session. It was there I sat. One could hear the approach of an individual long before they were actually seen. The steps reverberated, some louder than others. Elizabeth Hartselle, an associate attorney to Mr. Laurence, made her arrival more pronounced than most. Stiletto high-heeled shoes echoed a rhythmic beat as she turned the corner. Ms. Hartselle could not have had more than a couple of years experience as a legal professional, she was young and attractive. Her role as a member of my legal team was to support Mr. Laurence in the courtroom. Providing a second set of eyes and ears and organizing and fetching documents and exhibits. Her role this morning was to serve as my mental health counselor.

I had arrived early to avoid the rush and anxiety of being late. Waiting outside the courtroom, Elizabeth began to describe the rush of emotions that I had likely felt and may possibly experience. Her relative youthful status faded as she demonstrated wisdom well beyond her experience. One insight she shared that hit home was, Isaac, a partner in the law firm has said time and again that a trial is like a heavy weight boxing match; you deliver a few blows and you take a few – the goal is to be the last one standing. And with that she asked if I was alright?

Deadlocked; a standstill, two competitors equally matched, staffed and equipped. I couldn't assess momentum; which side has it, does it even exist. Optimism was replaced with frustration and both seemed to occupy the same place at the same time – a strange variation of multidimensional physics – a courtroom *Alice In Wonderland*. The situation reminds me of an antiquated statute that is on the books in Kansas: When two trains approach each other at a crossing, both shall come to a full stop and neither shall start up again until the other has gone.

I am convinced that the tie breaker may come in the form of expert witnesses. The defense has two surgeons waiting in reserve and the plaintiff has one. Expert witnesses provide a supposedly third party perspective – a dispassionate point of view that will lend credence to an argument. An expert witness is an authority, who by virtue of education, profession, publication or experience, is believed to have special knowledge of a subject beyond that of the average person, sufficient that others may legally rely upon that opinion.

The expert witness plays an essential role in determining medical negligence. Courts rely on expert witness testimony to establish the standards of care relevant to a malpractice suit. Generally, the purpose of expert witness testimony in medical malpractice is to describe standards of care germane to a given case, identify any breaches in those standards, and if so noted, render an opinion as to whether those breaches are the most likely cause of injury. In addition, an expert may be needed to testify about the current clinical state of a patient to assist the process of determining damages.

In civil litigation, expert witness testimony is much different from that of other witnesses. In legal proceedings involving allegations of medical negligence, "witnesses of fact" - those testifying because they have personal knowledge of the incident or people involved in the lawsuit - must restrict their testimony to the facts of the case at issue. The expert witness, however, is given more latitude. The expert witness is allowed to compare the applicable standards of care with the facts of the case and interpret whether the evidence indicates a deviation from the standards of care. The medical expert also provides an opinion - within a reasonable degree of medical certainty - as to whether that breach in care is the most likely cause of the patient's injury. Without the expert's explanation of the range of acceptable treatment options within the standard of care and interpretation of medical facts, juries would not have the technical expertise needed to distinguish malpractice which is an adverse event caused by negligent care or 'bad care' from maloccurrence which is an adverse event or 'bad outcome'.

The expert witness for the defense was called to the stand and sworn in by Judge Kent. Dr. Benjamin Arnold is a highly skilled surgeon with vast experience in performing all types of cardiovascular procedures, including coronary bypass, cardiac valve repair, and aneurysm surgery, he is also very adept at tackling the most complex surgical problems.

Dr. Arnold Testimony

Mr. Laurence asked Dr. Arnold to tell the court his past history and accomplishments. The doctor responded with little shyness as he threw caution to the wind and raised the bar of vanity. My mother had once told me that it is a poor frog who won't croak for one's pond; one should not be shy in defending one's values and beliefs. Well, I questioned the capacity of the pond as this frog began to reverberate. One may doubt his degree of expertise, but not because of lack of material to make an informed decision.

He began his self tribute by describing himself as a cardiovascular surgeon. And that he had practiced at the San Jacinto Heart Institute, St. Barnabas Catholic Hospital and Lone Star Children's Hospital. Where he was also active in teaching, holding appointments as Clinical Professor of Surgery at the University of Texas Medical School at Houston and at Baylor College of Medicine.

A Phi Beta Kappa honors graduate of the University of Texas at Austin, he had moved to Houston in 1968 to attend Baylor College of Medicine where he graduated with honors in 1972, and was named to Alpha Omega Alpha Honor Medical Society. Upon completion of a General Surgery Residency at Baylor College of Medicine Affiliated Hospitals, Houston, Texas in 1976, he completed a Thoracic and Cardiovascular Surgery Residency at Texas Heart Institute in 1978. Dr. Arnold served in the 1099th Army Hospital Unit of the U.S. Army Reserves from 1972 to 1978.

He continued his rant listing his certifications by the American Board of Surgery (1976), the American Board of Thoracic Surgery (1978), and the American Board of General Vascular Surgery (1983). He casually mentioned himself as a member of numerous professional and surgical societies, including the Society of Thoracic Surgeons, and the American Association of Thoracic Surgeons. Listing himself as a Fellow of the American College of Surgeons and the American College of Cardiology, he punctuated his accomplishments by inserting experience as having lectured in 11 countries and authored 240 articles in surgical literature. He sheepishly grinned as if his next accolade was his prized possession when stating he has enjoyed a national reputation in the field of cardiovascular surgery. He said, "I am listed in 'The Best Doctors in America' and was recently voted 'Houston's Best Doctor' in a poll of nurses".

His most recent experience, however, was much more grassroots in nature. Since semi-retirement he stated his activities ranged from sponsoring a healthcare center for disadvantaged youths in El Paso, Texas to 'filling in' for surgeons who elect to take a leave of absence; a service he called locum tenens. He also served as a volunteer surgeon holding the rank of Colonel in Iraq; where he performed front-line surgical interventions for war wounded soldiers.

His confidence was remarkable. His use of appropriate vocabulary at the precise time was profound. His voice was made for mass communications; not modern radio and television where political or social agenda coupled with sponsorship can make a 'nobody' an instant star. His voice was old-school. Deep and clear, the melodic tone and rhythm commanded attention. His weakest physical characteristic was a slightly receding hairline; the only noticeable mark of time's erosion. Maybe he was the tiebreaker; he had certainly been an icebreaker.

Mr. Laurence guided him through the details of the case; a daily dissection of what was done and missed: the details regarding medications, symptoms and intervention. The witness exposed Dr. Zopyros' lack of insight; his wanton disregard to glaring abnormalities. A common theme of Dr. Arnold's criticism of the good doctor's care was his charge as 'captain of the ship.' Over and over, as Mr. Goretti had pointed toward 'Them' and 'They', Dr. Arnold refocused the court's attention on the singular entity responsible for all outcomes – Dr. Zopyros.

Dr. Arnold did not shy away from calling it as he saw it. His indictment of the defendant was relentless. He began by; firstly, describing Zopyros' lack of response when he discovered a deep vein thrombosis had developed in conjunction with a drastic drop in the blood platelet count. Secondly, the unstable INR values that should have alarmed him of a severe clotting problem. Thirdly, a second admission that was the result of an additional heart attack that was caused by the clotting of the initial bypass grafts. Fourthly, a dire condition that was compounded by the surgeon's lack of acceptance of a suspected blood disorder that caused the clotting anomaly; and the lack on his part of interventional diagnostics to adjust the medications. And lastly, the stubborn, boneheaded decision to move forward with a surgery that was not urgent, utilizing anticoagulants that were unfamiliar. And the performance of a critically complex surgery without the appropriate monitoring devices to assure success was at best reckless and at the least wanton.

Dr. Arnold' next comment was chilling, "The surgeon is the captain of the ship. He is responsible for the souls in his trust. His decision to sail full-speed-ahead without the proper safeguards in place was negligent. He must have felt like the captain of the Titanic as the ship slipped un-recoverably below the waves. As the machine clotted and he realized that his arrogance had caused a death, he should have been sickened. Having reviewed the case record and comparing his actions with my experience and knowledge, I sensed he felt as though he were unsinkable. A real man would stand tall and take responsibility; a lesser male would seek an attorney. It is the captain's place to assume liability.

Mr. Laurence continued for several hours questioning the surgeon's actions and inactions; interventions and ignorance; attention and inattention. The strategy was brilliant; and the effect was lethal. The defensive was punch-drunk. The only collapse of this offensive would be a self-inflicted wound – a ceremonious falling on the sword. Mr. Laurence wrapped up his questioning of the expert witness and was about to give up Dr. Arnold to Mr. Goretti when Isaac caught his attention.

Isaac, a partner in the firm, had been observing the case from the visitors section of the courtroom. His place on the team was that of a scout. He not only scrutinized the opponent to identify strengths and weaknesses, he also evaluated the plaintiff's performance. It was 4: 55 – five minutes before the five-o-clock hour and minutes until the end of the day. Strategically, it was important to leave the courtroom on an emotional highpoint, it was critical to filibuster – to prevent Mr. Goretti from undermining the successes of the afternoon session. Goretti had demonstrated on several occasions a talent, no, a genius for twisting evidence to support his desired outcomes – a strange alchemy of facts and fantasy that he would use to cast as a spell on the court. Isaac knew this all too well and grabbed Mr. Laurence by the arm and unceremoniously spun him around. The ferocity of the action was twofold; the obvious was akin to pulling someone from the path of an oncoming bus – no time to be polite – just save the life. And secondly, the exploit created an opportunity to provide mentoring in hopes of avoiding a blunder in legal strategy.

I overheard Isaac's admonishment of Laurence and I saw Laurence's facial response. He knew Isaac was right – his pride had been bruised. Quickly, Laurence asked the judge if he could continue his direct examination. The judge smiled and agreed to the request. He, too, had presided over many cases where Mr. Goretti had the last word at the expense of his opponents. This was totally alien to me. The anger of colleagues, the positioning of the opponents and the judge's amusement of the goings on; all were activities that were an obvious orchestration to further an agenda.

Mr. Laurence continued his questioning of the witness. The questions were not focused on clinical topics; instead they were more personal in nature. Questions related to remuneration for legal services. Five hundred dollars per hour for deposition time, one thousand dollars per hour for court time and two hundred dollars per hour for reviewing medical charts; numbers that raised the eyebrows of the blue collar workers of the jury. As uncomfortable as it was to disclose this information, it was easier for the jury to accept it coming from the plaintiff. Mr. Laurence blended what may have appeared to be a money loving witness with the activities of a charitable doctor; one who donated his time and efforts to assist the poor and needy.

Even though the clock had struck five and arguably time to adjourn the Judge in a sense of fair play allowed the defense one line of questioning before retiring for the day, Mr. Goretti did not miss the opportunity. I felt as though my body language was obvious; the clock was moving slowly as the hand approached the closing bell. Mr. Laurence was wrapping up his cross examination of Dr. Arnold and I wanted the day to end on a wave of momentum.

Mr. Goretti had the reputation of defending his clients by discrediting his opponents. He particularly had a bad taste for expert witnesses - doctors who he would characterize as fallen angels; a backdoor insult and demonetization of these reprobates. Having a couple of minutes to unload on Dr. Arnold, I sat nervously, waiting to see on what horse of the Apocalypse he would ride. As Goretti approached the witness stand his voice was much different than that I and Dr. Zopyros had experienced. With me he had been stern and polite. With his client he had been sympathetic and professional. With Dr. Arnold, however, he raised the volume of his oratory to the point where his voice failed him. He used inflammatory words accusing the doctor of being a hired gun and a liar. One statement for the benefit of the jury, all comments were for the juror's ears was, "Would you agree that if a man believes money can do anything, would that man do anything for money?"

Mr. Laurence objected and it was sustained. The inference had been made, nonetheless.

Goretti wrapped up the session with the encouragement of the Judge to move on and asked Dr. Arnold a final question. A question whose answer would leave the juror's wondering if this surgeon is all he had made himself out to be. Goretti with his back turned to the witness and facing the jury while donning a sinister smile asked, "How many jobs, surgical positions, have you applied for within the last three years – and how many offers of employment were made?"

Dr. Arnold responded by stating he had worked consistently, as much as he had desired as a locum tenens. And that those employment applications were still pending.

Goretti was more than prepared and shot back a response with visual proof displayed on the screen that was damning. He had secured legal documents where Dr. Arnold had testified in other trials that he was declined employment at several institutions within that time reference. And in one of the documents he had defined locum tenens in layman's terms as a 'rent-a-doc'.

Goretti ended the day by asking Dr. Arnold, asking the court, "Are we to believe the rant and ravings of a rent-a-doc that can't seem to find full-time employment?"

Mr. Laurence objected and it was sustained.

Mr. Goretti said that will be enough for the day.

Judge Kent, as customary, reminded the jury to be back in their seats at 8:30 AM the next morning and to not discuss or research the case with anyone.

The judge's sense of fair play can be interpreted as stacking the deck. To permit Mr. Goretti two minutes at day's end to undermine Dr. Arnold's four hour testimony hardly seems just. I have heard of referees in sporting events giving the all star the benefit of the doubt - is that what is happening here? Could the judge himself be intimidated by the firm? At this point I have become a cynic. After all I was a born again believer in the medical profession prior to my mother's experience. I had been involved in medical scenarios involving other family members where medical professionals communicated, cooperated, were open, and candid; with my encouragement. This experience caused me to backslide and fall from grace. I made my way home as did the participants. Today had been exhausting.

I arrived early for the continuation of Dr. Arnold's cross examination. The halls were empty and the only sound was from the street – muffled traffic noise, an occasional horn, and a traffic cop's whistle. I glanced through the courtroom window to see if anyone had any less sleep than I and to my surprise Mr. Goretti was sitting at the defense table. I watched for a moment and decided to wait on reinforcements before entering.

The jurors made their way to the seats; the legal teams were present as Judge Kent entered the courtroom. Making his usual welcoming comments, he called Dr. Arnold to the stand. Reminding the witness that he was still under oath, Judge Kent pointed toward the defense and said, "Go!"

The slight modification in protocol caught me off guard. The patient and genteel judge did not seem to be as accommodating. The sequence had the sound of one shooting skeet; pull, aim and boom. I heard the word 'go' now I waited for the explosion.

Mr. Goretti was more in character as the morning session began. His mannerisms were mechanical. He strategically asked several technical questions regarding basic medical protocol. Who is responsible; when and where. And what is important to consider; how and why. Having observed Goretti mannerisms, I knew the difference in him going through the motions, so to speak and when he wanted to make his point. He would assume a position behind the witness and place the temple tip of his eyeglasses in the corner of his mouth and roll his eyes as the witness responded. The choreography reminded me of a shark circling its next meal - the arching of the back and the closing of the eyes signaled the impending kill. He then carefully positioned himself and asked a series of critical questions.

Low key and without tipping his hand that he was ready to make the kill, Mr. Goretti acted confused and asked the questions, "Do medical professionals sometimes differ in their opinions?" "And do they sometimes differ if their assessments?" "And do they sometimes see the same game from different seats in the stadium; that is, is it possible to come to a different conclusion utilizing the same diagnostic data?" All of which Dr. Arnold agreed.

Mr. Goretti summarized the testimony by stating, "It is possible and sometimes probable that doctors of equal experience and training can arrive at different conclusions while reviewing the same information. Is it fair and accurate to presume this could happen?" Dr. Arnold agreed. "Can doctors that are equal; arrive at different conclusions?" Dr. Arnold agreed. "Is it then safe to say that reasonable doctors often disagree?" Dr. Arnold agreed.

Mr. Goretti smiled and walked toward the defense table, took a drink of water and asked his associate for a document. From my vantage the piece of paper looked harmless, after all, what else could happen? And as I had feared it was more closely akin to a lethal injection. As Goretti turned to confront Dr. Arnold I felt like I was watching a public execution. Frozen, unable to interfere with what I knew was about to happen, I watched, although a part of me wanted to leave.

Mr. Goretti approached the witness stand and asked the witness to read the document. The document was a CV - Curriculum Vitae. A Curriculum Vitae is a résumé, a document containing a summary or listing of relevant job experience and education, usually for the purpose of obtaining an interview when seeking employment or to legitimize one's professional experience and knowledge. Its purpose today was to hang the witness with the same rope he had spun. A curriculum vitæ is Latin meaning 'the course of life.' At this moment I became ill; what had Goretti uncovered. What in the course of Dr. Arnold' life had he found suspect!

Goretti began by asking the usual questions. Is this your CV? Is it current? Would you like to disclose any inconsistencies? Is it accurate? I grew more ill by the moment; for heaven's sake come clean if there are any problems. Dr. Arnold took the document and confirmed it was his and that it was accurate. For reasons that were unknown to me at the time, my heart sank. I sensed trouble on a grand scale.

Mr. Goretti focused his attention on the credentials; the board certifications. Inquiring as to those he knew were in good standing to present a sense of fair gamesmanship, he closed ranks on his original target – the board certification that was not. Goretti asked the doctor if his Board Certification of General Surgery was current. Arnold shifted his weight from one hip to the other and responded that it was. Goretti's demeanor changed from the amenable legal counselor in search of the truth to a man possessed; charged with destroying the doctor's credibility – in this case my expert witness. I knew who would win this exchange of blows.

Goretti pushed the status of the Board Certification. Firstly, is it current? Secondly, if not, what is the status? Any answer would compromise the integrity of the witness and Goretti had positioned himself into a no-lose situation. The certification in question was one that the doctor had allowed to lapse. He had not filed the necessary application to renew his membership, nor had he submitted the required fees for certification. Dr. Arnold was at least subject to an inconsistency; at worse he had perjured himself. Arnold had the look of the vanquished; Goretti the look of the victor. Jurors were smiling as Goretti took this hired gun to the mat.

Hired gun; Goretti did not let up. To add insult to injury, he asked the witness how much does it costs to sell a colleague 'down the river?' Have you chosen a career of testifying against reputable doctors to make money instead of working for a living yourself. How could you expect the ladies and gentleman of the jury to respect your opinion when you lied under oath?

With each passing moment, Arnold's stature shrank. The once tall standing tree that cast a long shadow was now pruned of its branches and plucked of its leaves. Goretti then restated the costs the plaintiff had to bear to have this 'hired gun' testify. Five hundred dollars per hour for depositions; a thousand per hour for courtroom testimony; travel expense – for what - to have a suave and glib physician pose as a peer to Dr. Zopyros? Goretti paused as if to make sense of the madness. He said, 'I am not sure what to say, or how to feel. This is an enigma to me. How a defense attorney would secure the services of this deadbeat or how an educated physician could sell his integrity to make a buck!'

Mr. Laurence stood and objected and made a motion to strike the comment. Goretti stated, "I'm sure you do. I withdraw the statement, Your Honor."

There was silence in the court as Goretti made his way to the defense table. A long silence that begged for the void to be filled and filled it was. Mr. Laurence as a part of his redirect attempted to salvage his witness; one last opportunity to rebuild lost credibility. Laurence's un-played hand was non-medical and originally seemed like a legitimate response to the doctor's apparent hunger of money. Disclosing the doctor's marital status confirmed his financial situation – his wife is the daughter of an oil magnate. Her personal wealth with no strings attached, no in-laws to interfere, cash on the barrelhead, totaled a net worth of $625,000,000.00. The plaintiff's argument that the doctor did not have to be a 'hired gun' to exist fell on deaf ears. This did nothing but further alienate him from the fixed income members of the jury.

The morning session ended. Judge Kent instructed the participants to return at 1:00 PM. I heard very little of his canned speech and did not notice that those around me were standing as the jury exited the courtroom. I had closed my space around me; to the point where I stared at the floor and replaced the sound in my ears with white noise – tuning out comments of encouragement and other dribble.

Alice escorted Dr. Arnold from the courtroom and they made their way to the parking lot and then to the airport. I watched ten thousand dollars of supposed expert testimony leave the case and my life and with that I had to ask myself, "Did he improve my chances, did he leave things in better shape than he had found them?" I did not want to think about it too much; the thought of it made me sick. A doctor that seemingly can't find a job, a doctor that misrepresented himself on the stand; a doctor that committed an act of apostasy by agreeing with the defense that doctors can disagree and still be ethical; this would be my memory of the expert doctor. At this point I feared that it would not make a difference that his technical testimony was sound and that his criticism of Dr. Zopyros was well founded; all would be suppressed in the juror's mind because of the character of the messenger – a small tree with a big shadow.

CHAPTER 7

Fraud and Incompetence

Secrecy is the badge of fraud.
Sir Chadwick John (b. 1941)

———————

Returning to my position in the courtroom, I was more than relieved that the day would end with the testimony of Mr. Swindle. His deposition leads me to believe that there were many irregularities and inconsistencies that occurred prior to my mother's death. Certainly I was confident that setting aside shady doctors on both sides of the aisle, the truth could be revealed by a staff underling of Dr. Zopyros. Perhaps he would expose Dr. Zopyros for what I suspected him to be; a rogue and arrogant surgeon.

Testimony of Mark Swindle

I was finding it difficult to maintain my enthusiasm. The doctors' testimony was a draw – both sides gaining ground only to lose it to clever maneuvers. The expert witness was a major disappointment, not so much in substance of his message as in the content of his character. At best, the trial was even and in this case as in baseball the tie goes to the runner. The question was; who is at bat?

Two witnesses remained to be called by the plaintiff; two perfusionist that performed critical tasks during the surgery. Both had been deposed and inconsistencies and remarks were recorded that would lead one to believe that clandestine activities had been perpetrated. One perfusionist, Mark Swindle, was waiting with his attorney in the hallway near the entrance to the court room. He is employed by Shades Mountain Perfusion and contracts his services to the hospital. His responsibility was that of the lead technician and as it happened he transferred responsibility during surgery to a colleague.

The second perfusionist was not present. Attempts to locate him two weeks prior to the trial had been unsuccessful. The attempts were made by both official means; the county sheriff and by unofficial means; legal assistants watching the home. The reports were that either no one was home, or no one would answer the door; the messenger could see someone peering through the side window and would not respond. Richard Head had not made himself available and had sent a message to the court on the day he was scheduled to testify that he was away hunting. Hunting in Western Canada and if the court could wait three weeks, he would be glad to accommodate the request. Mr. Goretti delivered the message as he had delivered the message from the hospital that the subpoenaed medical chart had been lost. Mr. Goretti was the deliverer of much bad news.

Mr. Swindle took the stand. Mr. Laurence asked the usual barrage of questions; most of which dealt with what is a perfusionist. As the witness began to respond he was interrupted by Laurence three times; each regarding volume. The judge finally asked Swindle to slide forward in his chair and lean forward toward the microphone.

The most pronounced physical feature of Mr. Swindle was his hair style. Being a small man in stature the exaggerated crew cut seemed to be an attempt to increase his height. That in its self may have had some effect until he spoke. Sheepish and shy, it was difficult at times to hear and understand his responses. Defensive body language of crossing the arms and a continual stare at his personal attorney for head-nod approval, he would not win anyone with his charm. He was a want-to-be medical professional lacking the right stuff to make it happen; a peripheral staffer that desperately wanted a title.

Swindle continued with his definition of a perfusionist. He went on to say that a perfusionist is also known as a clinical perfusionist. A perfusionist is a trained health professional who operates the heart-lung machine during cardiac surgery and other surgeries that require cardiopulmonary bypass.

A more thorough explanation of a perfusionist is that one is a member of the cardiothoracic surgical team which consists of surgeons, anesthesiologists, physician assistants, surgical technicians and nurses. The perfusionist's main responsibility is to support the physiological and metabolic needs of the cardiac surgical patient so that the cardiac surgeon may operate on a still, un-beating heart. This is accomplished through the utilization of the heart-lung machine, as well its associated components of an oxygenator, filters, reservoirs and tubing. The perfusionist is solely responsible for the circulatory and respiratory functions of the heart-lung machine. In addition, there is a spectrum of physiologic parameters that are constantly monitored by the perfusionist that ensures that the circulatory and respiratory needs of the patient are being met and allows the cardiac surgeon to focus on the actual surgical procedure and less on the immediate needs of the patient.

Laurence's questioning led Swindle to describe every detail of a bypass surgery. Who performs what function and why; who records the events and when; where are ancillary functions conducted and by whom; who is in charge of what; an exhaustive chronicling of each tedious detail. As Swindle described the workflow, a nuts and bolts approach to the procedure, Laurence constructed a flowchart on a whiteboard. Major functions were established as key indicators and written with blue markers. Handoffs of responsibility; lab work, communication of important data and exchange of personnel were written with green markers. Connecting the dots for each listed task was a line indicated with a black marker. Pictured before the jury was a two dimensional representation of what should occur in an operating room; an outline of the standard of care. What was missing was the sensual aspects; smell, touch and sound. Laurence then turned to the testimony to corroborate what was done with what was described. Laurence resurrected the ACT and TEG tickets and values. The presented workflow suggested that lab work should be performed with certain regularity. And the lab values should be documented in the appropriate areas of the patient's chart. Questioning the witness as to when the test were performed, Laurence used a red marker to indicate a deviation from the workflow. Untimely performance and recording of lab values were the norm, not the exception. The board suddenly screamed of inconsistency. Swindle had to agree that if the test were performed at a frequency that would fall within a best practice standard, the chart did not indicate so. In fact, he volunteered that data, lab values and times, were entered after the coversheet had been removed; long after the patient had died. The carbon-copy approach to documentation was designed just for this purpose; a check and balance approach to proper documentation. And proper documentation had not been the standard; in fact it seemed to be an afterthought. Mr. Swindle requested to see the original chart; of course it was missing.

Laurence continued with his red marker. He next asked Swindle key questions regarding his involvement. When did he administer the Hirudin; did he perform any baseline testing; why did he leave the surgical suite? Swindle, as a senior member of the perfusionist team at the hospital, transferred the responsibility of monitoring the clotting of the patient's blood to a junior assistant. Laurence asked why he would make such a decision, considering the uniqueness of the surgery and the lack of experience the team had using alternatives to Heparin. The attorney, red-faced and agitated, asked, "What was so important that would require you to leave the surgery?" Swindle, with his head down, avoiding eye contact with anyone said, "I went to lunch." Laurence asked that he look up and answer the question. This drew an objection from Goretti that the witness was being badgered – the judge overruled and told the witness to speak clearly. Swindle repeated his response and sighed heavily.

Laurence placed a red mark on the workflow representing the time Swindle transitioned the perfusion responsibilities to a subordinate and took a lunch break. The attorney then asked, "What time did you return from your break?" Once again, the witness did not make eye contact. Laurence looked toward the judge and before he could utter a word, His Honor once again admonished the witness to focus and answer the question. After much hemming and hawing, Swindle responded by telling the court that he did not return after lunch. He did not return until he was paged some two hours later. Laurence then drew a red line marking the time the experienced perfusionist was not attending a critical surgery. At this point the whiteboard was red; as if it were bleeding. It was a symbolism that did not escape me and hopefully did not escape the jury.

Mr. Laurence made a gesture to Ms. Gee and she rose and left the court room. She returned as quickly as she had left with another whiteboard. Positioning the whiteboard to the left side of the existing displayed workflow, Laurence began another line of questioning. A series of inquiries regarding 'who knew what and when did they know it' questioning.

I am not sure who heard him, or if it would make any difference to a juror's perception of the evidence, but when Laurence asked Swindle, "When Dr. Zopyros contact you regarding the patient's allergy to Heparin?" Swindle under his breath said, "Jesus!"

The additional whiteboard was segmented with black tape into seven columns. Each column's header listed a date and the corresponding day. The first column displayed: Friday, March 22; the second column: Saturday March 23; and continued until the final column, titled: Surgery Day. The two boards would list the noteworthy events and actions of a medical team in disarray.

Laurence waited for Swindle's response. Once again he glanced toward the judge. His Honor responded, "Mr. Swindle?" The witness began to speak; monotone, mechanical and without emotion, as if he were in shock. The testimony revealed that Swindle left the hospital around four o'clock the afternoon of Friday, March 22. At that time he received a call from Dr. Zopyros. Swindle said that, "Dr. Zopyros called and the subject of the call regarded a patient that had an allergy to heparin. And the allergy had caused a previous CABG to clot and a redo surgery was required. He then asked if I would return to research alternatives to Heparin. I then returned and began to research alternative anticoagulants and discovered Hirudin to be the best option." Laurence then asked in researching Hirudin, did he contact anyone, personally, regarding its use. Swindle responded, "I did contact the President of the Perfusion Society of the Americas, Abraham Hillsdale, to discuss details in using this alternative." Laurence followed with, "When did you make this contact?" Swindle responded, "That same day, Friday, March 22."

Mr. Laurence wrote the words: HEAPRIN ALLERGY with the red marker in the March 22 column. He then wrote with a blue marker the words: RESEARCH HIRUDIN. He requested the progress note for Saturday, March 23. Displayed on the screen, the attorney asked Mr. Swindle to read the section where Dr. Zopyros remarked the patient has a blood clotting disorder. Mr. Laurence then took the red marker and wrote the words: Blood Clotting Disorder under the March 23 header. Below that with a blue marker he wrote: CONTINUED HEPARIN.

Continuing, the progress note for Sunday, March 24 was displayed. As before, Laurence asked Swindle to read the order for a blood clotting workup. Once again, with the red marker, the words: CLOTTING WORKUP was written under the March 24 header. Below that with a blue marker were: CONTINUED HEPARIN.

The progress note for Monday, March 25 was presented and as previously done, Swindle read that a Heparin allergy test was ordered. Laurence then took the red marker and wrote the words: HEPARIN ALLERGY TEST under the March 25 column. Below that written with a blue marker were the words: CONTINUED HEPARIN.

The progress note for Tuesday, March 26 was displayed and the attorney pointed to the documentation that Heparin was still given to the patient. With a blue marker the words were written: CONTINUED HEPARIN. Then on Wednesday, March 27, the progress noted documented a Heparin allergy. With a red marker the words were written: HEPARIN ALLERGY POSITIVE under the March 27 column. And with a blue marker below was written the words: DISCONTINUE HEPARIN.

Laurence stepped back as if to take a look at his masterpiece, he then panned the array of data and positioned himself next to the witness. Turning to the witness, he asked, "Is it your testimony that Dr. Zopyros discussed the Heparin allergy with you on Friday, March 22?" Swindle responded that the doctor had mentioned a patient's allergy. It had been the doctor's testimony that he did not suspect or anticipate a Heparin allergy until the test result was returned on March 27; five days after his conversation with Swindle.

Laurence continued by asking Swindle, "When did you communicate to the doctor your recommendation to use Hiridun?" Swindle responded, "That same day, Friday March 22." The doctor had testified that he did not conduct any research regarding the use of Hirudin until Wednesday, March 27. Laurence knew before asking the question that it would draw an objection and that it would be sustained, but the point had to be made. He asked Swindle, "Do you think it to be unethical and negligent to wait until the last minute to 'bone up' on a new surgical procedure when there were five days to prepare?" As expected, Mr. Goretti blew a gasket and the judge reacted in kind.

Mr. Laurence asked a similar question, "Do you think it to be negligent and reckless to have five days, ample time, to secure the necessary equipment, an ECT machine, to monitor a surgery performed using Hirudin and do not?" Goretti once again objected and was answered with different a response. The judge overruled and the witness was required to answer. The doctor had previously testified that there was not enough time to request an ECT machine. The delivery of the machine takes five days from the vendor. The surgery was deemed urgent and when the allergy was confirmed on March 27, time had run out; not enough time to request the machine. Swindle's testimony now cast doubt on that reasoning because the doctor knew at least five days prior to the surgery of the allergy; obviously enough time to secure the machine.

To recap the testimony, Laurence moved through each day on the whiteboard; pointing out key items – the red items. As he moved from day to day, he erased the data; stating, "Gone, a missed opportunity to do the right thing!" Then he moved to the workflow whiteboard and continued the same approach, "Lab should have been performed and was not - gone; perfusionist goes to lunch and should not - gone!" Goretti objected, Laurence continued; erasing each step as he had done on the date and day grid. Finally making his way through the workflow where the words MACHINE CLOTTED written in red was the single entry remaining – he did not erase that event. The presentation was straightforward, but had an underlying strategy. The need for the jury to have a diagram of events was understandable, but Goretti had a reputation of using the plaintiff's exhibits and proof sources against his opponent; Laurence knew that tactic and erased the presentation. So, the masterpiece he had created that had been his ally would not become his Brutus. Goretti would have to reconstruct the piece of art – and sequels don't play well.

Laurence wrapped up his interrogation of Swindle by asking, "Who did you call in an attempt to locate and secure an ECT machine to monitor the effects of the Hirudin?" Swindle response was vague. He said that he had contacted a colleague at a local hospital with no success. Laurence then asked, "Did you contact the University Hospital?" His response was short, "No." Laurence asked, "Why not?" The witness did not answer; the attorney did not press for an answer. The non-response spoke volumes for the haphazard approach the perfusionist took in preparing for the surgery.

The attorney teased the witness by telling the court that he had completed the direct examination; and as Mr. Swindle made his exit from the stand he asked the court for an additional line of questioning. The request was granted and Laurence asked Mr. Swindle, "Were any parts of the bypass machine coated with Heparin?" Swindle's response was expected. He stated he had requested from his vendor Heparin-free tubing. "What about the oxygenator?" He responded, "That, too."

Mr. Laurence then asked, "So, it is your testimony that the patient was not given Heparin directly through injections, or indirectly through inappropriate equipment?" The witness responded that to his knowledge, no Heparin was given. Laurence explored another line of questioning regarding the training of the perfusionist prior to surgery in the use and monitoring of Hirudin. The attorney asked, "Is it a normal practice of you to leave mid-surgery to have lunch?" Swindle answered, "No." Laurence then asked, "Had you planned to leave this surgery to have lunch?" Swindle answered, "No." Laurence then asked, "If you did not anticipate leaving the surgery, does that mean that your replacement was not trained in the use of Hirudin?" Swindle was noticeably shaken. He rambled on and on about the expertise of his staff and that after the research had been done and the plan enacted, any perfusionist could step in. Laurence repeated, "Did you train your replacement prior to surgery?" The witness whispered, "No."

Mr. Laurence then took a deep breath and focused on a spot on the ceiling; waiting for what had been said to sink in. He continued recapping the previous answers to his questions. And with his final question, he opened the door of doubt in each juror's mind, "How do you know your replacement did not administer Heparin during surgery. And how can you be confident in your response since the replacement was not trained?" Swindle simply said, "I just know!" Laurence asked, "Were you there at the time?" Swindle responded, "No." Laurence, "Can you trust the chart as an accurate record of actions and interventions? Swindle said, "Yes." Laurence asked, "What has changed? You said earlier that some data was entered long after the death of the patient. Which data? Where would your associate document a critical mistake?" Goretti objected and the judge overruled. Swindle said, "There was no mistake!" Laurence turned toward the jury and said that the witness was not there and how could he know for sure. With that statement, Laurence ended his session with Swindle.

It would be interesting to observe Mr. Goretti' cross examination of the Mr. Swindle. Goretti began by entering into a long diatribe regarding the accuracy of memory. He then turned toward the witness and asked, "How long ago was it that you had this discussion with Dr. Zopyros about a Heparin allergy?" Swindle responded, "A long time ago, over five years." Goretti continued, "Would it be safe to say that you may have your dates wrong; that you may have meant the discussion occurred on Monday and not Friday?" Laurence objected and judge allowed the question. Swindle responded, "Uh, sure. That could have happened. That would explain things." Goretti continued his explanation of memory that the recalling of events is more important than the details of date and time. He then summarized that the discussion occurred on Wednesday, March 27th, not Friday, the 22nd and that prevented the procurement of the ECT machine.

This rant was hypocrisy. Goretti had nailed me to the wall regarding dates and times that I misquoted from my diary; he offered no excuse then. Now, as an act of convenience and self efficacy, he allowed the witness wiggle room to maintain his integrity. He ended by saying, "After all, who amongst us has not forgotten an important date in their lives?" I looked toward the jury and all were on board with Goretti as evidenced by the nodding of their heads in agreement.

Goretti then asked Mr. Swindle, "What would you have done differently from your associate in the later stages of the surgery?" Swindle answered, "Nothing! Not one thing!" Goretti then said, "So, it really didn't matter who was there, circumstances were what they were, correct?" Swindle said, "Absolutely."

Goretti then said, "No further questions, Your Honor."

I was completely taken aback. The cross examination was short. No dissection of medical detail; no philosophical arguments; no overt theatrics – just enough discussion to mask the truth with a coat of cosmetic incredulity. What was his strategy?

Mr. Laurence as a matter of protocol is allowed to re-direct the witness. He stood and positioned himself between the witness and the doctor. While facing the jury, extending both arms and pointing to both parties he asked, "Which of you is ultimately responsible for the results in the operating room? Who is captain of the ship? Mr. Swindle with hesitation responded, "It is the surgeon, Dr. Zopyros!"

Mr. Swindle was excused from the witness stand and he left the courtroom with his attorney. The only sanction he was likely to face is his close association with the defendant. He and Dr. Zopyros will mostly likely team up again on a number of surgeries. The tensions in the courtroom will haunt them; I am sure they will not forget this date.

The day's session had ended and Judge Kent directed the jury with his usual instructions to go home, keep silent and return on time the next morning. As the last juror exited, Judge Kent asked if there were any motions. Mr. Goretti asked that the subpoena for Mr. Head be quashed. The justification for the release was the inability to serve the document; the witness was away on a hunting trip – camping in Western Canada. Attempts to serve the subpoena prior to the trial had been unsuccessful. Judge Kent granted the motion and with no objections, the session ended.

Something about Head's absence, his convenient exit from the state, did not settle well with me. Too many odd happenings had occurred to make this a coincidence. A missing chart, a missing witness and a defense attorney's matter-of-factness concerning the lost made me suspicious. The more I observed the more I grew to suspect the integrity of the trial-by-jury method of justice. I can only imagine the happenings of uncivilized courts.

I walked with my legal team to the executive parking lot. The daily price to park seemed more like extortion than a fee. Nonetheless, spirits were upbeat, the younger team members showed more enthusiasm than did the older. In fact, Isaac made a point to tell me there are still many hurdles. I am a realist; a feet-on-the-ground kind of person, but still I need a few minutes to bask. And with that, I made my way to a local tavern to spend some time with old friends; the college variety – time to get caught up – and medicated.

CHAPTER 8

Rush to Judgment

Don't ever try to swim against the mighty tide of justice.
Pirates Cove

———————

The jurors gather each day prior to a session in the Jury Room located at the rear of the courtroom. The door to the room in reference to the wall seemed proportional and it was only when a juror passed through the opening that its scale became apparent. The frame raised over nine feet in height through which a table and leather-bound chairs were visible. This portal seemed to remind each person that passed through it that the decisions made here are much larger than any one person. It became more apparent each day that this was as a refuge for the jury, a place to hide. Each juror would carry food or drink, backpacks, books, pillows; it looked more like a slumber party than a somber event. No one from the Defense or Plaintiff parties was allowed to go into the room – at any time. Laughter and loud conversation could be heard beyond the door; there was a high degree of irreverence in their behavior; a blatant lack of respect. This further concerned me regarding their integrity and their willingness to serve.

I had taken my place to await the beginning of the fifth day of trail. The original agenda listed the planned testimony of two expert witnesses for the Defense. My understanding was that this would consume the entire day and that the sixth day of trial would be closing arguments. Alice Gee, Mr. Laurence's legal assistant, leaned and whispered in my ear that there had been a development. Usually this meant something major. I had a catch in my voice as I asked what had developed. My mind raced through several possibilities. Naively, I supposed they had seen the error in their ways and wanted to settle. Had there been a personal emergency with the judge or jury – one juror had already been excused because of a medical emergency. I could not imagine all the possibilities. Never would I have guessed that Mr. Goretti would make such a bold move – if this were poker, he called our hand, time to show the cards.

It was Mr. Goretti's option to call expert witnesses to support his client's case. The names were listed in the discovery phase of trial preparation and plaintiff depositions had been taken. Having read their depositions neither of their testimonies would inflict serious harm to the plaintiff's case. In fact, Dr. Player of Tuscaloosa seemed to support key items in the breach of Standard of Care that was a pillar for our arguments. Additionally, if he were to testify Mr. Laurence would be in a position to enter into evidence a written protocol that was not followed by Dr. Zopyros, further damaging the Defense' credibility. Dr. Marks of Decatur was listed as a possible witness for the Defense and his deposition indicated that he did not have any experience with a case similar to the one being tried. His testimony would have had no more relevance than that of a Monday morning quarterback critiquing Sunday's championship game – all talk, no glory. Dr. Marks was not a problem. What was Mr. Goretti's strategy?

I have learned from my limited experience with this trial that one supports their case by either building credibility for their side or by destroying credibility of their opponents. Often the easier of the two options is to chip away at the opponent's credibility. The practice of law to an outsider is a dirty business. Exposing the truth seems to be secondary to self efficacy and winning. I certainly will give closer attention to any legal case I hear or read about in the future.

The Defense elected to not call their expert witnesses to the stand. This served two strategic purposes; one was to limit the Defense's exposure to a breach of the Standard of Care discussions that would certainly be supported by testimony and two, and just as effective, rush the Plaintiff into an unrehearsed closing argument. Mr. Goretti had played this perfectly. Goretti had sent Mr. Laurence an e-mail as to his plans to not call additional witnesses; this to satisfy his obligation to play fairly. The e-mail was sent at 7:30 AM; minutes before Laurence left his home. Goretti had presumably completed his closing argument document the previous day and waited for Mr. Laurence to stumble at the finish line. Mr. Laurence made a significant play himself, he moved that the second Perfusionist' testimony be read into record from the deposition taken several weeks earlier. Mr. Head had been subpoenaed to appear in court as a witness for the Plaintiff. Many attempts were made to serve the subpoena without success – he was not to be found. Word had it that he was hunting big game in Canada – strange how the hunter becomes the hunted. Mr. Laurence's move served two purposes, it allowed the jury to hear Head's testimony and it allowed him time to prepare for the closing argument.

Mr. Laurence read the questions as he had once asked them and Ms. Hartselle read Mr. Head's response into the court record.

Laurence: Where did you attend college?

Head: Several, multiple schools and then military service.

Laurence: Did you graduate?

Head: No.

Laurence: Where did you learn to be a perfusionist?

Head: Perfusion school at Prairie View Heart Institute

Laurence: In your study to become a perfusionist, did you ever study either at Prairie View Heart Institute or any other places of employment the acceptable methodology to go about perfusing blood during cardiac surgery without the use of Heparin?

Head: No.

Laurence: Was Ms. Carroll's case the very first time you had been involved in any type of heart surgery without Heparin?

Head: Yes.

Laurence: Have you ever observed a non-Heparin surgery prior to Ms. Carroll's case?

Head: No.

Laurence: Prior to Ms. Carroll's surgery had you been in attendance for any in-service or continuing medical education classes that discussed how to appropriately perfuse blood in a non-Heparin cardiac surgery?

Head: I don't recall.

Laurence: Have you ever been involved prior to Ms. Carroll's case where the heart-lung machine completely thrombosed, clotted?

Head: No.

Laurence: Can you remember whether, or not, Mr. Swindle reviewed his research efforts with you regarding a non-Heparin surgery with you prior to March 28.

Head: I don't recall.

Laurence: Well, after the machine clotted and after the patient died, did you ask him, Mark, if he did research on how to manage the surgery without Heparin?

Head: I don't remember having a conversation.

Laurence: When you took over for Swindle, did you know that the case was a non-Heparin surgery?

Head: Yes.

Laurence: So, before you walked in and started assisting with the surgery by managing the perfusion of the blood, did you find out what you were supposed to do in a situation that you had never been exposed to before?

Head: I asked at that point, when I took over for Mark, what I was supposed to do.

Laurence: As you walked in at 12:10 PM, you asked, what are we supposed to be doing, right?

Head: That's correct.

Laurence: Do you recall if Dr. Zopyros discussed the perfusion plan with you?

Head: I don't recall.

Laurence: You don't remember if you had a conversation with the surgeon?

Head: No, I don't recall.

Laurence: What did Mark Swindle tell you what you were supposed to do?

Head: I don't recall.

Laurence: Do you remember walking into surgery?

Head: I do not. I have been in hundreds of surgeries; one is like the other.

Laurence: This isn't a typical case, though, is it?

Head: No, sir.

Laurence: Is this the only surgery in your career where the heart-lung machine clotted?

Head: Yes.

Laurence: And this case does not stick out in your mind?

Head: Every person is important, but no, it does not stick out in my mind.

Laurence: After taking over for Swindle, do you remember adding Hirudin to the heart-lung machine?

Head: I don't remember.

Laurence: Did anyone add Hirudin to the heart-lung machine? You may review the chart.

Head: I didn't add any.

Laurence: After you took over for Swindle, how many tests did you perform to monitor the clotting of the blood?

Head: I did not perform any tests.

Laurence: From 12:10 until 2:08 PM, no tests were performed to monitor the blood?

Head: Not by me.

Laurence: Okay, when the tests were performed, what were they? You may look at the chart.

Head: Let's see, well, a TEG was performed.

Laurence: What is a T-E-G?

Head: A Thrombo-something.

Laurence: You don't know?

Head: I am not sure.

Laurence: What is Ecarin Clotting Time?

Head: I can't remember.

Laurence: Who actually conducted the Ecarin Clotting Time test during Ms. Carroll's surgery?

Head: Barb Swindle, Mark's wife.

Laurence: How did she know how to do this test?

Head: I am sure Mark called the company.

Laurence: What company?

Head: The TEG Company.

Laurence: How many whole blood Ecarin Clotting Tests were performed on your chart for Ms. Carroll's surgery?

Head: It looks like six.

Laurence: According to Mr. Swindle's testimony, ACT tests were performed to monitor the blood. Show me where the Ecarin Clotting Time tests are recorded in the chart?

Head: (no response)

Laurence: Mr. Head, it has been four minutes since I asked that question. I'm just asking you if there's anywhere on this documentation that you can show me where the information is documented that an actual Ecarin Clotting Test was performed?

Head: I think it is the same as the ACT.

Laurence: Is that your answer?

Head: Yes.

Laurence: In your post operative research, did you remember reading, or discovering, the need for a special piece of equipment to monitor the use of Hirudin?

Head: I don't recall.

Laurence: Would it be fair to say that you and your group relied upon Dr. Zopyros as to whether to go forward with this surgery, or not?

Head: Yes, absolutely.

Laurence: Do you recall the point at which the heart-lung machine clotted?

Head: Yes.

Laurence: What were you doing at the point you realized that the machine began to clot?

Head: I told the surgeon that the machine was clotting and asked him if he wanted to set up another machine.

Laurence: Okay. What did he say?

Head: Go ahead and set up another machine and then he said, wait, never mind.

Laurence: You were not originally scheduled to participate in the surgery, were you?

Head: No

Laurence: Why did you have to relieve Swindle?

Head: I don't remember.

Laurence: Do you remember who paged Mark when the machine clotted?

Head: No.

Laurence: Was the heart-lung machine, or any of its parts, primed with Heparin?

Head: Not to my knowledge.

Laurence: Was there any pre-operative testing of the patient's blood and how it might react to Hirudin? Please refer to the chart, if necessary.

Head: I did not perform any test and I don't see any listed in the chart.

Laurence: So, you and Mr. Swindle went into surgery without having any testing to show how Ms. Carroll's blood would react to Hirudin, right?

Head: I don't know the right answer, I just don't know.

Laurence: I am not trying to trick you. It either happened, or it didn't.

Head: I suppose the TEG value of 1400 would allow the surgery; that it would be safe to move on.

Laurence: Are you looking at the chart that lists the time as 1400. Mr. Head, that's not a test value, that's a time – 2:00PM. So, my question is again, were there any pre-testing of the patient's blood and the reaction it might have to Hirudin?

Head: I can't answer that!

Laurence: Is there one documented in your records?

Head: I can't answer that!

Mr. Cooper (Head's personal attorney): I think he is trying to find out from you, Mr. Head, is whether there is any record in your chart that indicates that some blood test was done before Ms. Carroll ever went to the operating room that showed how her blood might react with Hirudin. He wants to know if that documentation exist, or does it not exist.

Head: There may be, I just don't know.

Laurence: Do you know how to read your chart?

Head: I may be missing it, I can't find it – I just don't know.

Laurence: How many years experience do you have as a Perfusionist?

Head: Thirty years.

Laurence: Based upon your thirty years of experience, what do believe happened that caused that machine you were operating to clot.

Head: I don't know.

Laurence: That's all, Your Honor.

I watched the jury as Ms. Hartselle read Head's deposition. She made every attempt to be engaging and theatrical in her reading, entertaining, even. I listened intently and in this sanctuary of law and justice I was reverent and respectful. The reading was appropriate, in context and needed - this to complete the story. The vicarious testimony contained many points to support the Plaintiff's case. The jury looked bored and indifferent – one juror slept, others looked away. I felt no optimism at all – fate rested in this group of slackers.

The reading of Head's deposition made things perfectly clear why he was not on the stand. His absence looked more like an orchestrated nonevent instead of a scheduling conflict. How someone with his acumen could be allowed to conduct a critical aspect of the surgery without supervision is beyond belief. My mind raced with sordid scenarios - a theater of the mind where conspiracy, greed and lies were center stage and rationalized as situational ethics; a production where the lead character of weak moral constitution uses a cape to cloak the truth to save himself and his career. Could Swindle have anticipated a bad outcome midway through the surgery and made his exit. Transitioning the failed experiment to an underling to shoulder the responsibility; after all, I have seen that happen in the business world. I could not find peace with the realization that the death of my mother was caused by the inexperience of a stooge; the puppet of Mr. Swindle. My body shook with anger!

CHAPTER 9

The Closing Arguments

Your argument defends an ideology; mine defends the truth.
Mason Cooley (b. 1927)

Judge Kent instructed the jury regarding closing argument protocol. This is the part of the trial where all of the cards are on the table. The introduction of new evidence and the cross examination of witnesses is no longer permitted. Each side knows what the other knows and how each plans to sell their story to the jury. As the judge explained the rules the jury for the first time seemed interested; they leaned forward in their chairs and lent an ear. First Mr. Laurence would present the closing remarks for the Plaintiff, followed by the Defense. The Plaintiff would then be allowed to rebut the Defense's remarks. The burden of proof rest with the Plaintiff, the principle is if you believe something to be, you believe more than me, tell me what you know. So, Mr. Laurence will be in a position to present his case and respond to Mr. Goretti's closing. That afforded me some comfort.

Plaintiff's Closing Arguments – Mr. Laurence

Mr. Laurence began his closing with the traditional, "May it please the Court, counsel, ladies and gentlemen of the jury?" He then opened his three-inch binder and continued, "On March 28th, 2002, Myrna Sue Carroll, a 60-year-old lady that had begun enjoying the twilight of her life, died while on the operating table undergoing cardiopulmonary bypass surgery. She died when the heart-lung machine that was keeping her alive completely clotted, and her heart stopped beating..."

One could sense that Mr. Laurence's oratory would be lengthy, filled with detail and agenda. The jurors had the look of interrogated prisoners. Blank stares, withdrawn body language and heavy sighs. Their short-lived enthusiasm faded as the diatribe began. The judge had assumed his usual position – reclined, with an emotionless face. He avoided eye contact as much as possible in fear of possibly influencing a juror. The exceptions to his countenance at this time were closed eyelids. I hoped the jurors were not looking to him for motivation. Mr. Goretti paid little attention to Mr. Laurence as he organized his notes for his closing statements. The court reporter typed the attorney's narrative while gazing at something beyond the room. The mood of the court room was that of intense boredom. Either one's mind had been made regarding a decision or, one has heard this before and does not care to hear it again. Frankly, I found myself a member of the later.

To hear the details of my mother's death at the hands of an inept system where bureaucracy and arrogance struggle for control was more than I could stomach. And to hear Goretti trumpet the heroics of a group of doctors that had their experience and skills taxed well beyond their abilities would tap the area of my brain and consciousness that harbors territoriality and aggression. Mr. Laurence's rant could damage my well being, Goretti's propaganda could damage the well being of others.

Looking for a distraction, I focused my attention on the railing that bordered the jury box. A pattern imbedded in the wood grain on the corner post resembled a face. The image caught and held my attention. The more I concentrated on the image more detailed became apparent. I was not completely sure what was real and was my imagination. The longer I focused the less attention I paid to those around me. The sounds of the court chamber faded and the revival-like presentation of Mr. Laurence became muted. The realization of a still, unbeating heart and the memory upon first hearing of my mother's death took my mind to a much different time of my life.

A time when the only pressure a child faced was the fear of disappointing one's parents, a time when eternity was confined to a single afternoon, a time when the universe ended at the railroad tracks - a time when death was limited to the loss of a goldfish. A time when telling the truth was not a conscious decision, it was a part of one's character; a time when one's most important playmate was one's imagination, a time when it was taken for granted one's parents would live forever. In a sense, much of who I was at that time is gone and in another it defines me. And the person who could chronicle my life is gone. The mother who could recall the most insignificant detail in my learning to walk and talk is gone. The woman who sensed my struggles in adolescence is gone. The parent who proudly watched as I was the first female coed to receive the engineering award at graduation is gone. And with her leaving the planet, I am less than whole.

A juror interrupted my escape with a productive cough just as Mr. Laurence barked, "At the beginning of this case, I told you that we were going to prove to you that she died as a result of the failure of Dr. Zopyros to diagnose an allergic reaction to Heparin that she developed after her first surgery, failure to treat that allergy appropriately, wrongfully rushing her to surgery, and then choosing to do the surgery the wrong way..."

I know in my heart that Mr. Laurence is correct. That is, it was the responsibility of the medical team to assess and implement a treatment plan. And the medical team, Dr. Zopyros, was not attentive to many warning signs that should have been noticed. And as a result tragic mistakes were made. No more tragic than the responsibility that now I have placed on myself.

The demon that haunts me to this day is an overwhelming feeling – an instruction – to get a second medical opinion prior to the second surgery. It is as if something, or someone, was directing me to a much needed course of action. In retrospect, I did follow that intuitiveness and made the request of the staff to contact the most notable cardiovascular surgeon in Birmingham. Fate played its hand and Dr. Ocean was out of town, on vacation with his family. That reality coupled with the news that mother had experienced a third heart attack and I abandoned the most basic innate trait of humanness – my sixth sense. Instead of pressing on, securing the second opinion of another surgeon, I simply lost touch with what I have now learned as a fundamental truth; one is either reacting in fear or acting in love. I was afraid of losing her love and my fear may have cost mother the ultimate price.

I have a recurring dream where she comes to me dazed and confused. Although no words are spoken in the reverie, the meaning is clear – why did this happen? Mother had complete trust in the doctors and their abilities, she had reliance in me that I would manage the details and she had a deep faith in God that she would recover. I can understand why she is puzzled.

Mr. Laurence dropped his writing pad on the desk to emphasize a point in his narrative. I snapped my attention toward him as he said, "As I mentioned to you, the definition indicates that if you have a Heparin antibody test and a thrombosis, without a doubt, that's the definition of HIT. On March 6th, after she underwent her first surgery on March 4th, she developed what's known as a DVT. That's a deep vein thrombosis. And the deep vein thrombosis, if you will pull it up -- the deep vein thrombosis is in evidence that you will see in the record is not just a normal DVT..."

I was both frightened and thrilled to see my mother in the CICU recovery room after the first surgery. The tubing that provided her the needed oxygen was taped to her face and descended into her throat. The anesthesia had disabled her ability to breathe on her on; her diaphragm was paralyzed by the intense medication. The recovery unit was anything but quiet. The gasping sounds of the respirator and the continuous beeps and clicks of the equipment were extremely unsettling. Monitoring machines and IVs circled her bed while extending their tentacles into her body. My presumption was that the ancillary extensions of life were necessary and yet my focus shifted to the heart monitor and the movement of her eyes beneath her eyelids. She was in there, somewhere and soon to be well and home with her family. Any inconvenience, any measure of pain, any amount of time to weather the treatment would be OK with the expectation of a long and normal life thereafter.

The day following the first surgery she was moved to a private room and it was there she was to begin her road to recovery. Much of the day was spent with her in good spirits – sore from the surgery and somewhat nauseated from the anesthesia she nonetheless engaged in conversation. Her voice was coarse as if suffering the effects of a cold. I later learned the coarseness was the result of the oxygen tubing that irritated the vocal cords as it was inserted into the lungs. The conversations seemed to take on a more philosophical tome than that of an expected casual tenor. In her reflection of her experience she seemed to be providing me with life's lessons. One topic introduced the subject of personal shortcomings. She said that there are people that refer to shortcomings as faults as if a person has completed their growth an unable to adjust their life's course. Shortcomings or faults, whatever one wants to call them, are aspects of life which we can change who we are. And having faults in itself is not a damning condition; it simply means we are human. She directed a life principle to me that I live by to this day, it is we don't live our lives we create our lives. A conscious act deciding what one will become; daily, event by event; moment by moment. Humans are in control of what they become by what they think, what they say and what they do. She said that things seem to come in threes; the Father, the Son and the Holy Ghost – the Soul, the Mind, and the Body - Thought, Word and Deed. So in recognizing our 'aspects' we enable ourselves to create new lives as we mature – and we constantly mature and evolve. Our souls provide us with thoughts, ideas and inspiration that seem to come to us as a result of coincidence – and coincidence does not exist. Our mind then converts those thoughts into words so that we can construct a map to guide our actions. So that, then our bodies can act out the soul's instructions in the form of deeds – to create our soul's intent. Mother noticed my furrowed brow and interpreted that as a request to simplify her lesson and she said, "Follow your heart - that is your soul talking to you." And the first aspect of anyone's life that needs constant re-examination is gratitude – we all have reason to be thankful. I could not agree more. Mother was alive and on the road to recovery.

The instructions of the medical staff were to have mother take short walks the day after surgery. Her first trek with my assistance was a short walk to the bathroom. And it was this simple act of taking a few steps that signaled an ominous event on her horizon. The left leg began to hurt and cramp, its color changed from a flesh tone to a deep purple. The anomaly extended from the knee to the ankle. At the time, I did not foresee this as a critical occurrence; I simply didn't want her to experience pain. Ultimately, this signaled what was beginning of the end.

The attorney continued by saying, "And so what happened? She was discharged from the hospital. She was released on Coumadin, which you heard from the witness stand is not indicated for someone that has a Heparin allergy. And her blood levels went all over the chart; all over the chart. Sometimes she was much coagulated, sometimes she was not..."

Mother was discharged on a Saturday morning. I was at the hospital with her husband to drive her home. She was remarried and Pop was unable to drive or care for himself due to two medical conditions. One was a congenital heart malady which placed extreme physical restrictions on him and the other was a brain tumor that affected his ability to make critical decisions. Pushing her wheelchair through the sliding doors, mother's first breath of cool morning air after having spent eleven days in a stuffy hospital room was a treat. She valued the simple things; a fresh tomato from the vine, serving refreshments at vacation bible school or listening to a symphony of tree frogs on a hot August evening – she was well entertained with life.

The cloudless day created a palate of blue skies and green pines; a backdrop for a drive that she had taken many times. The narrow country roads were lined with small rural homes and freshly plowed fields waiting the spring planting season. Everywhere one looked, one saw life. Life in abundance as people made their way about their business or life in promise as evidenced by dirt fields that soon would bear its fruit. It was a happy time.

The neighborhood in which she lived was a typical rural southern community. Visitors did not need an invitation, a porch light, an un-pulled curtain or an open door was a signal to drop in and talk. And drop in they did. Friends and family kept her busy with discussion; reminiscing about the good old days and questions about her health. Food was delivered daily. The ladies auxiliary at the Baptist church was staffed with volunteers blessed with a mixing of good-heartedness and a degree of nosiness. They made sure mother was adequately supplied with food and support. The daily cuisine included favorites like collard greens, butter beans and fried corn with more recent additions to the menu such as Cracker Barrel's Hash Brown Casserole and any selection from Paula Dean's cookbook. Fried chicken, meat loaf and pot roast were featured items. And banana pudding, strawberry pudding and pineapple puddings were daily fare with an occasional coca cola cake thrown in to break the monotony.

Excursions from her home were short in duration and were limited to monitoring visits to mother's family doctor. Each trip took us passed the Tannehill Furnaces. As a child, mother would take my brother and me to the furnaces to picnic and swim. This is a site where Confederate troops produced armaments that were used in Civil War battles throughout the South. It is now a State Park. Back then it was nothing more than a trail that led to a swimming hole. The swimming hole was lined with willows and oaks that provided a constant shade. One oak was unusually large and nature had orchestrated a perfect branch that jutted out over the water. It was on this branch a large rope was tied to provide hours of entertainment as we would swing and drop into the cold water. The banks of the stream were red clay and a path that was rippled with tree roots led to the old stone structures where pig iron was made. Vegetation, vines and bushes, hid just enough of its walls to make any child weary to be there alone. Ghost of the antebellum south, the snapping of a twig, the sound of a squirrel making its escape was sensory overload for some adults. All in all, things were well. Except for the constant pain in her left leg.

The pain concerned me. She was discharged on the 9th and had several visits to her primary care physician to monitor the effects of the Coumadin. This drug provided a method to regulate the blood. This regulation was to moderate the viscosity – the thickness or thinness of the blood. I paid close attention to the lab results. The monitoring visit on the 18th indicated the blood was becoming too thick – a propensity to clot. The nurse at the local clinic was troubled by the resulting value and faxed the results to Dr. Zopyros. This was the second ominous sign that she was not getting any better.

Mr. Laurence became extremely charismatic as he continued by saying, "She comes back into the hospital within two weeks of completely having all three grafts that had been put in place completely occlude, completely clot. This, you heard from the evidence, is extremely rare. It doesn't happen. It doesn't happen; except when certain conditions exist. And I asked Dr. Zopyros to name each and every potential cause for all three grafts to clot within two weeks of him performing the surgery. And if you remember what the surgery is, we showed you how they take veins out of the legs -- and they're called conduits -- and they clean them out, and they completely go around the clogged part of the heart. They make sure that these veins are completely clean. He listed for us about six or seven potential causes for there to be a triple bypass graft occlusion within two weeks of surgery. And we eliminated, in his testimony, each and every single cause except for one: A coagulation problem with the blood. That's very important because that means that he knew as of the time that she came back in on the 21st, late that night, and the 22nd, when she had her heart catheterization, he knew that she had a complete occlusion problem that wasn't caused by these other things, but it was caused by a coagulation problem. What was the coagulation problem? It was an allergic reaction to Heparin…"

Laurence's remarks took me back to that night. I was awakened at 2:00 AM on the 21st with Pop pounding on my bedroom door. He was trying to tell me that mother was sick and her chest was hurting. I ran past him, pushing him from my path, to her room and she explained that she was unable to sleep because of pain – pain not in her leg but in her chest. I immediately called for an ambulance. My mind returned to the development of the DVT and the nurses comment regarding the lab result of the 18th – could the thickening of the blood have caused the DVT and the abnormal lab results. And how could that happen when one is taking a medication to thin the blood.

Prior to this occurrence I had given the medical team the benefit of knowing more than I regarding the practice of medicine. And in my thinking I knew that the doctor's technical knowledge was far superior to mine, but I was not as confident regarding his ability to 'figure things out'. His wheels moved far too slowly for me. The recurrence of chest pains and the ultimate diagnosis of a second heart attack made me suspicious of his analytical and diagnostic skills. My immediate concern was mother's wellbeing and to insulate her from my wariness regarding the quality of care she had experienced. In retrospect, she sensed my distrust; we did not discuss anything for several hours. The DVT, the thickening of the blood and another heart attack – this should have captured someone's attention; it consumed my thoughts!

The attorney continued, "So what happened? We know that she is very abnormal. She has clotting that has occurred in now six different veins in her body. We saw the definition. If there's a thrombosis while you are on Heparin, you should be suggestive of a HIT allergy. And now, as of the 22nd, we know that not only have three veins in her leg clotted without explanation, we know that three vessels, the vessels in her heart, have completed clotted. That should send off red lights and sirens everywhere. And if you believe the testimony of Mark Swindle, it did. Dr. Zopyros simply did not have the appropriate reaction."

"So what happened next? Dr. Zopyros also, in his note from the 24th, indicates that there needed to be a clotting workup. This note is inconsistent with his testimony that he was unaware that there was a Heparin allergy. Let's take a look at it; the progress note from the 24th -- on page 34. The progress note from the 24th indicates, 'Have recommended repeat CABG with workup of clotting.' What does that indicate? That indicates that as of the 24th, Dr. Zopyros believed that there needed to be an analysis of the clotting problem that she was having. That's not normal. You do not normally do a clotting workup, according to the evidence that we've heard."

Sunday afternoon, the 24th, Mother and I had a discussion regarding the next step. Pop sat quietly next to the window and watched the traffic on I-65. The day before, Dr. Pantheras had made a comment that disturbed us. His rationale for the cause of the three bypass grafts clotting and the second heart attack could have been the results of a mistake made by Dr. Zopyros. A colleague of Dr. Zopyros was questioning the surgeon's actions. In my mind, if medical team members are breaking ranks and no longer represent a singular voice, it was time for a new team. Mother remained intrepid and I became more belligerent. The surgeon had recommended a second surgery and we insisted on having a second opinion. In hindsight, if the definition of insanity is doing the same thing and expecting different results, then Dr. Zopyros was insane. A formal request was made for a second opinion before moving forward with the surgery.

On Monday, the 25th, Dr. Pantheras ordered a test to determine if an allergy to Heparin exist. We were not made aware of the concern and she continued to receive daily doses of Heparin as an intervention for additional heart attacks. Dr. Pantheras had been the most accommodating with respect to disclosure of medical facts. He, however, did not share this information. I suspect that he had hoped the test would have been negative and move on to other possibilities. Of course, if the test were positive, well, Pandora's Box of finger-pointing would be up ended.

Mr. Laurence continued, "...now, let's take a look at why that is. We know that she's coming in with three vessels completely clotted. We know that she has unexplained clotting in her leg, unexplained clotting in her heart. And the decision is made to rush her to surgery. And according to his testimony, he then finds out on the 27th, oh, my goodness, she has a Heparin allergy or an antibody, and so, therefore, we're going to have to use a different product that is not anything that I've ever used before. It's not anything that I've been trained on. It's something that I'm going to have to research tonight on the Internet, and I don't feel the need to tell the family about any of that. But the reason why that's important is because the very explanation that he has sat up here and given to you as to why he did not violate the standard of care for going to surgery with a patient that was positive for a Heparin antibody is because she was sick. She was sick. But she was sick because they were continuing to give her the drug that she was allergic to."

Thursday morning, the 27th, mother and I sat quietly in her hospital room. I was reading a medical journal on coronary disease and she was working a crossword puzzle. We were interrupted by Dr. Pantheras with the news that he had ordered a Heparin allergy test the previous Monday and the results were positive. Mother and I looked at each other and I asked what that means regarding the surgery. And not unsurprisingly, he said that an alternate blood thinner would be utilized during the second bypass surgery. Before I could follow up with another question, he said that Dr. Zopyros would be in soon to discuss the options. He then walked to mother's bedside and removed her oxygen and said, 'That makes you look like you are sick – you are not that sick – you don't need it!"

At the time, this information seemed to pale in significance to the other problems she faced. That is, two heart attacks, uncontrolled clotting and now an allergy to a much needed medication. Dr. Zopyros then entered the room to discuss the second surgery and alternatives to Heparin as an anticoagulant.

Dr. Zopyros cut to the chase by stating the inability to use Heparin in bypass surgery was not alarming, just an inconvenience. And that it meant that other drugs would have to be utilized and that Hirudin would be the choice. Anticipating our next question he volunteered that we should not overly concern ourselves because he had been exposed to the use of Hirudin in heart surgery and that experience occurred at Duke University in North Carolina. Mother and I knew of Duke University's reputation because of recent research and discussion regarding my nephew's selection process for college studies. We later comforted each other with the wonders of medical science and the doctor's training at Duke. Same surgery, different drug and the surgeon's familiarity with the amended procedure set well with us at the time. I did ask the mortality risks regarding a redo CABG using an alternate blood thinner and his response was immediate and reactive – 10%. He instantaneously explained a 90% survival rate – we were encouraged by his disclosure.

I glanced toward Mr. Laurence and he was showing physical signs of exhaustion. Two hours of pounding the details of the case was taking its toll. He wiped the sweat from his brow and his clothes were darkened by perspiration. He nonetheless continued his delivery, "Dr. Zopyros admits from the witness stand that it was his responsibility, once he decided to go to surgery, to determine what agent to use, what equipment to use, and to monitor the blood appropriately. Obviously, the machine clotted. There was no explanation from Dr. Zopyros as to why the machine clotted. It's obvious that either one of two things happened: Either Heparin somehow got into the system, or there was not enough Hirudin infused into her body and into the machine in order to adequately anticoagulate her blood."

Since the failed surgery, I have learned a lot about bypass surgery, blood chemistry, monitoring standards and medical protocol. At that time, however, I simply did not know what to ask. And when I did ask a question, how was I to know if the response was credible. At 2:15 PM on the 28th of March, 2002, an assistant surgeon gave me an update of the surgery. His report was wrought with clinical problems. He emphasized the attempts of the surgical team to repair the holes in the lining of the heart. Why were there holes in the heart? No one mentioned the possibility of holes! What are her chances? The assistant surgeon responded that the holes are characteristic of re-do surgeries. And because it is a re-do surgery her chances of survival were 50%.

The assistant surgeon turned and disappeared behind the swinging doors that lead to the surgical suite. I turned to make my way to the surgical waiting room. What happened to the 10% chance of death – the 90% chance of living? It was at that time the emotional eruption that I had avoided overcame me. Instead of returning to the waiting area, I ran, uncontrollably at times, to the professional building that was connected by an elevated crosswalk to the hospital. I burst through the doors of Dr. Pantheras' office. The lobby was full of patients awaiting their turn with the doctor. The receptionist immediately took me to an exam room; I was certainly a disruption. I told the doctor of my conversation with the assistant surgeon and he called the surgical suite for an update. The call was brief, extremely short. He looked and me and suggested that I allow him to escort me back to the surgical waiting room. Dr. Pantheras did not say another word – the meaning was clear.

Reliving that experience resurrected the emotional strain of that afternoon and I began to cry. Ms. Gee presumed I was moved by Mr. Laurence's comments and she leaned toward me to offer consolation. The act was effective in that it brought me back to the present just in time to hear Mr. Laurence say, "So, ladies and gentlemen of the jury, we believe that the evidence shows and the literature that we've looked at shows that she had an allergy to Heparin. And that based on the evidence that was in front of Dr. Zopyros as of the 22nd, the 23rd, the 24th, the 25th, the 26th, and the 27th, the evidence showed that she had this allergy and that he should have stopped the Heparin and should have given her something else to reverse it. He should have never gone to surgery, according to the literature. He should have waited and tried to treat her conservatively and given her a medication to see if she could have gotten past this period where she had the Heparin antibody instead of trying to perform this extremely risky surgery that he had never done and had never practiced and for which he didn't have the right equipment."

"Lastly, we have to prove to you that Ms. Carroll died as a result of the violations of the standard of care. What do the defendants say? The defendants said she died because, according to the operative note, her heart lost contractibility. She bled to death. The surgery was complicated and, during the surgery, I nicked some lungs, and I nicked some other parts of the heart, and there was bleeding everywhere, and because of the bleeding, she was going to die anyway. It really doesn't have anything to do with the fact that I didn't have the right machine or that I've had no experience in administering Hirudin to a patient during surgery or that I'm trying to operate on a patient who's got a Heparin allergy the day after I find it out, allegedly. Or that the literature mandates reversal drug therapy to surgery."

I looked at each juror as Mr. Laurence presented his case. What ownership do they have in this process? Why should they care about mother, or me? What value do they place on their role? What value do they place on my mother – on anyone's life?

Mr. Laurence placed a value on human life from a judicial perspective, "Wrongful death, is unique in Alabama. It's not what you would think. Intuitively, you would look at the value of the life by how much Ms. Carroll would have earned or how much she would have enjoyed life or how much she would have enjoyed spending time with Vicki and Vaughn. Legally, that's not important - we do not look at life that way. Alabama law says that in a wrongful death case, you look to whether or not there's an amount of money that will preserve human life. It doesn't matter whether you are a wealthy person or a person that is not of many means. There's not a specific value on a person's life. But what you, as the ladies and gentlemen of the jury, have to do is to use your collective reasoning and determine, as what the judge is going to tell you is called, punitive damages. Damages that look to how much money will it cost to prevent this from happening in the future to other patients – this in support of the preservation of the human life."

"There's no hard and fast rule for that. And it's up to you, the ladies and gentlemen of the jury, to come up with an amount that you believe will prevent these types of things from happening again. And that's hard. When I'm trying to come up with an amount to ask, it's hard because there's no hard and fast rule.

"But, ladies and gentlemen of the jury look at what's happened in the case. We've had a patient who relied and trusted on a doctor, who developed obvious signs and symptoms of an allergy that went unnoticed and untreated. And then when the decision was made to go forward with surgery, there was a disregarding of the fact that there was no experience, no history and no equipment. There was an arrogance and lack of humility there that cost Ms. Carroll her life."

"And so when you're back there and you're asking yourself how much money we should award in this case due to the violation of the standard of care, I'm going to give you a range."

"If you think there was a violation of the standard of care in this case for a failure to diagnose the HIT early enough, failure to postpone the surgery, failure to properly monitor the blood, I suggest to you that there should be an award between 1.5 and 3 million dollars. That amount is simply a suggestion from me. It's a suggestion because you're allowed to award less than that; you're allowed to award more than that. If you find that there was misconduct in this case, that there was lying or that there was a cover-up or that there were untruths, then you can award the upper end of that, or more."

"And I'm not asking for a specific number because we trust you. Vicki and Vaughn trust you that if you make a determination that there were a violation of the standard of care, to award an amount that you see fit."

"And, ladies and gentlemen, after you've heard all of the evidence and the testimony like you have and after you hear all of the closing arguments, I trust that you'll go back to the jury room and find that there was a violation of the standard of care here, a violation that cost Ms. Carroll her life, and render a verdict in favor of the plaintiffs in the case."

THE COURT: All right. Thank you, sir. Now we will hear from counsel for the defendants.

Defense's Closing Arguments – Mr. Goretti

"May it please the Court? Counsel made some remarks, but before I get into those, I want to say this: You have heard for the last hour accusations and charges of dishonesty and now arrogance on the part of Dr. Zopyros. I'm going to address those in a few minutes. But I want to say this: It's pretty fair for us to keep in mind the credibility of somebody who's making those accusations. And in a few minutes, you and I are going to go together and see exactly how honestly Mr. Laurence has tried to present the evidence in this case - because we've got some issues with that.

"Now, you guys have been here over a week, and I want to say thanks for this: I'm not going to say thanks for being here. I've heard lawyers say that to juries. But the truth is I bet none of you wrote in and asked to be here. Y'all got a summons that said be here. So the system can bring you in, the system can put you in a jury box. But the system can't make you pay attention and listen carefully. And you guys watch us; we watch you guys. And one thing that's become apparent to the Court, to me, to everybody, it is each of you has paid very careful attention throughout this case. And that's important because I'm going to tell you something, that's not always true of all jurors. And so for that, we thank you. Because all we can ask of you in the end is that you do your best to reach a fair and equitable decision."

"The case will be turned over to you in not too many minutes. You'll be charged by Judge Kent with reaching a verdict."

"Now, the word 'verdict' is a significant and instructive term. It is Latin and it means strictly speaking and true statement. And so what a jury, any jury like you, is charged with doing is finding the truth and making a true statement with your verdict. The law, or our system, rather, in turn gives you two tools to arrive at and speak the truth. You have on the one hand the evidence that you get from the witness stand and, in this case, the medical records. And then on the other hand, the law that His Honor, Judge Kent, will give you in a few minutes. And in putting together the law with the facts, the truth emerges."

"So what I'd like to do is talk for a few minutes about the law that is important in a case like this and then talk about the facts and see, when you put those together, what that truth is that emerges."

"Now, I'm not going to presume to stand before you and tell you everything that Judge Kent will tell you about the law in a few minutes. But there are a few things that bear underscoring."

"Can we see Number 1, please?"

"Some of this you've already heard. This is the law of Alabama. The first bullet point is that the burden of proof is on the plaintiffs. In other words, Mr. Laurence bears a heavy burden. He bears the burden of proving each and every one of his claims to you. His Honor will tell you that. His Honor will tell you that he has to prove each of those claims by expert testimony, which is a real issue in case. We'll get to that in a bit."

"Let's see the next one."

"He talked to you about the standard of care."

"Let's see Number 2. He will tell you words either precisely this or real darn close to it: The standard of care for a cardiovascular surgeon like Dr. Zopyros is that level of reasonable care, skill and diligence as other similarly situated cardiovascular surgeons follow in the same or similar circumstances. And this term right here – reasonable care - is huge. Andrew must act reasonable."

"Let's go back to Number 1."

"He'll also tell you that the burden of proof is that Mr. Laurence prove his claims by substantial evidence. And the definition of substantial evidence is significant."

"Let's see Number 3, please."

"He may tell you precisely this: That substantial evidence is that character of evidence that would convince an unprejudiced thinking mind of the truth of the fact to which the evidence is directed."

"Let's go back to Number 1."

"He must convince you. So the burden in this case is for Mr. Laurence to convince you of what? That under these circumstances, Andrew acted unreasonably. He was not reasonable."

"What else does the law tell us? Well, he's already talked to you about alternative methods. And what does that mean? Well, he'll tell you and I think you've seen in this courtroom that doctors don't always agree on the best way to handle a given situation. That doesn't mean one of them is wrong. What it means is that medicine is not a perfect science and that doctors have to make judgment calls. Sometimes good doctors disagree on the best course of action, but both can be and are often within the standard of care if there are alternative methods of treatment."

"Let's see the next one."

"His Honor will tell you that doctors do not and cannot guarantee success, which only makes sense. Every doctor who's testified to you, even Benjamin Arnold, has told you they have had unexpected bad outcomes, including death. And that's not malpractice. Because medicine is not a perfect science, doctors can't guarantee success."

"Let's see the next one."

"His Honor will talk to you about sympathy and emotion. I addressed sympathy in my questions to you back a week ago, last Tuesday afternoon. I didn't address emotion. I want to talk about both of them right now. I told you then and I tell you today, it would be a natural and normal thing for all of us to feel sympathy for Ms. Anderson and Mr. Goodson. They lost their mother. Anytime anybody loses a parent under any circumstances, it's a sad and sympathetic situation. And I tell you and the Judge will tell you that you should not ever feel sympathy. If that's the fact, then we wouldn't want you in a jury room. The ability to feel sympathy and act on it, some philosophers have said sets us apart from animals. And that's a wonderful thing. So emotions like that are things for us to recognize and embrace and rejoice. But, we also need to recognize those feelings, and for the time you're in that jury room, and only during that time, take whatever natural feelings you might have like that and set them aside. That's the point. For that time only, you set them aside because your calling is a higher calling than the dispensation of sympathy. You're called to dispense justice."

"His Honor will also talk to you about emotion. See, that can't influence you. And I'm going to tell you what: From the beginning of this trial until the very end of it until less than five minutes ago, Mr. Laurence has done nothing but try to inject emotion into this case, particularly the emotion of anger. He's called Dr. Zopyros every dirty name you can probably think of; this in an effort to do what? This in an effort to make you angry. Why? So he can ask for an outrageous number – a large sum of money like he did."

"Let's see the next one."

"Before I go there, let me tell you something. The judge is going to tell you that emotion should play no part in the verdict. He'll talk to you - Judge Kent will - about credibility of witnesses. And what does that mean? Well, it means just what it says: The credibility or believability of witnesses. You are asked to determine who in this courtroom has been believable and credible and who has not. And that's pretty darn important when we get to some of the witnesses in the case; in particular, Dr. Arnold."

"Finally, His Honor will tell you - and this may be the most important instruction any jury can get from any judge in any case - is use your common sense. Apply the knowledge that you have gained over the years of walking around and living in this world and apply it to this case."

"Now, with those points of law in mind, let's talk about the facts of this case…"

Mr. Laurence's closing statement consumed over two hours and, now; Mr. Goretti will certainly feel compelled to volley an equal but opposite perspective. Goretti has used two methods of engagement that does not rely on the facts of the case, at all. The first method is the demonization of his opponents by attacking their character and morality as in the examples of Mr. Laurence and Dr. Arnold. And, secondly, to continuously ask where 'Them' and 'They' are and why aren't they sued. Cloaking his client's vulnerability by mudding the waters with his own spin of conspiracy, Goretti is able to confuse the juror. Confusion that is centered on: Who are really the bad people – "Them' or 'They', Dr. Arnold or Mr. Laurence? And 'the safety in numbers' strategy; to introduce as many characters as possible – thus the predatory shark is confused by schooling fish, unable to focus on a single kill. So, on whom does the jury focus their attention – are there too many moving targets?

Mr. Goretti continued his assault on 'Them' and 'They' as he continued his remarks, "We begin with the opening statement. I heard, you heard, I guess, two dozen times, 'They' didn't test for the platelet antibody, they gave Heparin. It wasn't until I stood up and showed you that the 'They' was not Andrew, that all of these other doctors were involved, that none of them thought there was a Heparin antibody issue after the first surgery. And, in fact, when she came back to the hospital, it wasn't Andrew - who started Heparin; it was somebody else. So is that putting the evidence out there fairly? And then the very next witness - the very first witness, Ms. Anderson, takes the stand, and I think you'll vividly recall this. Mr. Laurence misleads her in asking about blood tests. Remember he said, do you recall something about blood being taken on the 6th? Oh, yeah, they came in, and they said - they said it was out of whack so they had to retake it. And then he puts up for you and for Ms. Anderson Number 12 and says, well, how do you explain that there are no platelet blood tests on the 6th? How does one explain that? And I want to tell you something. I think I made a mistake at that point. Because I thought Ms. Anderson and Mr. Laurence had come up with this together. And I was wrong, and I'm sorry. Because I now know having seen how the evidence was presented that, in fact, Ms. Anderson was being misled by Mr. Laurence, just like you. And it wasn't until I pointed it out in her diary that she wrote the magnesium/potassium results were out of whack."

"And let's see the next one."

"And lo and behold, there it is on the 6th: The Potassium and Magnesium tests."

"So I want to tell you something, I think I probably was a little harsh on Ms. Anderson at that time because I thought they probably had done that together. Now I know it's not true. He misled her just like he misled you on that."

"And we've got the 'They', we've got the 'Them', and we've got this. He puts on Dr. Zopyros. And he puts up a chart that says here are all of the ACTs from the slips. Now, according to the perfusion record, there was only 18 minutes between the first and second ACT, but the slip shows almost two hours. The chart he had so carefully constructed was inaccurate. The chart didn't contain the first ACT from the perfusion records."

"Put that back up."

"And what did we look at? We looked at the time for the first ACT, times for the second ACT and the third one. And they all matched up perfectly. But he had had those records for long enough to construct that chart. He had had Ms. Anderson's diary. So we have the 'They' and the 'Them'. We have him misleading his own client on the stand, and then we have this ACT chart."

"What's next? Well, Dr. Zopyros, you say you relied on Dr. Iapetos' report. You couldn't have. It was dictated a month later; somehow, by the way, implying something sinister in the fact that a cardiologist, not Dr. Zopyros, dictated a report a month later. And what did Mr. Laurence ignore, but Andrew pointed out to him?"

"No, sir, Mr. Laurence, there was a report - this is a full-page handwritten report that was there on the 22nd. I saw that. But then finally - then finally, after the 'They' and 'Them', after misleading his client, after his chart misrepresented the time intervals for the ACTs, after that, he pulls out one more trick. He says I'm going to prove that this guy is lying. I'm going to prove to the jury."

"Remember, he said, Dr. Zopyros, you said it would be below the standard of care to give Heparin on the 28th. And you did it, didn't you? You gave Heparin on the 28th, and you're not being up-front with this jury. Well, who was being up-front with whom at that point?"

"Let's see Number 14. Here it is."

"Remember so clearly him standing up here like this; bending, stretching and pointing. He says there it is on the 28th. Lovenox, you gave it. It's in the billing records. You haven't been forthright with us. He's been deciphering and studying on this for gosh knows how long. He said they were billed for Lovenox on the 28th, he must have given it."

"It's a credit. It's a credit! Lovenox was not given and Mr. Laurence presented the bill as if it were administered..."

Mr. Goretti's theme of 'Them' and 'They' was relentless. Every opportunity to insist that there were others that corroborated in mother's care was not missed. Every opportunity to poke holes in Mr. Laurence's character was seized. And one final character assassination remained that of Dr. Arnold, the expert witness for the plaintiff.

Mr. Goretti paused, smiled and then openly chuckled as he continued, "First of all - and I could spend an hour talking about Benjamin Arnold, but a few highlights will be sufficient. He's a guy that can't get a job. He left Connecticut in 2000. We don't know what the circumstances were, but since then, what has he been doing? He has been working locum tenens, going all over the country filling in for doctors who are on vacation. As he admitted, yeah, I'm a temp. I'm a rent-a-doc. He's applied for real positions, he said, at three or four different places, and each time was rejected. But he can't get one job. He can get a job testifying. And he admitted that he makes $120,000 just from initial reviews, trials and depositions. That doesn't include the other time he spends, talking with lawyers, reading additional medical records, reading depositions. So it's $120,000 plus per year."

"Mr. Laurence says, well, this case isn't about surgical critical care, so that doesn't make any difference if that's on this his CV. Yeah, it does. Yeah, it does. If somebody is going to misrepresent something, maybe they'll misrepresent a lot of things. Mr. Laurence put his CV into evidence; we exposed him for what he is."

Goretti's demeanor was much more relaxed. Laurence moved quickly with exaggerated jolts; raising and lowering his volume for effect. Goretti moved slowly and spoke softly. Laurence was often offensive in his delivery – Goretti was anyone's favorite uncle.

Mr. Goretti symbolically signaled the end of his oratory by closing his binder and placing it in his briefcase. He then removed his presentation flipchart from the easel. He instructed his assistant to power off the projector. He then turned toward the jury with open hands and said, "So we take all that together, and what's the truth that emerges? Here it is. Here it is. This case dramatically, dramatically illustrates the precarious and difficult position surgeons like Andrew Zopyros have to deal with. Think about this for a second: Ms. Carroll is in the hospital. She's had two heart attacks: One in the hospital. She's had mitral regurgitation, a severe diagnosed. She no longer can be on Heparin. Everybody thinks she's at risk for sudden death. He's got one or two choices here. He makes it along with some other doctors who agree. He can say, as they suggest, let's just put it off. Let's try to keep her on medicine. Or let's take her to surgery using the equipment that we have available. Either way, either way, there's a risk of what? A patient like this might not survive. And you better believe -- you better believe that if a doctor like Andrew Zopyros said, let's just wait, I don't want to operate, and then in two or three days she has that heart attack and she dies, there will be a Benjamin Arnold who will come in and say, you know..."

Mr. Laurence: Your Honor, I object. That is completely an improper --

Mr. Goretti: No, it's not.

Mr. Laurence: -- argument as to what would have happened had he waited.

THE COURT: I'll sustain and ask counsel to wrap things up.

Mr. Goretti: "Sure. You can see the position that Andrew Zopyros is in. Because, you see, lawyers are the very best second guessers in the world. Show us a situation where something goes wrong, and we can Monday-morning quarterback. But in the real world of surgery folks like Dr. Zopyros have to make decisions based on what they think are best for their patient at that time. Reasonable doctors can reasonably disagree. These reasonable doctors - Pantheras, Allen, and Zopyros - all felt, in their judgment, the best and most proper course is to go to surgery. And that's what they did."

"This is not a man who's dishonest. This is a man who cares for his patients and makes difficult decisions. And he made a difficult decision in this case, doing what he thought was best for his patient, doing what was reasonable in every regard."

"Mr. Laurence has asked you to award an outrageous sum of money to send a message. Well, I agree, a message ought to be sent. But the message is this: The message should be we recognize that medicine is not perfect. We recognize that doctors have to make difficult choices. We recognize that in situations like this, there's no perfect solution. There are risks no matter which way you go. And so when a doctor, an honest and a good doctor, makes a reasonable decision and does what he in his heart thinks is best for his patient, we're going to recognize the law can't guarantee success. And he's done his best. He's acted reasonably. That's all we can ask for."

"That's the message that ought to be sent with the verdict on behalf of Andrew Zopyros."

Mr. Goretti, "Thank you, Your Honor."

THE COURT: All right. Thank you, sir. We'll hear a brief rebuttal from the plaintiff, and then we'll break for lunch, ladies and gentlemen.

CLOSING ARGUMENTS BY Mr. Laurence:

"I will be extremely brief. I could go through a number of different documents and articles, but what I want to talk to you about in the rebuttal is this: Whether or not a doctor made a hard decision is not the law. Damian Goretti told you that you couldn't play on emotion and sympathy, and he stood up and tried to do the very thing that he said you couldn't do. He tried to play on your sympathy that we naturally have for doctors. We respect doctors because of the very urgency that they have with our very lives."

"But the sympathy that he just tried to create is not the law. The law is that doctors are just like everybody else, that when there is a negligent act, they have to be responsible for it just like every other human being in our society. And when there is a negligent act, just because he can hire lawyers that can come up here and yell and scream at experts and then tell you that the doctor deserves a break because he had to make a hard decision, that doesn't mean that Dr. Zopyros is above the law. What it means is, if there was a violation of the standard of care that caused a death, and then the law says there should be a verdict for the plaintiff."

"And the one thing that I didn't hear Mr. Goretti talk about at all, at all, was an explanation that - let me back up. What he didn't describe to you accurately at all was that there really was a Heparin allergy that was causing the clotting. He stood up here and in one hand tried to accuse me of doing something wrong, and then in the other hand, tried to tell you with a real quick slip of the tongue that there's a difference between an antibody and an allergy. And the antibody, she had, but the allergy, she didn't. She had six different large veins clot, and they missed it. The very sick condition that she had was created by Dr. Zopyros. And he tried to point the finger at me and say that I referred to 'They' and 'Them' as those who were responsible for the Ms. Carroll's death. I'll point out that there are two entities sued in the case. It's Vulcan Clinic and Dr. Zopyros. That's plural. That's "They."

"And he wants to on one hand belittle me and our clients for making a lawsuit that we're allowed to bring into this court for suing a doctor. But then he points throughout the trial and says, we didn't sue these other doctors, we didn't sue these other doctors. Well, let me ask you this: Where are they? Where are they? He's standing alone in this courtroom. There's not one doctor that came and stood up and testified on his behalf and said his conduct was proper. Not one. The only doctor that came into this courtroom and said, 'I did everything right,' was Dr. Zopyros, himself. All of the doctors that you saw Goretti point to, they're not here. And they live in town, and they work with him, and they could have been here supporting him, and they did not!"

"Don't you think that if they would have supported his conduct in the case, they would have been on this witness stand standing up for him? They didn't support him. Don't you think that the expert witness in Tuscaloosa would have been here if Goretti had thought he would have been helpful to their case? He wasn't. And that's because the literature in this case - the literature is what says the standard of care is in this case, and every single thing that we showed you was directly out of the primary source of literature in the United States, saying that when you have thrombosis on Heparin, you have to think of HIT, and he didn't. And when you find out that there's HIT, you can't go to surgery, and he did. When you find out there's HIT, you give a reversal medicine, and he didn't. And when you do have a surgery that you have to do with an alternative, you use the ECT machine if you pick Hirudin. That's what this book says, and he didn't do any of those things. And so he can get up here and point at me, and he can accuse me of being dishonest, and he can accuse me of doing things that are improper, but that's simply a case of a lawyer attacking the messenger. When you can't fight the message, attack the messenger."

"The truth is the judge did not throw out any claims dealing with the second admission as to whether he did or didn't diagnose HIT early enough. He found there was substantial evidence that should go to a jury. He found that there was substantial evidence for which it should go to the jury as to whether they should have gone forward with the surgery or used an ECT."

"So don't be fooled by the disdain and bewilderment of Damian Goretti. He's jumped on Vicki Anderson. He's jumped on me throughout the entire trial. He's jumped on Benjamin Arnold. But when lies came out of Dr. Zopyros' mouth, he put his arm around him. Andrew, did you see that? Is it just a printer problem - a printer problem? Did it just roll to the next page? No. Those paragraphs aren't even on the next page, and he's trying to represent it's okay. It's okay. But attack Vicki Anderson because she didn't read her notes right; come on!"

"He wants to attack Dr. Arnold and me. But when Mr. Swindle, who doesn't remember properly the day that he was told to investigate the Heparin allergy, he puts his arm around him and says its okay. It's dishonest!"

"The point is that it doesn't matter whether you're a doctor or a normal human being that is not a doctor. We're all under the law of this state. And the law says that if you violate the standard of care and you cause a death, then you're held liable for it."

"And when you took an oath to be a juror that took some courage, and it's going to take courage in the jury room to make the right decision. And we trust that the right decision in this case will be consistent with the evidence and the literature, that there was something wrong that made her clot her leg. There was something wrong that made her clot her heart. They shouldn't have gone to surgery. They didn't have the right equipment, and they went anyway. Because there's something that caused that machine to clot for the first time in the history of his career, and it's because he wasn't paying attention to what he should have been."

"Thank you"

As with the opening remarks, the tale of two patients continued. Mr. Laurence continued to hammer home the conspiracy theory regarding medical records and 'who knew what and when did they know it', scenarios. He continued to call attention to Dr. Zopyros' poor judgment in performing a first-time surgery without fully disclosing the risks to the family. At this point I stop being critical of the coaches or the players, I became a cheerleader. Let's score, pull the game out at the end and go home. I began to believe it – to believe we might win. I had to. Just as my mother was intrepid living her last days the least I could be is supportive of those who have worked tirelessly to present her case. Present the case in a meaningful style to strike a nerve in a couple of jurors, so that they could lead the others to do the right thing. I expected some consideration for my mother's sake!

Mr. Goretti on the other hand stuck with the 'Them' and 'They' argument, projecting onto the screen the name of doctors who could have made a difference and did not. Strange as it may seem, he was implicating other doctors as having performed malpractice acts. These doctors are also insured by the same company that employs him as a staff attorney. What sense did this make? Except that the window of opportunity to name them as defendants had closed – the statute of limitations had expired. To hell with their reputations, just win at all costs, their standing in the community was collateral damage in presenting a warped and twisted tale to allow a slippery escape by the good doctor. Contradictory, isn't it, doctors being the demigods of the modern world and he is allowed to blaspheme the group to save the one!

Judge Kent announced a recess for lunch and instructed the participants to return at 2:00 PM at which time he would instruct the jury before allowing them to deliberate. I could not eat.

CHAPTER 10

The Verdict

*My life has appeared unclothed in court, detail by detail, death-bone
witness by death-bone witness, and I was shamed at the verdict....*
Anne Sexton (1928–1974), U.S. poet. "Talking to Sheep."

Waiting to take my place in the courtroom, I watch the jurors return.
Each juror had a look of renewed enthusiasm; a smile on their face
and a bounce in their step. The odds were against me that a decision
would favor my efforts. Just like students on the final day of school,
they were on their best behavior. Power in the hands of the weak
most often results in acts of convenience. As the school bell rings
to signal the end of the last day; no matter what has been learned,
no matter what lessons need to be remembered, no matter what
contribution has been made to leave things better – we're going
home – all is right with the world! The jurors sensed that they would
soon be home.

As I took my seat Mr. Laurence turned and placed his hand on
mine and said that regardless of the outcome it has been a pleasure
representing you. With that a sense of finality set in. There was
a tingle in my spine, a sense of falling; I knew that the end had
come. I responded simply by saying that I had always believed in
his abilities. And I had. He fought the war on several fronts; one

front being judicial protocol where one's hands are tied in many ways with regard to what is allowed as testimony. Another front being Goliath – Mr. Goretti's firm with its unlimited resources and experience simply would not concede a point. Another front being public sentiment against lawsuits with the roots of that sentiment planted in the Holy Scripture. And the final front being financial; his firm funded the legal cost of the suit. Surely he had fought a good fight and had kept my faith. I once visited his office and a small statue of Saint Laurence held a position of prominence on his desk. I asked Mr. Laurence's administrative assistance the importance of the figurine. She said it was a gift from his mother as a reminder to remain humble in his endeavors. She continued by giving me a brief history of the saint. St. Laurence when asked by his superiors to hand over the fortunes of the church he presented the sick and the poor. He was burned at the stake.

Judge Kent began his charging of the jury - a judicial act that is intended to keep the focus of the jury on what is important, legal and relevant. At the conclusion of the presentation of evidence, the judge read to the jury a set of instructions that must be followed in deciding the case. Included in those instructions was the law as it currently existed for medical malpractice cases. The jury was instructed that they must follow the law as it is given to them by the judge even if they disagree or do not like the law. In fact, at the beginning of the process when the jury was initially sworn in, each juror swore an oath to apply the law as it is given to them by the judge.

Prior to the judge instructing the jury, Judge Kent held what is known as a jury charge conference with the attorneys from both sides. This so that each side can submit jury charges to the judge for what they believe the law states and which, if read to the jury, they believe would be most beneficial to their clients. The judge reviewed the charges submitted by both sides and picked which suggestions would present the most accurate and balanced statement of the law to the jury.

In addition to the instructions regarding the burden of proof the plaintiff had in proving all aspects of the case by a preponderance of the evidence, the jury was instructed regarding several other general statements of the law. One statement was that an error in the physician's judgment does not mean malpractice was committed. Another statement was that just because another physician would have done something differently in the care of the patient does not mean that the defendant committed malpractice.

Instruction that supported the plaintiff's position was a statement that the patient does not have to prove with certainty that the patient's outcome would have been better if not for the malpractice, but only that the malpractice deprived the patient of a chance at a better recovery. Moreover, the jury should not decide the case based on the sheer number of expert witnesses one side presents, but by the quality and credibility of the testimony presented. His directives were simple enough…consider the evidence, discard opinion and come to a unanimous decision.

We rose as the jurors filed past the plaintiff and defendant to deliberate the evidence of the trial. I made an attempt to make eye contact with each as they passed. No juror looked at me; in fact their exaggerated body language was rigid and awkward, most looked away or at the floor as they passed. One juror – the sleeping juror – actually placed her hand over her brow as if to shade her eyes from the sunlight. I wondered if she were ashamed, I was embarrassed for her! It was Tuesday, November 13, 2:21 PM.

Mentally exhausted from wrestling with the emotional currents of trial arguments and overwhelmed with nervous energy, my mind once again wandered. In my research I had read that as many as 220,000 deaths per year occur as a result of mistakes made by physicians and hospitals: 106,000 of those deaths were a result of adverse reactions to medications; 12,000 of the total received inappropriate surgeries; the numbers were staggering. Botched surgeries, missed diagnoses, failure to act timely; these are some of the reasons for unnecessary death. And all due to an arrogance that originates from society's proclamation of these individuals as untouchable. It is as if the profession has a stranglehold on humanity that if we attempt to hold them accountable they will withhold their services.

I can't help but wonder if another industry had similar statistics. What if comparable numbers were the case for, say, commercial airlines? Flight mishaps that result in 220,000 deaths annually; a jetliner crash each day; a life lost every two minutes in the course of a twenty four hour period, and no questions asked. And with that, public acceptance that those in charge of making decisions that affect the lives of others is unequivocal; a belief that those in charge are doing their best and should not be questioned; and that tough decisions merit special accommodations. The practice of medicine must have strict and enforceable rules that regulate how care is tested, delivered and maintained. Physicians must perform under the same scrutiny as the least of us.

I found a quiet place to reflect on the thirty one days that marked the end of a life.

Astonishingly, three heart attacks and two open heart surgeries that occurred within a month. Within this timeline the development of a suspicious, severe Deep Vein Thrombosis that was dismissed as unremarkable. An allergy to Heparin that was undiagnosed until it was too late. The doctor's continued denial of the existence of Thrombocytopenia. Abnormal lab values and a surgeon's first attempt at what, for him, was experimental surgery without the proper protocol and equipment. All of these points alarmed me then and now. Each point had the impact of the sound of a hammer striking an anvil to shape its subject. Clear, loud and real; these events were distinctive and disturbing. Collectively, they should have set off many alarms to those in whom we entrusted her care.

Even though my mother was the victim of seemingly everything that could go wrong, she never stopped living. The Tale of Two Patients still bothered me. The day before the bypass pump clotted, she was walking, sitting, working crossword puzzles, eating, engaging in conversation; no indication of a woman at death's door. Fear may have possessed her; she did not let it show. I tried to be like her. Strange as it may be, I still draw strength from her courage. The text on her grave marker states, 'To live in the hearts you leave behind is not to die'. She still lives in my life.

Ms. Gee motioned for me to return to my seat. The jury has reached a verdict. The time was 2:40; nineteen minutes in deliberation! How could they have had time to elect a jury foreperson, re-read the judge's charging of the jury, take their seats? The jurors made their way from the Jury Room in single file to the Juror's box. Each took their seat and looked toward the judge. No one looked at the plaintiff or the defendant. The judge asked for the written decision from the foreperson, before opening the envelope he asked if the jury was unanimous in its decision – each juror nodded in the affirmative - and did anyone have anything to state prior to the reading – they all nodded in the negative – with that communication he opened the envelope.

As the judge read the verdict, I did not know where to look. Should I watch the judge, no he is the messenger. Should I watch the jury, no they are predictable. Should I watch the defendant, no he looking toward the ceiling, and beyond? Should I watch Mr. Goretti, yes he is the one to watch. He sat their flipping through a writing pad with a slight smile on his face. We had delivered several blows to the defense and never were we able to compromise the doctor's armor. The armor was his god-like persona, his altruistic image in sacrifice to save his patients, his status as an honorable family man in the community; all of which heavily influenced the juror's minds. It was as if I were asking for the death penalty.

Reading the preprinted form that the jurors were instructed to submit, His Honor simply stated that the jury finds in favor of the defendant. Simple, quick and void of passion, the trial was over. The judge looked toward the jury box and offered his gratitude for their time and excused them.

Immediately after the verdict was read the jurors hastily gathered their belongings and rushed from the court room as if they were rock stars leaving the stage. The defendant and his attorney exchanged smiles, handshakes and back-slapping. The doctor's wife bolted by me to join the celebration; his daughter stood and applauded her dad.

My legal team busily began packing their supplies and support documents. I moved away and waited to have a word with Mr.

Laurence. Finally, Mr. Laurence and Ms. Hartselle approached me with their apologies for the verdict; up-hill battles, public sentiment, complex medical issues, all were dimensions of the conversation. He also mentioned that his legal team would review the court documents for a reason to appeal. Appeal? I don't want to mount that horse again. One that has thrown me repeatedly!

I was alone in the courtroom. Noise from the street below, muffled conversation from the Judge's chambers and occasional footsteps from the hallway reminded me of life outside of this room, outside of this appalling experience. I left the courtroom and took the elevator to the basement. Exiting through the freight door I walked up the ramp and crossed 21st Street. Standing on the sidewalk, I watched the doctor and his family saunter to their car and leave the lot. As I followed the car, my eyes made a complete circle of vision. Office and judicial buildings walled the area and dozens of people made their way about their business. I had experienced the worst possible ending to my quest. It was time for me to go home.

It was well after midnight and this was a day I will never forget. I looked intently at the last glass of the bottle of pinot noir; the past few hours had been a time of self-medication and reflection. The evening had been spent either flipping through photo albums which brought nostalgic, bittersweet anguish. Or, rehashing the trial and reliving the hospitalization which caused self-indicting anger. Across the room, two leather chairs bordered a table that was positioned next to a reading lamp. On that table was an onyx chess set. It had been a focus of my attention for several hours as I mused. For the first time, in a long time, I did not have a plan. Forget a plan, I didn't have a mission. I knew in my mind that I could not accept this as a final chapter. Even though I lacked imagination as to what to do next, I hoped inspiration would find me.

Tired of sitting, I walked to the table and picked up a pawn. I had learned this game as a child, the pieces, the movements and the strategies. Even though I didn't win all of my matches, I was nonetheless competitive. I knew my way around the board. Holding the pawn, I began to mull the players in the trial. I placed a pawn to represent myself on the table and another pawn to represent the doctor. Placing the pieces as if to have them face-off in competition I wondered what pieces would represent the attorneys? Would the bishops work? No, after some thought I determined they are pawns, as well. Which piece would be best suited for a juror? Although I had been told by my attorney that the jurors are in control of the decision, they were not in control of the process. A pawn seems appropriate for them, too. The Judge, what piece is best for His Honor – a King? No, he doesn't have that much control or power; he, too, is limited by protocol. Perhaps a bishop is best suited for him – one that manages the edicts of the king. A bishop and a few pawns; certainly not an imposing cast of players; pushing the remaining pieces from the board something seemed to be missing. Where is the King; who is in control? Who was in control of the dynamics of the trial, the lawsuit, the law, and of public sentiment? No players represented on the board.

Returning to my glass of wine, the nagging thought of the missing player stirred me. Like having a word on the tip of your tongue, it was there and real. I then took a pad and pencil from the desk. I had planned to record my thoughts of the trial and maybe outlining the events would jog my memory. Across the top of the page I wrote Trail: Day One. Underneath the heading, bullet point number one: Pre-trial Motions. The first pre-trial motion was presented by Mr. Goretti. He insisted the relationship between the defendant, the expert witnesses for the defense and himself be barred from trial testimony. Why was he so passionate about having that information barred from trial testimony? Was there something there that I could use? The pieces began to come together in my mind. And it was that connection where I found the inspiration I needed. The malpractice company that covers the doctor also covers the expert witnesses and employs the attorney. What other influences does the company exercise? Political, do the lawmakers in Montgomery bow to the company? And public relations, which personalities in the media are the voice for the company and to what extent does the company go to in its efforts to influence public opinion? Under the table dealings, who is on their payroll? Does the company have a hunting lodge in Western Canada? If so, does the company exile potentially harmful witnesses to hide the truth? This entity was the major player; the unseen player – the King on the chess board. This is the one who controlled the dynamics of the trial, the lawsuit, the law and public sentiment and the one about which I knew the least.

This was my next mission; what is the King's dominion? I accessed the company's website and found nothing more than public relations dribble. I wanted the unadulterated scoop on what it does, how it does it and why. For this I would need more than promotional material. I would need an expert witness; someone on the inside. How would I do that?

PART II

The Reckoning

So comes a reckoning when the banquet's o'er,— The dreadful reckoning, and men smile no more.

John Gay (1685–1732)

CHAPTER 11

The Kingdom

In the animal kingdom, the rule is, eat or be eaten; in
the human kingdom, define or be defined.
Thomas Szasz (b. 1920)

As the traffic passed the intersection of Zelda Road and Chestnut Street, I waited for Amanda to arrive. My need for her was insight; to provide an intimate perspective into the inner workings of the Kingdom. An insider's distinctive viewpoint would shed light on the seamy underbelly of the malpractice insurance industry. As I was downing my third cup of coffee, a tall, thin lady walked into the coffee shop. She was wearing a heavy coat, woolen scarf and gloves as if it were a winter's day in Minnesota; the temperature that morning was moderate at the very least. Was she cold or in disguise; heavens, I am making too much of this. Making the presumption she was my contact I stood to introduce myself. Before the introduction could be made she asked, "Are you wanting information about the agency?"

I had found Amanda by watching the employees of the malpractice company. The staffers would walk from their offices to the snack bar located in an adjacent building. I observed their comings and goings for a couple of days so that I would be a familiar face in the crowd. Approaching several and introducing myself, I posed as one who knows someone that is looking for a candidate for employment. A candidate that has insurance experience and could they help me. Most said that they were satisfied with their current employment; some said nothing at all and distanced themselves from me with an obvious nervousness. I realized that my presentation was suspect as I was not getting past the introduction. So I modified my approach by asking if they knew someone who had recently resigned their position. And if that person may have regrets leaving their job. Most could not help or would not help. One gentleman on the other hand did know a person. And he was willing to share her name and current employer's phone number. His eagerness to assist was borderline flirtation; a possible tit for tat exchange. I got the tat; he did not get the tit!

Care had to be taken in approaching her with my needs. Having one name to call, one opportunity to sell, a single shot in the dark; the presentation had to be crafty. I called Amanda and asked if she would meet with me to discuss the workings of the company. Remuneration was the bait for her time and information and continuing studies was my reason for needing her. As it happened, she confided that money was a motivating factor. She was late paying several financial obligations. Her request was to meet as soon as possible.

It was a Saturday morning, a few days since the verdict. I really did not know where to start. My recent exposure to legal protocol was much more a lesson in frustration than a tutorial in harvesting information. Approaching her and the subject would be simple and direct. Tell me and the world what happens inside the walls of the company. With that she began to answer. Noticing the voice recorder she stopped. She turned in her chair and shifted her focus toward the window and asked, "Why are you recording me". The recorder made her extremely tense and guarded. Two minutes into my interview and she had raised her guard. Startling her, I resorted to courtroom theatrics. Jumping to my feet, I tossed the small recorder into the trash can near the door. Returning to the table I said, "Let's keep this relaxed." This surprised her; to throw away a perfectly good recorder was an extravagant action in her mind. She was impressed with my passion for what she possessed - her knowledge of the industry. And my actions may have given her the perception that this was important and cost was not an issue. I never presumed her to be unintelligent. She proved that by being very descriptive and slow-speaking. After all, I was paying her by the hour! She began by saying, "Let's discuss what is not obvious to most people."

She began by defining an insurance company's core competency and that is to acquire money to invest; plain and simple. Investments in stocks, real estate, whatever; the goal is the accumulation of funds - lots of money. And malpractice companies secure their investment funds from physicians. Doctor's cannot practice, or at least should not practice medicine without this professional liability coverage. They are assessed and rated on a risk scale. The ranking on this scale governs the cost of coverage; an unambiguous straight forward formula and resulting fee schedule for covered services. When a physician is sued for malpractice there are costs in defending the doctor; legal fees, loss of production time and payment of awards if the case is lost or settled out of court. This, more often than not, is justification to raise the premiums; to increase the amount the doctor must pay because he is a greater risk. And if the premiums are not increased for the offending doctor, other doctors carry the burden in increased costs. Most people are led to believe that litigation costs are the primary reason why premiums increase annually. What is not commonly understood by either the public or those that work in the industry is this scenario is not the primary reason rates are increased.

The insurance companies through propaganda and legislation promote a deception that malpractice lawsuits are out of control. And that the cost of this out of control trend is driving up the price of liability coverage for all physicians. Thus squeezing the medical industry's profits and making it difficult to make ends meet for the practitioner. Now, lawsuits do place a minimal financial strain on the insurance companies, but this strain is in line with the general increase in healthcare costs and inflation. For example, studies have indicated that the trend in the 1990s showed that premiums increased at 4 percent annually. This increase matched or exceeded the payout to medical malpractice plaintiffs. Then as 2000 rolled around, things changed. Payouts dropped to 1.6 percent annually and premiums increased disproportionately. Why? Because of a slumping stock market after September 11, 2001, returns on invested money dropped significantly. Premiums physicians had to pay for coverage increased in some cases as much as 25 to 50 percent in a single year. So, to lessen their investment losses, the companies simply raised the rates they charged the physicians.

The fallout from the suspicious rate increases was manifested in political pressure to place capitation on awards; tort reform on medical malpractice claims. The pressure was fueled by doctors leaving their profession and creating gaps in public health coverage. This exodus of physicians inflamed public sentiment and inconvenience is the mother of necessity. So, what began as losses in the stock market resulted in the creation of a movement where healthcare providers must be protected from the evils of the litigators – the trial lawyers. The goal of this movement was to create a utopia where the public has low-cost, or no-cost healthcare and the profession of law takes a back seat to what is really important; an unregulated medical industry. The insurance companies looked on as a civil war waged. The warring factions represented those who sought to hold an industry accountable for its actions and those who would allow the industry carte blanche to charge ahead unchecked. In the middle were the patients, providers, third party payers; all who struggled to make healthcare work.

The patients were at times without adequate medical options, the providers were forced to rely on lessening profits and the third party payers were pressured to increase reimbursement to improve provider income. The vicious circle hurt one group more than the others; the increase in reimbursement caused more harm for the patient as higher healthcare costs were passed on to the consumer. The increased costs were in the form of escalating premiums and larger co-pays, co-insurance responsibilities and deductibles. And unlike the third party payers, the physicians were unable to pass on the increase in professional liability coverage to the patient; provider contracts limit reimbursement to a negotiated fee schedule. So, the malpractice industry basked in the warmth of an economic niche where their clients bought their services as a required component of conducting business. And as efforts to limit the medical industry's exposure to an ever increasing number of law suits, the malpractice companies kept a low profile as the public's pressure on the Federal and State lawmakers was intensified.

She went on to say that the company defends its economic agenda by asserting that reduced return on investments does not cause an increase in medical malpractice premiums - because the rates that can be charged are regulated by the state. Of course, there are different rate schedules based upon the outcome of a physician's risk assessment and the insurance company can't raise the rate of a physician without re-classifying the doctor's risk rating. So, when the assertion is made by the company that its revenue potential is fixed based on state laws, the risk rating of the doctor is the variable and it is defined by the company. If more money is needed, the stricter the company is on those that commit indiscretions; and as the risk rating increases so does the amount that is charged for professional liability coverage. That is why malpractice costs have increased as much as fifty percent in a single year; the reclassification of doctors who made mistakes. The argument of fixed income does not have merit.

She continued by describing what she called the wooing process; attracting physicians as potential clients. The medical industry at the physician level is paradoxical. From one perspective it is easily seen by the lay person as an obvious network of closely related disciplines; a good-ole-boy club of men and women professionals that confide in each other; sharing the risks and rewards. Medical disciplines that are integrated and homogeneous. A network that is standardized and stalwart. The practice of medicine is seen as a thriving economy; a model of western capitalism.

On the other hand, each doctor feels as if he or she is alone on an island. Solo providers or small groups that are unable to negotiate with third-party payers find themselves having to do more with less. No economies of scale exist to leverage purchases for supplies and equipment. The public's perception of the physician is that money is not a problem. Big houses, country club memberships and fast cars are more indicative of their lack of frugality than their net worth and financial savvy. So, when a sales rep appears at the door offering a service to protect the doctor from potential financial ruin, he believes it is an offer he can't refuse. He agrees to pay for protection; legal protection; this in hopes of eliminating one potential nightmare.

The primary marketing ploy of the company is the concept that the company will never settle a law suit; the company will 'fight the claim to clear the doctor's name'! The company is proud of its long-standing record of tough defense. It boasts having hundreds of millions of dollars in reserves; this to cover any judgment and legal defense cost. The sales reps pitch the experience of the claims team. They emphasize the medical, legal and industry background of each staffer. They also brag about the success of the seasoned attorneys that represent the doctors and how they never lose a case. This combination of administrative and legal expertise provides the prospect with a high level of comfort – a confident swagger as a sales rep once said.

Added to this, the company promotes another vital feature. One that provides special assistance to a doctor if he 'thinks' a complaint may be made against him. This service consists of an attorney that mentors the doctor through the early stages in the development of a potential lawsuit. This mentoring is to provide the physician peace of mind that nothing will be missed – no surprises. Its actual benefit is not intended for the doctor at all. It is a risk management tool for the company. This tool dictates early intervention to minimize the company's exposure regarding liability concerns; it encourages the doctor to 'come clean' so to speak. It also serves to monitor and manipulate the doctor's actions to avoid legal blunders. So, what on the surface appears to be hand-holding benefit actually becomes a handcuffing experience.

Another feature of the company in the recruitment of a physician is the advisory committee. This committee is staffed by physicians representing multiple specialties. The collective experience of this panel represents hundreds of years of expertise. This entity is offered to the doctor as a resource that is available to assist the claims and legal teams in researching and preparing legal defenses. This collection of caring colleagues is perceived by the prospect as a helpdesk for solutions to problems that may find him. This tribunal is the personification of a living and breathing library of wisdom and acumen; a collection of self-ordained high priests. What is not shared with the prospect is the fundamental role of this committee.

This role is to serve as judge and jury. When a complaint is filed against a doctor, he may very well find himself in front of this authority defending his actions. At this time, their collective experience and knowledge is not a refuge for the doctor it is an inquest, an intimidating and humbling experience. The doctor does not have the luxury of legal counsel; this peer review is closed and private. His efforts in defense are either to save his coverage – he could be dropped; or to save a rate hike – the cost can skyrocket. Rarely do the blemished escape sanctions; the latter being the most common form of punishment.

A feature that is closely related to this committee is its persuasive power to recruit expert witnesses. If an expert witness is needed to support a doctor's defense, the company's client list of physicians is quite extensive. The physician / witness resources are more than willing to help a doctor in need. The prospect is comforted in the knowing that this big, happy family of colleagues will drop what they are doing to assist. What is not communicated to the prospect is if a physician does not volunteer to become a witness, other forces can be brought to bear. Those doctors that appear before the tribunal to save their coverage and rates are more susceptible to acquiesce. Once again, the underlying truth is that the company will exert undue pressure. This pressure is placed on the physicians that stand before it in defense of themselves. The pressure is to say anything on the witness stand to assist a colleague. For the doctor's trouble and effort in assisting, a courtesy may be extended and an indiscretion forgiven; a dollar of future insurance costs saved. This approach is a well understood dynamic that is never the subject of conversation.

A doctor is persuaded by the features and benefits. These features and benefits are centered on the promise of support for the doctor through critical times. Critical times are foretold as an event that will happen, regardless of the doctor's caution. The support is defined as an expert team of professionals that have the doctor's best interest at heart. Sold on the fear of losing one's practice and on the security of the closed ranks of the organization, a doctor is foolish to decline the offer. An offer than can't be refused.

The doctor submits an application for protection. This is the doctor's authorization to permit the company to delve into every nook and cranny of his personal and professional life. Digging for dirt and buried skeletons, no detail escapes this scrutiny. No awards are given for discovered merits; penalties are assessed for the most minor fault. Accompanying the application are documents to support educational and licensing status of the physician. Education credentials must list the schools and the major and continuing education credits. All licensing both state and local have to be verified.

With an application for insurance, a history of the doctor's 'prior acts' is researched. Background checks are performed to establish moral turpitude and medical acumen. Prior acts are any complaints, inquiries, criminal or civil actions; medically related, or not and law suits; settled, or tried. A comprehensive listing of the doctor's personal and professional life; details that would include substance abuse, cruelty to animals, spousal abuse, office hours, office location, services performed, anything that could be defined as a risk. The company looks for any reason to adjust the amount that is charged whether it is industry related or not. Agreeing to the application process is the tip of the iceberg; financially surviving the scrutiny is titanic.

A doctor's specialty is examined when researching what services are provided by the practitioner. If a doctor is not credentialed, or trained to perform a service that service is carved-out. And if a complaint is filed regarding a non-covered service, the doctor is back on the island alone, no support from the company. Often a doctor may, in an attempt to generate additional revenue, perform popular medical procedures. Those procedures that appeal to the vanity of a patient and provide a needed increase in cash flow are often too tempting to ignore. And temptation is defined as a weakness, an emotional shortcoming, when assessing financial risk.

The facility where the doctor practices medicine is inspected to make sure that optimal conditions exist to perform covered services. No stone is left unturned. On-site inspections are conducted. This bricks and mortar approach provides another variable to allow the company to opt out of coverage when convenient.

All in all, the company looks for what they call risks in insuring the doctor to protect the company. In reality, the company will insure anyone that can, or will pay the premium. The extreme risks are in effect self-insured as evidenced by what they are required to pay. The doctors know they can't, or shouldn't practice medicine without coverage. And hospitals require proof of insurance before privileges are granted to practice within their confines. The doctors endure the scrutiny, holding fast to the illusion - the illusion of a coalition of physicians working together to provide mutual legal protection.

The information from my informant has been interesting. Catchy phrases like, 'fight the claim to save the doctor's name' and 'the big, happy family' is a bit trite, but not condemning. And the fact the company gouges the doctor for more money, well, what is unusual about making a buck. If the doctors are not willing to pay the company's price why not go to another company? Her answer was revealing, to say the least.

The company knows that many times it would be more cost-effective to settle; the money versus the aggravation factor. But in the big picture the company closes more sales because the prospective clients - the doctors - feel more secure with the aggressive approach in defending all complaints. After all, there is a belief held by each physician that regardless of a mistake that might have been made, their integrity will be preserved when reviewing the complete record; the record of who they are and what they do. Their arrogance is a product of the process they had to endure to become physician. While the average person was learning interpersonal skills, humility and politeness; the doctors were exiled to their studies and residency where the traits of condescension, superiority and egotism were ingrained. Then when the company fights a law suit by going to court the expenses are then passed on to the doctor; naively he thinks this is better than settling at a fraction of the cost. He is now a higher risk and reclassified as such. The doctor's appearance before the committee is his only opportunity to appeal the reclassification – battles are never won in that theatre.

Then there is more, with this considered a prior act – on the books, if you will, a court record – no other company will insure him at a standard rate. The option of moving to another company would require the purchase of a tail policy. A tail policy would cover any complaints prior to signing with the new company. Then, the cost for the new coverage will be extremely elevated because the doctor is now a higher risk. So, even though the cost to stay with the company is much higher than before, the doctor stays and pays - the pain to change being greater than the pain to stay the same. This relationship represents a type of symbolic coitus between an entity of superior size and an unwilling recipient – a painful experience. The doctor is damned to spend his existence with the company that fought to clear his name. There is also an added, unspoken pressure to cooperate if the company should need a hired gun to support a colleague's case; an arm twisting, slap in the face experience. There are many prisons without bars; the most harsh being a self-imposed detention. The company creates a dependency. A dependency in the sense the doctors have few, or no, options to exercise - nowhere to go without major penalties.

Amanda not only provided answers, she also interjected questions that I did not think to ask. If the doctor can't leave what are their options internally, the committee? Do any of the doctors complain? Do they have any recourse? As I listen to her I found it difficult to believe that in a society of options, in a world of point-and-click solutions, one does not exist for this scenario.

She continued by explaining they do have an option that is certainly not made public; but is as obvious as the nose on the face. Their recourse is to sue the company. Close the gap and play their game!

Why would a doctor sue the company? This caught my interest. Since the verdict, I have been at a loss as to what avenue I could pursue for closure. I feared that my one and only chance was the trial. Getting the case to trial was a feat within its self. Winning the trial was, in retrospect, a long shot. Now, this may be a ray of hope.

Hypothetically, she said, "Let's use an example of a doctor that was sued for wrongful death. Let's presume the plaintiff has a strong case and competent legal counsel. Let's also suppose the company's in-house attorneys have to expend great resources and effort in defending the case and the fees mount. Let's also imagine it cost half a million dollars to provide the defense. An innocent verdict does not make everything OK; in fact it is just the beginning for the doctor. It will take many years to re-pay the legal fees with inflated premiums. It does not matter what he may have paid in past premiums, those days and monies are gone. Publicly, the company will assert the legal expense is part of the doctor's basic coverage, but why do they raise the doctor's insurance costs? A savvy doctor will then ask the company what would have been the cost to settle the case. And if the doctor feels that it would have been less to settle, then he may have a case to sue. If the company says that was not an option, the assertion is, why not and legal malpractice is suspected.

Amanda noticed my puzzled expression and before I could ask the obvious question she responded, "Sue for what?"

She said, "There is a concept, a legal principle called Informed Consent."

I lifted my hand as if to ask for a moment to absorb what I had just heard; informed consent! I quickly typed the words Informed Consent into an online search engine and Wikipedia displayed the definition. Would it apply to this situation?

Informed consent is a legal condition whereby a person can be said to have given consent based upon an appreciation and understanding of the facts and implications of an action.

Implications? Had the company fully explained the implications of a trial?

The individual needs to be in possession of relevant facts and also of his reasoning faculties, such as not being mentally retarded or mentally ill and without an impairment of judgment at the time of consenting to the relevant facts.

Had the company explained its benefits for going to trial? Has the cycle come full circle? The case against Dr. Zopyros was in large part due to lack of informed consent; he did not tell all that he should have told prior to the surgery that killed my mother. But how does this apply here?

"In our pretend case', she continued "the company did not tell the doctor of the ramifications of going to trial; or the option of settling, which the company does not extend to the doctor. The doctor loses in any scenario; the question is by how much. Another angle to consider is how much money will the company make if it goes to trial from a marketing perspective; the company will not lose any money from an expense standpoint – that deficit is passed on to the doctor. A decision for the Defense is a public relations victory for the company; it is not in the best financial interest for the company to settle. So, informed consent applies because the client – the doctor – was not given an option; a choice in his future. And the company – the attorney – profits from this lack of disclosure. The doctor, in fact, becomes the topic of conversation for the next sales presentation, 'fight the claim to save the doctor's name'!"

Lack of informed consent is the charge and a legal option is the avenue, what can he hope to get from suing? Where does the money come from; the doctor, other doctors, higher cost of medical care, where? Does he sue for money? Does he sue to reinstate his low-risk status? Sue for peace of mind? What is the purpose?

Lawyers are bound by ethical rules and standards, both written and unwritten. Sometimes lawyers forget that they are in a fiduciary relationship with their clients which requires them to act with the highest level of trust and integrity known in the law. Sometimes, they can act greedily and unethically without regard to their client's best interest. Often, violations of ethical rules involve a conflict of interest for the lawyer. Conflicts of interest arise in many different kinds of circumstances but lawyer conflicts usually have a basic dilemma: The lawyer's advice may not be truly independent, because the lawyer is either representing two or more sides in a matter or the lawyer's interest are in competition with the client's best interest. Violations of ethical rules may give rise to actions against lawyers.

Legal Malpractice is the failure of a lawyer to render competent professional service to a client. If the client is damaged as a result of the failure, he or she may have a claim against the lawyer for legal malpractice.

All insurance companies have insurance; coverage to cloak this type of scenario. It is not a secret that an Error and Omission policy exists that protects the company from those things that are missed or forgotten; or as in the previous example, orchestrated. This concept always reminds of the movie *Contact*, based on a book by Carl Sagan. The astronaut, Dr. Eleanor Ann Arroway is given a pill, a lethal dose of poison, to take if something goes badly. The pill is not for the known possibilities; plans are in place for those scenarios. It is for all of the unknown possibilities; for all of the bad circumstances that can't be anticipated. The unknown or unanticipated scenario in our example is a clever client – the occasionally smart physician that can put two and two together and arrive at the correct answer. This pill, a pill to provide protection for the company, in the real world is the Errors and Omissions policy (E&O) that is underwritten by a much larger company.

This presented a significant turn of events. Instead of the doctor telling one to take a pill and call the next morning; the company takes a pill and hopes the doctor goes away!

This industry is a food chain; a sequence where the smaller in absolute numbers is consumed by the larger. The patient is dependent on the doctor, the doctor dependent on the company, and the company dependent upon the perceived need for its product – a strange symbiosis linked to litigation and trial lawyers. For without the trial lawyers, the malpractice insurance industry would not exist. This process is driven in a bizarre way by fear of the masses. That is, the lesser in the food chain is the masses – the patients representing the larger in total numbers – the smallest in the chain is the single entity, the company. The company fears the doctors and purchases E&O insurance, the doctors fear the patients and purchase malpractice insurance, the patients fear the accessibility to the doctors and secures health insurance. This balance is predicated on a presumed need based entirely on fear. So, to fight the system, one must not be afraid to get hurt. After all, the absence of fear is the quintessential definition of a bully. And each level exerts its leverage to maximize fear and in turn its control.

At that point I had lost track of time. The possibilities seemed real and within my grasp. How could this information be of use to me in my goal of winning my case in an appeal to the public? A tragic death blended with corporate leverage has the sound of an epic tale of power and corruption. How can what I have experienced and learned be exposed for what it is? A proxy is needed to fight the battle and extreme pressure is needed for motivation.

I thanked Amanda for her time and placed two, one hundred dollar bills in her hand for a couple of hours of what was casual conversation for her and a needed stratagem for me. As I walked along the boulevard a unification of theory and application jelled in my mind. I now knew what to do and how to do it – a detailed plan that requires painful leverage and the manipulation of a predictable pawn. I had to create an implication – an adverse implication for going to trial; one that has merit and one that would cause verifiable consequences. The strategy is clear, no need to enhance it, it is simple and direct. The pawn lives as an acquitted man, without fear of appeal. The leverage requires an exceptional effort – the learning of new skills and the most powerful weapon one possesses. Political activists have often said that a creative songwriter has more influence than the most popular politician.

I reached my car an opened the trunk and look for it, where was it? She could help. I'll make the contact today. As I got into the car and made my way to the corner, Amanda waited at the bus stop for her transportation. I stopped and through the lowered glass of the passenger door, I asked a final question; one that I thought had little relevance, but one that my curiosity would have nagged me to resolve.

I asked why she was overly sensitive to recording the meeting. She said it is difficult to explain and even harder to believe; but the company has been known to go to extremes to protect its interest; extremes that could be deemed as unethical or illegal. Anticipating my next question, she said the extremes can be excessive intimidation.

Pressure to force compliance with the company's directives. Or it could anything that seems to be a random act or coincidence. Everything is possible. Contemplating her comment, I did not notice the bus behind me. It then sounded its horn as if to imprint the message deep into my mind. I sped away without saying another word.

CHAPTER 12

The Missing Link

*It is easy to ignore responsibility when one is only an
intermediate link in a chain of action.*
Stanley Milgram

The pieces were beginning to fall together. The unwillingness of
society to believe that doctors can be deceitful, a general disbelief that
an insurance company can be scheming, and a naiveté that a legal
firm can be unscrupulous painted a picture of classic corruption. The
missing piece was the missing witness, could this be a coincidence?
Or, a random act as Amanda suggested? I suspected this missing link
to be weakest link in the doctor's defense.

The deposition of Richard Head, the perfusionist that relieved
Mark Swindle for lunch on the day of the tragic surgery, was at
best inconsistent. His inability to answer basic questions was
presumed to be extreme nervousness, or abject stupidity. And one
could understand the former and could not offer apologies for the
latter. His absence was clearly orchestrated in an attempt to not
compromise Mr. Goretti's case.

Many attempts had been made by several sources to serve him a subpoena, and with no success. Mr. Head and his wife never answered a knock at the door, or ventured out into public. Family made deliveries of food and supplies and shadows were observed lurking beyond sight when strangers peered through the windows. And with the trial in the distant past, it was now time to once again knock at his door and hear his story. Having made the purchase of a recording device that was cleverly hidden in a pen; I keyed his address into the GPS. The estimated time of arrival was fourteen minutes. Fourteen minutes from either completing the tale and closing the loop, or experiencing another setback. For some reason deep inside me I knew something edifying was soon to happen.

Arriving at the residence, I sat in the driver's seat for a few moments to gather myself. I had a catch in my voice and a knot in my stomach. Fear overcame me. Not so much from a standpoint of confrontation as much as the uncertainty of what may happen. So much time and effort had been expended by so many people to get to this point, a time and place where the willingness of a person to be humane could the difference in closure, or continued torture. Climbing the steps to the front door, the sound of dogs barking could be heard from inside the home. And suddenly the barking was behind me. The dogs stood between me and my car and blocked my path for retreat. My first thought was that Head had released the animals to scare me away. And it was at that moment, the door opened and I introduced myself. He then said I know who you are and I have been expecting you.

The home furnishings were soiled with dog hair and urine. And the distinct smell of mustiness permeated the air. So far, the man of the deposition and his dwelling were consistent; cluttered and unkempt. Beyond the sensual marking of the dogs was the evidence of a person who had lost their way. Whiskey bottles that were mostly empty were scattered about as if to have one within arm's reach. And reading material that one would define as tabloid journalism encircled key sitting areas. What happened next was surprising. The conversation began by the announcement that he had retired after the trial. And the reason was based on a medical condition that affected his balance and speech. Even though his speech was affected by the malady, he was not the bumbling idiot that the deposition would suggest. A thought came to my mind that his unwillingness to talk when he should have at the trial had affected his ability to speak now; it was as if fate had overtaken him. He, however, recalled detail and offered thoughtful rationalization for his actions.

After a few minutes of exchanging pleasantries, I leaned forward and made an embellished statement. I lied. And that troubled me to some degree and yet I had been the victim of so many lies, I felt justified. I simply had to know. I made the statement that a junior member of the surgical team had made the comment that Mr. Head had been thrown under the bus and was being made the scapegoat for the acts that were performed in the surgical suite. He reclined in his chair. Looking toward the ceiling to gather his thoughts, or to pool his tears, he rubbed his hands through his graying hair. He then said that a nurse in an attempt to console him said you can't save them all.

He began his tale. The hospital paging system located him in the cafeteria. The message was from his partner, Mark Swindle, that he needed assistance – stat – in the open-heart surgical suite. When he arrived the patient was unstable, bleeding from incisions and oozing from tissue, he pushed Swindle aside. The situation was desperate in that the management of Hirudin had not gone well because of the inability to monitor its effects. And the available blood supply was exhausted. The confusion in the room was reduced to yelling and finger-pointing. The disorder was broken when the shrill voice of a nurse restored focus.

With too much Hirudin in the patient's system, the situation became unsustainable. Hirudin's half-life of eighty minutes and the limited blood supply on hand limited the time necessary for the effects of the anticoagulant to wear off. The combination of events made the condition untenable. It was then the perfusionist, Richard Head, told the surgeon that the bleeding had to be controlled and Dr. Zopyros gave the order: Give the patient the Heparin.

Head then moved his arms in a manner as if to calm me. He expected me to explode with emotion. I was in shock. In a strange way, I felt better. Felt better knowing the truth. His rationale for suggesting the use of heparin even though Mother was allergic to that drug was to create a reverse effect. That is, her allergy to the anticoagulant did not make her blood thinner, it made it thicker. And thicker is what was desired to reduce the bleeding.

After a few minutes to recover my thoughts, I asked why the defense made such a concerted effort to deny Mother had Heparin Induced Thrombocytopenia. Head's response made me angry at the judicial process. The reasoning for avoiding the acceptance of that condition would make it easier to defend the use of Heparin in a moment of crisis. That is, if the truth were ever made known then giving the patient with that condition Heparin would be inexcusable. It would be manslaughter.

I walked toward the fireplace. Above the mantle was the head of a deer. The name plate below the unfortunate creature was Richard Head, Alberta River Valley Hunting Lodge November 2007 Alberta, Canada. That was the same month and year of the trial. I turned and asked if he were an avid hunter. And had he been hunting the week of the trial. Before he could respond, I told him of an acquaintance; a person that had helped the defense by compiling and managing the exhibits during the trial. I told him the name Rob would not mean anything to him, but he had acquired a sizeable medical debt that was burdening him. And a friend of mine that worked in the billing office of the medical facility had made arrangements to have the debt forgiven for specific information. And the information was that the attorney's, through an independent third party, had made the necessary arrangements to get you out of town. His first response was as much a reaction as it was an explanation. He admitted that it was true and said that he did not have a choice in that decision. I didn't admit to him that Rob had not made any comments. I had once again lied.

Richard head's deposition was scattered and suspect because he was a terrible liar and actor. His response to questions had been scripted by Goretti's team. And yet, even with rehearsals, he was never comfortable with that role. The presumption that Swindle's departure from the surgery at a critical time was not an act of irresponsibility, it was one of dismissal: Head had been called to save the day! And with Head's lack of familiarity with Hirudin, he went with what he knew: Heparin. There were a lot of accusations for weeks after the botched surgery. And a protocol for the use of Hirudin was developed six months later.

The opportunity to appeal the decision expired thirty days after the verdict. Still, there had to be a strategy to expose those that had wantonly abused two trusted institutions. The medical and legal professions are staffed with honest professionals making honest livings. But, policing the ethics of each requires its members to recognize and sanction those who practice outside the standards. And when there is a need to preserve the integrity it often requires a purging; a cleansing of the dirty and corrupt. And that begins by making the dirty and corrupt known, publically.

CHAPTER 13

A Most Powerful Weapon

*The most potent weapon in the hands of the oppressor is
the mind of the oppressed.*
Stephen Biko (1946–1977)

———————

The hum of the engines and the constant vibration of the plane
provided a relaxing mix of stimuli as I finally found some time to
unwind. The plane was not sold-out and there was room to prop
my legs on the seat next to me. Forcing myself to ponder more
pleasant thoughts, I found some pleasure in the coming holiday
season. Christmas had always been a time for family and work took a
backseat to shopping, baking, parties and bowl games. An unspoken
and well understood meaning of this time of the year was instilled
in me from my childhood. I was taught by my Mother that one
should live their life from their epitaph, backwards. That is, do the
things and live the life that would provide the pastor that conducts
your funeral with ample resources of good things to say. And that
foundation began with a cornerstone of faith and a framework of
family. The principle on which I was taught to live my life is a
variation of the Golden Rule. I was mentored by Mother to use the
Boy Scout Rule in my daily experience; to leave the campground in
better shape than I found it. What she meant was to make people,

places and things better as having had contact with me. That is why I do what I do; that is why I will not tire in my efforts. Mother would have the energy of a child, hyper in her enthusiasm for opening gifts and making merry. Things would never be the same.

The flight attendant announced that the plane was on final approach to Bush Intercontinental airport and the cabin must be prepared for landing. The usual dialog of seatbacks and tray tables in their upright and locked position and the passing of an attendant to gather all beverage items and discarded materials disrupted my nap. In two hours I was to meet with an author of books of local interest in the Houston area. Contacting Judy TwoBears had not been much of a problem; persuading her to hear my story and assist me in chronicling my mother's experience, was. She was apprehensive, uneasy that I may be overwrought and out of control and this being a probable waste of her time. After all, grief is a strong emotion that can cloud one's judgment and fade over time. Reckoning, however, is a goal that demands resolution. And resolution has been a five year marathon.

Deplaning and winding my way to the baggage area I waited for my luggage and more importantly the boxes of documents and research material I had spent five years collecting. Even though I felt confident that the information was safe; the flight was nonstop from Birmingham, I still did not breathe a sigh of relieve until I saw the five boxes. The containers were printer paper boxes that were given to me by my legal firm. Each container was packed tightly and overly taped. The overuse of tape in itself was a self indictment of insecurity. Fear that I may lose something; I had lost too much already.

A sky captain assisted me as I hailed a cab and made my way home. I live in a suburb of Houston. Kingwood, Texas is not unlike most suburbia environs; complete with shopping malls, a bit of crime and a sense of community. Turning the corner into my neighborhood a rush of emotion overcame me. A part of me wanted to throw the luggage into the garage and forget everything and sleep for three days. That would have been feasible if I were not haunted by a waking nightmare. Instead I placed the luggage inside the front door, the boxes into the Jeep and made my way toward Sugarland for my meeting. Sugarland is a community that was founded in the 1800s and was not surprisingly a sugar plantation. Today, it is a fast-growing community southwest of Houston. Kingwood on the other hand is northeast of Houston and the geography made my commute time unpredictable; traffic and road construction made the trip irritating. I finally made it to the exit that MapQuest listed as the preferred route. And with surprising ease I found the residence of Ms. TwoBears.

The home was a simple craftsman style structure. It was a dwelling that had a gabled roofline, a porch, flower boxes and shutters; a style more akin to a cottage than the ranch style homes of the neighborhood. The landscaping was genuine, not cold and scripted. Much effort had been spent on the appearance. The curb appeal looked less measured and planned and more the work of intuition and feelings. I walked to the front door and as I approached it, it opened with a greeting from an intriguing person, a welcoming from a leathery woman with deep eyes to enter her home.

Entering the home everything in my field of vision was real; earthy objects. No plastics, no synthetics; wood, stone, handcrafted items was not just a theme it was the backbone of the furnishings. I perceived that she was a no nonsense kind of person; a person who sought a simple explanation to problems – a person that that avoided psycho-babble. How would she respond to the medical complexities of my mother's illness, the legal technicalities of the trial or my sense of reckoning in the pursuit my goal? I was not interested in having her write a book about tree-huggers in Alabama; I wanted to right a wrong. She asked me to sit and make myself comfortable.

I began to discuss my situation when she interrupted me with an apology and asked if she could make a request. I nodded and realized that I should speak only when spoken to. There was a writing pad and pen on the table; she took both and placed them in my hands and asked me to define myself in one word or one sentence and take my time. Puzzled and dazed, I had not planned for this turn of events. Define myself, in what context, who I am now, or then? I looked toward her and she was staring through the window, into the garden. And without looking toward me she said that I must find my center. My center; I am not into this kind of thing. I had not anticipated a New Age lesson in meditation. With closer observation of the surroundings, I saw books and literature on meditation and prayer. We sat there for an hour before I wrote my answer.

'I am a message that must be heard, a tale that must be told'. I gave her the pad and turned and walked toward the same window that had held her attention the entire time of my contemplation. This seemed so corny and a waste of time. I felted somewhat embarrassed. She then exited the room and was away for quite a while; long enough to make me feel uneasy being alone in her home. Was she somewhere laughing her ass off or was she simply taking care of other things. Returning with a tray with what looked to be a pot of tea and two cups; she sat on the sofa and asked me to join her. Pouring the tea she said that she could not write my book.

I felt as though I had failed an exam and would have to repeat first grade. My heart raced and I felt flushed. She took my hand and said she would not feel comfortable finishing a book that I had started; a book that I had started? What could she be talking about – that was my reason for contacting her; she is the pro. She took the cup from my hand and placed the writing pad in its place and pointed toward my definition of myself and said here is the first sentence of your book – finish your definition – write who and what you are - and call me.

Strangely enough I felt energized by her directive; encouraged by her cleverness. She had planted seeds of thought in me without any psycho-babble, without measurement or calculation. She accomplished this with intuition. And intuition was a star by which she guided her life's course. I felt as worthy to write my book as her garden was to demand attention of passersby. I thanked her and made my way home via Highway 59. In route I called my office and left a voice mail to my supervisor that I was taking a leave of absence and a follow up call to human resources with the same message.

Organizing my thoughts and without over complicating them, I spent the entire evening outlining how I wanted to tell my story.

Having kept a daily log, a diary, I wanted to use the same format for the book; a format that documents each day of the trial with legal notes and medical details. And to make the reading possess a sense of humanity, personal experiences and feelings of both my mother and me would be added. Writing for effect and reviewing for content and grammar, I slept very little and worked without interruption.

Writing was not difficult. The format would be in a diary structure based upon the trial. Utilizing courtroom manuscripts, I chronicled each day's testimony. Inserting exact quotes when needed and paraphrasing when the attorneys were redundant, I prepared the backbone of the book. Starting at a high level representing the broad strokes of the brush, more detail was added to each level with each passing. Each added level of detail representing ever smaller strokes. This completed, the document provided a comprehensive listing from the medical and legal perspective. It was a document full of facts, but much like a portrait without a face. What was missing was the passion. What was my perspective?

With each day of trial activities listed, I proofed the document for exactness. Technically it was correct. It was not readable, however. It did not capture one's imagination; in fact, it could be a cure for insomnia. Recalling what Ms. Two Bears had told me, I used the book as a template to define myself. Creating an electronic copy of the file, I then added my detail.

Over the years, I had spent thousands of dollars on books, online medical subscriptions and seminars to learn the medical aspects of mother's condition. Hundreds of hours consumed in providing documentation to the legal team. And still, this paled in reference to the emotional energy that was spent during the last thirty one days of her life. Each day of hospitalization was a tome unto its self; each memory a chapter.

I recall the day prior to her death, she was alert. Sitting next to the window working a crossword puzzle she was busy doing things that are not typical of a person at death's door. A person that could not wait for other medical options as the doctor had claimed. With all of the problems she had to occupy her thinking, she found time to mentor me regarding business relationships. I suppose most

VON GOODWIN

people would have withdrawn, circled the wagons and reflected on their personal problems. Certainly this would be an understandable reaction. My mother had a different approach to life.

With my emotions tempered by time and equipped with years of research, I wrote the treatise. A discourse of a life that in some respects faded as fate played its hand - a sermon of a life that in other respects had become larger than life itself. I felt that I was not so much writing a dissertation as much as having it dictated to me. The words flowed and the message grew stronger; no one can avoid accountability. The book with the added detail was at the very least engaging. In fact, it is a fitting testament of a life that was lived to its fullest and ended prematurely. A blending of medical terminology, legal protocol, and technical jargon; with hopes, fears and conversation, it now had the feel of real time. A voyeuristic perspective of intimacies that only mother and I would know. Fittingly, the book was finished in thirty one days.

For me to write a book was noteworthy, to have that writing survive literary criticism was wishful thinking and to have a publisher underwrite the cost was, well, not an option I had considered. I had no fantasies that this effort would compete for shelf space at the major bookstores. Candidly, that was not a part of my mission. To profit financially would be secondary. The goal was to make my story known to the public; to make my resolve known to the doctor.

I made arrangements to meet with Judy Two Bears. She had asked me to contact her upon completion of my 'definition'. Sitting where I had started my book, she took the transcript and placed it on the table next to the herbal tea. I had expected her to immediately flip through the pages and read excerpts and give expert feedback. She continued her casual conversation with subjects ranging from gardening to end of the Mayan Calendar on December 21, 2012. My nervousness did not go unnoticed.

Taking my hand, she said that her review of my book was not necessary. How could she make a critical assessment of what I have lived; and the book was a part of that epic – an epic of living the questions. The drama of the hospitalization, the quest to find the answers, the resolve to find accountability and need to record that passion is personal and private. The attempt to make it perfect based upon some lofty literary scale would have the vanity of elective cosmetic surgery; exaggerated parts here, stuff removed there; a complete makeover of reality; that in itself is defined in its purest sense as fiction. And fiction is not your tale.

A knock on the door interrupted her course in enlightenment. Ms. Two Bears left the room and returned with a guest. She introduced the gentleman as an old friend; one that had assisted her in many of her publications. He sat next to me and removed the manuscript from the table. He flipped through the pages and stopped to review passages. I watched his facial expressions as he read. Some readings resulted in a furrowed brow, some caused a protruding bottom lip, and others a raised eyebrow; I became more nervous by the moment. He turned and asked a couple of statistical questions, "How many words and how long did it take for me to write the book?" I immediately responded 31, thirty one days. And I opened my laptop and provided the answer to the first question; ninety eight thousand words. Ninety eight thousand! I hadn't even considered the word count as a condition. I asked if that was in line with other books. Ignoring my question he asked, "How many books have you written prior to this?" I now felt ill; this would certainly fail my efforts to get it published. I responded, "None like this one." He then tossed the book onto the table and reached for the tea Judy had prepared.

Taking several sips before he acknowledged either Judy or me, he then turned and introduced himself as Tom Lott. Tom is a third-generation owner of a small publishing company located in Corpus Christi. He began a long-winded oratory, one that I imagined he had performed many times. Beginning with how competitive the industry is, how small the margins are, pardon the pun, with regard to profit and how difficult it is to speculate on unproven authors. He went on to say that his guarded temperament came naturally; his rationale centered on an event that happened almost one hundred years earlier.

He went on to describe the events that would shape his caution. In the early morning hours of Sunday, September 14, 1919, a hurricane made landfall in Corpus Christi after gathering strength in the Gulf of Mexico for two weeks. Crowds packed the North Beach area for their last weekend of the summer season, most continuing to ignore the last-minute evacuation warnings of police officers, firefighters and soldiers from Fort Brown.

The rapidly rising water blocked vacationers from escaping to higher ground. As the water rose, people climbed to their rooftops and tied ropes to themselves and their children so that they might not be lost. A giant wave of water carrying oil from ruptured tanks on Harbor Island, timber from Port Aransas and cotton bales from a dock in Corpus Christi crashed down on North Beach, sweeping its victims into the black waters of Nueces Bay.

On Monday morning the sun rose on a scene of terrible destruction. Though the official death toll was 284, estimates place the actual number, including those lost at sea, at one thousand. In the ensuing days, the survivors worked together to rebuild their homes, rescue the injured and bury the dead in mass graves, some containing more than fifty bodies, using farm implements as undertaking tools. A month later the bodies were removed to Rose Hill Cemetery in Corpus Christi and other sites as requested by friends and family members.

Property damage and crop losses were estimated at twenty million dollars. The great storm of 1919 was the worst disaster to hit Corpus Christi in the twentieth Century. So, Ms. Anderson my family has endured great loss and even though I did not suffer firsthand, I do carry a fear that bad things can happen. The building that houses my offices and publishing equipment was one of few that were not destroyed in the deluge. My great grandparents and my father experienced the storm and its effects from the roof; my great grandmother was swept away. This is a memory that haunts me and has affected my business and my personal life to this day. So, I avoid storms; both man made and acts of God.

He leaned forward and re-filled his cup. Taking a moment to enjoy a couple of sips, he then said that Judy had previously enlightened him regarding my quest. He continued by saying, "His sympathy for my plight should in no way affect his business decision, but this is what I suggest." With that, he mapped out a plan to go to print with my book; generate twenty thousand copies, share the production cost and the proceeds, and orchestrate its distribution. Initially, I was taken aback that an offer, any offer, was suggested. Excitement gave way to prudence when I realized I didn't know the production costs. I didn't know what to expect. I cleared my throat and asked, "What do production costs mean in actual dollars?" Tom smiled as he realized my excitement had suddenly derailed. He stood to adjust his belt and took a deep breath and said, "Ten thousand, your cost." I did not know the business, was it a good deal and was it a fair deal? What questions should I ask; should I question at all? Buying time, I stood to adjust my belt. Judy sat between Tom and me, eye level to our Texas standoff. She then said, "Good Lord, Tom, sit down and Vicki take the deal, it is good and fair!" With her clairvoyant comment I extended my hand and agreed to the terms.

He called his office and gave his partner the details of the conversation and made an appointment for me to meet with his legal department to dot the I's and cross the T's. He then instructed me to convert the document from Microsoft Word to Quark and if I had any problems, Debbie in technical support could assist me. With that, he handed me his card and made his way to Hobby airport for a weekend in Vegas; I guess taking a gamble is not that foreign to him, after all.

A few weeks later, a box was delivered to my office. Its content was twenty four copies of the book. I glanced at the calendar, the date was February 26; the date of my mother's first heart attack and hospitalization. Six years ago the thirty one day epic began. My timeline was on schedule. I dialed the number of the doctor's office to make an appointment to have a conversation with Zopyros; a non-medical consultation. The receptionist was extremely inquisitive and guarded concerning my desire to see the doctor and asked what was it regarding? I realize that I may have been too crafty in my approach and I quickly shifted my tone to that of being concerned about my health. Her mood changed as well. She asked what problems was I having and I simply replied, "I have a chronic condition of the heart." I then requested the last appointment of the day to accommodate my schedule. The appointment was made, March 28 at 4:00 pm and the stage was set for the confrontation.

CHAPTER 14

The Confrontation

*A good plan, violently executed now, is better than a
perfect plan next week.*
George S. Patton *US general (1885 - 1945)*

My flight arrived the morning of the appointment, the scheduled
confrontation. Securing a rental car I made my way to the cemetery
where mother is buried. The drive was a forty mile trek that took me
fifty years into the past. The site of the grave was near the area where
mother had spent her childhood; an old mining town that had seen
its best days. Vacant storefronts, homes in disrepair and disabled cars
supported by cinderblocks were testaments of better times. The only
business that seemed to flourish was that which serviced the soul;
the churches were many in numbers and well kept. A cynic would
find some fault in this anomaly; I on the other hand felt a degree of
comfort that some things should never change.

Arriving at the cemetery, I opened the iron gates that were flanked
by old brick columns. An official bronze marker attached to the
right column celebrated the historical significance of the graveyard.
Graves of soldiers from the Civil War, Spanish American War, the
two World Wars, Korea, Viet Nam, Desert Shield and Desert Storm
and the Iraq and Afghanistan conflicts were scattered about as if

sentinels standing their watch. Other graves whose markers had lost their lettering to erosion were older, still. The gate rose twelve feet above the gravel road that had been the pathway for many visitors and mourners. Walking the path that I had trekked on March 30, 2002, the day of my mother's funeral resurrected many memories and emotions. The weather that day was fitting for a funeral, cold and rainy; everything that could agitate the senses did just that.

At the grave site, I expected there to be a need to perform maintenance; weeding, adjusting floral arrangements and the like. I was pleased to find the site clean and well kept. The marker was polished granite with the usual listing of name, date of birth and date of death. The exception was an inscription that I had anguished over for several months. It had to be appropriate, it had to be something she would have wanted and it had to be a source of comfort to me: *To Live in the Hearts of Those You Leave Behind Is Not to Die.* The area is bordered by the same polished granite with white stones that provide the groundcover; sharp lines and neat landscaping; exactly what mother would have wanted.

When I am fortunate enough to visit this place, I find myself talking aloud. Talking to whom? Myself, mother, God; I find it therapeutic in many ways. I am sure the locals would tell me that it is nature's way; God's way of helping us cope with our struggles. Maybe I should talk more; heaven knows that there are many struggles. My faith has been affected by this ordeal. One moment I expect to be reunited with my mother in a better place, one that she once told me about when I was a child And the next, a cynical 'I am not sure of anything' attitude that has found its way into my heart as a result of God's apparent apathy to my struggle. I am ashamed of the latter and long for the former. Long for a day when I am resolute in my standing with those things eternal.

Leaving the cemetery I stopped for a snack at the Cahaba Lily restaurant, a local hangout for teenagers looking for hamburgers and milk shakes. The eatery is named for a rare wildflower found on the shoals of the Cahaba River near Old Piper. The building did not have a consistent color scheme. The fact it had any paint at all was for practical purposes - protecting it from the elements.

The once paved parking lot was in disrepair, pitted with holes and unsightly. Vertically placed four-by-four pressure treated lumber provided the framework to support a tin roof that sheltered the picnic tables and the patrons from the rain and the sun. This outside dining experience was the local's version of al fresco. The screened walls were more than adequate in withstanding the onslaught of insects. If a flying pest were to breach the meshed encasement, a bug zapper was strategically place to lure the victim to a sudden demise. Effective as the screening was in providing a barrier for insects, it had little effect on environmental conditions. The heavy, humid air of summer pressed its way through the tiny openings to manifest itself as beads of sweat on the brows of the diners. The northwesterly winds and winter rains, however, created a bone chilling mist that resulted in many takeout orders. As unassuming as it was, it is the only place in town.

Parking the car, I walked to the screened door leading to the dining area. There were several diners, most of which were retirement age. The wrinkled faces of those I had grown to know reminded me of antiquated books whose covers were worn and tattered but whose contents were rich with information. The volumes represented by as many faces that looked my way as I entered referenced lifestyles whose subsistence was supported by lives of farming or mining. That's one of the depressing aspects of a community in decline, the loss of its youth. I saw a face I recognized. It was one of my mother's best friends. I told her of my efforts to write a book. She was still saddened by the events six years earlier and asked if she could purchase a copy; I gave her a book and spent some time explaining its contents.

She like most of her neighbors in that rural setting trusted the doctors and the facility where my mother had been treated. The facility had been in existence for decades. Neighborhood children had been born there, family members had been treated and recovered there and loved ones had appropriately spent their last days there. The circumstances of my mother's death still, to this day, created great concern among her friends in the community. Describing the trial and the theatrics of the defense resurrected suppressed emotions deep within her and she became angry. What little I was able to share with her in a short time, she was able to grasp the concept that the doctors missed accurately diagnosing her condition, ignored the symptoms and acted recklessly. She, like most people who have not experience courtroom protocol, insisted that I should sue them again, and this time do 'this' and do 'that'; she was full of good intentions.

I finished my lunch and began my exit strategy. The locals were without options to occupy their time with meaningful activities and when there is nothing to do, the only thing to talk about is nothing to do. And Annie was in high gear. As I was leaving, she took my hand and asked if I could give her a couple of minutes to share a story regarding mother. Of course, that was all she had to say. She continued with her tale of a conversation she had with mother two weeks prior to the first heart attack. Dining at a restaurant in Bessemer known for its Greek cuisine, mother had confided in Annie a fear, one of dying and leaving her husband to be on his own. Pop suffered from congestive heart failure, obesity and had an inoperable tumor in the right frontal lobe of the brain. He had been in and out of the hospital for years and mother's role as a wife had been transformed to that of a caretaker. His medical condition worsened on a linear scale and his faculties diminished at an exponential rate. Orchestrating medications, coordinating trips to the medical specialists, hiding the car keys, assisting with bathroom needs; all were exceptions in life for most people that had become daily responsibilities in her life. Annie's concern was did she know, did mother have some ominous feeling of her fate. At this point in my life, I could not discredit any supposition. I left her reading.

I drove through rural communities that were not clearly distinguishable; one from another. In fact, I could not tell the boundary between each except for my mother's stories. And that made each unique. More like a chapter break than that of a city limit. With each rise and turn in the road, landmarks triggered memories of my mother. Like road signs guiding my way, it was as if I were re-living her childhood.

I approached a narrow wooden bridge and that crossed a set of railroad tracks. The single-lane crossing could possibly make one claustrophobic if not for the fear of falling. The structure was support by a complex wooden frame, an edifice that was well over a hundred years old. Heavy timbers crisscrossed to create an arch that allowed the trains to pass underneath. The tracks marked the boundary between Woodstock and Green Pond. I stopped the car and stood where mother once stood. She had on several occasions recalled the story of the train wreck; the great train wreck that occurred in the early 1950s. It was from that vantage point on the bridge that she recalled the derailment that was considered in its day a great tragedy. The derailment killed seventeen people. And as tragic as that was, mother's remembrance of the event was the sense of urgency and helplessness that the locals experienced in their attempts to assist the dead and dying. It was an event that caused her to become an extremely charitable person.

Less than a mile from the train trestle was the old farm house where she lived with my grandmother. The small house is nothing more than an accumulation of rotting lumber covered by a thicket of 'sticker bushes' and weeds. She lived there with her mother and her stepfather. I walked on the same ground where she had played and performed chores as a child. A large oak tree stood tall as a monitor of the lives that it had sheltered from the oppressive summer sun. I know that there is uniformity in nature, everything is made of the same building blocks of life, and I leaned and placed my ear on its trunk wishing it could divulge its secrets. Listening, hoping that it would possibly fill in the gaps of my understanding. Secrets that mother never revealed to me. Secrets that suggested mother was not secure in her surroundings, I am still angered that she had to leave her home to live with relatives. My grandmother, the woman who was responsible for mother's well being as a child, did not make wise decisions. And her stepfather was not a source of security. He breached the ethics and morality of a caretaker.

Not too far from the farm house was the old school. The school is but a shell of the grand, white framed structure it once was. Once a tall A-framed building that was home to elementary school children, it is now a back drop for community softball fields. More recently used as a community center for meetings, it has become tired and wrinkled in its old age as the paint peels and the boards warp. I stood near the area where mother had told me of the story of innocence; a story of her and her classmates; a story of a child's misinterpretation and consequence. As mother told it, she could still see the man waving from the window of the small, single engine plane as it circled the playground. She and her friends returned the wave as if the pilot were simply teasing the children. Mother's recounting of what happened next had a great affect on her.

The children stopped waving as the engine sputtered and smoked. The plane then disappeared behind the trees. She later learned the pilot had died. The realization that the pilot wanted to attempt a landing on the playground did not have complete meaning until she was older. Her way of coping with the apparent guilt one might expect her to experience was the demonstration of wisdom beyond her years. She felt that guilt is an emotion that causes one to become a person they are not; and if our decisions create our life guilt, then, that affects who we become. She honored the sacrifice the pilot made in protecting the school children by crashing the disabled plane safely away from the school. She never shifted the focus from the bravery of the pilot to her feelings. To do so would have dishonored a noble act.

Highway 5 intersected with I-20. The road sign pointed south, for those wanting to travel to Tuscaloosa and north, for those wanting to travel to Birmingham. This fork in the road represented more than instruction to a specific destination, it represented something more symbolic to me. I was presented as a teen the option to take my life in any direction that I wanted. Mother reinforced in me the controversial concept that life is not lived, it is created. This concept was not readily accepted by her church-going friends, they felt that one's life had been predestined by a higher power, a calling to a predetermined lifestyle. And life was to be played as if on a stage, scripted by a preordained set of rules. She respected the values of others and kept her beliefs private. Her purpose was placed on spirituality, not religion. She was not given an option in her adolescence to create her life.

I turned the car in the direction that would create life, or preserve its memory.

Arriving at the professional office building adjacent to the hospital I gathered my canvas bag that contained the weapon – the book. I walked briskly as to not lose my bravado and to exhaust any nervous energy. Entering the doctor's office I signed in and the receptionist asked for my driver's license and insurance card. Even though I had not planned to misrepresent myself I did not anticipate having to fully register as a patient. I gave her my license and told her I would be self-pay today. This was unusual and she did not know how to respond and started to make her way to the doctor for guidance. I noticed the sign taped to the window that stated all co-pay money is due at the time of service. Stopping her I suggested that I would pay two hundred dollars and if that were too much she could mail me a refund, or if too little she could send me a statement. This was more than satisfactory to her, after all part of her performance evaluation I'm sure is based in part on how effective she is in collecting self-pay money. With that she gave me a four page registration form requesting demographic information, health and family history, a consent to treat form and a HIPPA compliance document.

Completing the forms with true and accurate information, I wondered if the receptionist would make the connection. I had listed my mother by name and the cause of death. I watched as she entered my data into the computer. She then took the registration forms and other documents and constructed a patient's chart. Brightly colored decals of letters and numbers were placed on the edge of the manila folder; AND1059 would be my medical record number. She then placed it in a tray and resumed other tasks. So far so good; no red flags, no alarms, what will the doctor think when he sees me. Will he see me? Will he make the association and recommend I see a colleague – as with my previous experience with the doctor, he was late arriving.

The door marked, Do Not Enter, opened and a nurse called my name and directed me to an area for triage. Weighing me, taking my temperature, measuring my height, she recorded my vitals and asked what brings me to the office today? It is customary for the nurse to ask for the chief complaint of the patient to give the doctor a 'heads up' so he can anticipate any questioning. With that I was guided to exam room number 3; waiting there I positioned myself so that I could maximize my effectiveness. I could hear a muffled conversation from the hallway; most words were inaudible, a couple were clear. He had made the correlation and my fear was that he would not see me. I rushed to the door and told him that I did not expect anything of him. I wanted him to hear what I had to say - I am here to inform. He stepped into the exam room and asked his nurse to witness the encounter.

My dialog began by addressing a comment that Mr. Goretti had made in the Defense's opening statement of the trial. The comment had always been in the back of my mind as having some degree of relevance and truth. I was accused of not having the integrity to discuss my mother's death with the doctor to find answers to my questions. I was accused instead of seeking litigation which suggested a less than honorable approach to the problem. So as not to make the same mistake twice, I told him that I was there to inform him of my intent to distribute a book to retail outlets in the Birmingham area about my mother's experience and the trial. This book is in a daily journal format – a diary – consisting of trial notes, medical records and my commentary. With that having been said I handed to him a copy of the book for his review. At that time I positioned myself between the doctor and the door. Under his breath I heard him whisper the title, "An Unprejudiced Thinking Mind – A Story of Malpractice." He flipped through the pages, pausing to read certain passages and walked toward the window as if to gather his thoughts.

His first response to me was he would have Mr. Goretti look into the legal aspect of the book and he would use any and all lawful options to stop the distribution. My response was that I had anticipated that reaction and two legal firms had reviewed the book and it is without reproach. In fact I would welcome the free advertising that defending a lawsuit would generate. I waited for the next volley; take the punch. He then asked how much did I want for the rights to the book and my story? I responded by saying that I had never wanted any money from my mother's death and I am not looking to profit from the book! In fact, if you had had the integrity to contact me after her death to apologize for the extreme measures you took, to perform the second surgery we would not be here today.

With a puzzled look on his face he then asked me why am I really here today? With that I asked if we could have some privacy for the next phase of the conversation. He excused the nurse and told her to clear the office and he would explain what he could tomorrow. We walked to his office. Positioning the chair closer to his desk, I peered over my glasses as I told him my intent. I began by stating the death of my mother was a result of many bad decisions on the doctors' behalf, yours included, and a reckless surgical procedure that you were ill-prepared and ill-equipped to perform. She died because of your arrogance; that is my determination, that's the way I see it and my opinion will not change. You misrepresented yourself and you withheld important information from my mother and me prior to the surgery on March 28. Informed consent; or better stated lack of informed consent is why we are here today. Under oath you testified that you did not think it to be important to tell us all of the details; well, I am much more accommodating than you are. I will share with you some details that may prove important to the both of us.

Your surprise, anger and frustration should not be directed at me, for like you I am a victim. We are both victims of arrogant deceit. I am a victim because you withheld vital information that would have affected my decisions and you because your attorneys withheld fundamental information that would have affected your decisions. Let me make this clear, your attorneys never told you that I would, or could, pursue other options for closure and they did not suggest you settle and place a gag order on me, did they? Why wouldn't they suggest settling? They would not offer that option because settling is not in their best interest. The attorneys and the malpractice firm that insures you stands to profit much more by going to trial and winning, or even losing, a case than to have people like me to simply go away. It is not about me or you as a matter of fact; it is what is best for them. The malpractice company raises the rate at which they charge you for malpractice protection because of legal expenses and because they can – you are now a greater risk. The legal firm has another win, another notch on their belts, and the sales reps for the company have another case that is won to boast about when entertaining another prospect. So, you have played into their hands by being a patsy in letting them defend your honor. Honor had nothing to do with it; manipulating a desperate man, was. Can you imagine a couple of attorneys sitting on a patio overlooking the city, sharing a bottle of Scotch, smoking a Cuban cigar, discussing what a chump you are?

The book will be promoted and distributed; in that effort I will become an evangelist, preaching my gospel of disclosure. Any kind of hindrance from you will be welcomed, as that will further my ability to promote this epic. As I see it you have two options and they should be obvious. One; is to do nothing and take the risk that I will be unsuccessful in promoting this book; and you can only gage my resolve by my past and not my potential. Have I demonstrated the characteristics of a quitter? Two; is to take the fight to your legal counsel and the malpractice company for not fully representing your interests; Mr. Goretti fully protected the company's interest, not yours. This will be your sermon to preach and perhaps you'll have a congregation that will listen. The time has come for you to make a stand. No longer can you use the defense of Them and They; it is You; and what will You do?

The doctor reclined in his high-backed leather chair and turned toward a portrait that hung behind his desk. It was an old image of a man that bore a striking resemblance to himself. I presumed it to be his father; a man who had created a life for him and his family as a first-generation immigrant; a man that most likely had uncompromising ethics and morals. I wondered if the doctor was drawing strength from his bloodline; I was tempted to suggest he talk to his himself, his father, or God. He stared at the portrait for what seemed a long time and turned and asked me to leave. I stood and turned toward the door; my work here was done. As I walked away he asked, "Legal malpractice? Is that what you mean? The doctor did not demonstrate an ability to think outside of the box. In fact, he was not getting it at all. I have spent much of my adult life training adults. Adults have a narrow attention span and if a hands-on application is not viable, an allegory is effective. Tell a story and make it fit.

Let's use a hypothetical scenario:

A doctor performs a risky surgery on an unstable patient; a patient whose condition is the results of the doctor's oversight. The procedure goes badly and the patient dies. The daughter of the deceased is overwhelmed with grief and dedicates her life in an attempt to gain an understanding of what caused the death. Let's say the doctor did not document his interventions properly and generally speaking makes a mess of the medical records and panics. Modifying records, short-arming informed consent, botching a surgery; the daughter found fertile ground in which to plant seeds of doubt in her mind and others When the doctor is served, presented with a charge of malpractice, he called for the help. Help arrived as a deacon of the judicial system; a trusted professional – an attorney. A litany of legal red flags caught the eye and the imagination of the doctor's attorney. And the attorney presented a doom and gloom synopses of the situation; one that caused the doctor fear and loathing. The doctor felt as though he had no options; options were not offered by the attorney and the doctor blindly accepted a sole recommendation. The difference in faith and fear is; God waits on the other side of faith; the doctor's malpractice insurance company on the other side of fear.

Preparing for the trial, the doctor is interrogated by the attorney; week after week, month after month – years pass. The doctor's confidence varied with the tides of emotions until the attorney announced his strategy. The strategy did not change the rules of the game - that is not allowed; rather the game itself would change. The doctor, at the insistence of the attorney, changed his interpretation of the events and shifted the blame to other medical providers; even changed the cause of death. The doctor was encouraged by the brilliance of the crafty lawyer and bought into the charade.

The attorney wrote the script and the doctor learned his lines and rehearsal continued until show time. The production was well received and the audience – the jury – returned with rave reviews. The story made sense and the performance was engaging. The doctor left the stage - the courtroom - a vindicated icon of the community. And the attorney rode into the sunset having righted another wrong. The doctor's family hugged and kissed; the daughter of the deceased wept; all was right with the world.

All was right until…until the daughter's grief was transformed into a reckoning. She, too, had the talent and ability to change the game. Calculating the required elements to make her plan work; to right this wrong was twofold. One, educate the doctor in real-world facts and conditions; the behind the scene dynamics. And two, create leverage – an adverse implication - to force a desired outcome; a reason to cause action. Not really that difficult when one knows the rules of the game.

The daughter gained an audience with the doctor to explain the real-world facts and conditions. The behind the scene dynamics were dependent upon the doctor being persuaded to go to trial; this effort at the hands of his attorney. This was the only option offered and was pitched by the attorney as a wise course of action. The doctor was influenced by the use of dialog that inflamed his integrity; buzz words that included honor, innocence and vindication, the defendant became embolden by the brainwashing. What was not so obvious to the doctor was the self-serving motivation of the attorney and the malpractice company to defend the case.

The malpractice company profits more by publicly trying the doctor's case than it would by settling out of court and out of sight of the public. The doctor becomes another case study for a marketing strategy that is driven by a firm policy of defending at all costs. And that has been a successful image clients, including the doctor, have been lured to for years. The 'all costs' aspect is what evaded the doctor when he agreed to initially commit to the company and later to go to trial. The expense of the trial would be at the cost of the doctor in increased malpractice premiums because he is now rated as non-standard risk. The doctor in effect was a puppet; suspended by so many strings – all controlled by the attorney and his association with the company.

The doctor was caught in a perverse triangle and ultimately the odd man out. The attorney was the maiden serving two suitors; one being the doctor and the other being the company. The attorney served the doctor's needs by defending the case and served the company's needs by defending the case; the difference was the intimacy. The attorney's conflict in serving two clients meant that one was mislead. And that type of cheating is by definition legal malpractice. The attorney's incestuous relationship with the company meant the doctor had been duped.

In our hypothetical scenario, the doctor became angry but lacked the courage or motivation to seek his on reckoning. The impetus to act came in book form; a chronicle of the deceased patient's ordeal at the hands of an incompetent surgeon. The daughter had constructed a damning account of the actions, inactions and blunders of the doctor and had the means and motivation to distribute the indictment. The doctor had to defend his honor and innocence and preserve his vindication. He assessed his options; crush the grieving daughter's efforts meant an ugly public relations nightmare or, become the victim and file a suit against the attorney and the company. The daughter added fuel to the fire by further enlightening the doctor that the company has a few billion dollars in assets and has its own professional liability coverage. The doctor saw the hand writing on the wall; the publicity of the book would have great effect regarding his status in the community and, with his back to the corner, he realized the need to become a hero and challenge the company and its unscrupulous practices.

The conclusion of the hypothetical scenario is that in the end, as it is at Christmas, we may not get what we want, but we get what we deserve. The daughter got closure and public awareness of her plight. The doctor got public vindication and a few thousand dollars to offset his loss of patients. The company got exposed for what it is, a manipulative storehouse of money, corruption and propaganda.

The doctor buried his head in his hands. His anguish was obvious. I turned to avoid seeing a soul in this much pain. In my attempt to orchestrate a makeshift resolution to my highest calling, I was at times overwhelmed with sympathy and charity. Planning and intuition, intuition and planning; at times I did not know if what drives my actions is a product of cunning or of choreography.

Cunning defined as a dispassionate and deliberate set of acts based on a set of objectives. Or, choreography defined as being led about by the music someone else conducts, an influence that was not so obvious. I was at that crossroad as the doctor agonized his circumstance. A part of me considered forgetting the entire plan and going home; letting him off the hook, so to speak. And, candidly, mother would have taken that high-road. What was still unclear to me was what the high road is?

I took a deep breath in preparation to offer a conciliatory truce and immediately my thought focused on the objective. It was as if at that moment that I paused to take my breath I stopped utilizing my critical reasoning skills and listened to a higher voice, a voice that spoke with crystal clear clarity. To simply let a wrong go unaddressed is far from taking the high road. In preparing for the trial, I interviewed several former patients and family members and discovered far too many anomalies. One patient had lost a foot to amputation as a result to a Heparin reaction the doctor did not recognize. Another patient that lived near Mother was discharged from the same facility, by the same surgeon, with the same symptoms. He, too, died, at home, after experiencing a suspicious clotting event where the bypass grafts occluded. His family was so distraught that God had abandoned them in a desperate time of need. They dismissed the death as the will of the Almighty and their faith suffered as a result.

The good doctor not only cost patients the ultimate price he also created a crisis in faith for others. My temporary insanity to release Zopyros from accountability quickly waned as I rededicated myself to my highest calling. That mission is to either force the doctor to make a career change or, to encourage him to improve his skills set. And that defined is taking the high road. Discipline overruled my temptation of charity and I admonished the doctor to do the right thing. I challenged his manhood. With that, I placed a listing of attorneys that were licensed to practice in Alabama on his desk. Before he could ask its useful purpose, I told him it was a list of cannibals; attorneys that sue attorneys. Just do it! The most successful were marked with a heart.

Before leaving, in an attempt to be fair, I informed the doctor that my next action was to file a complaint with the state medical board. And with that complaint a recording of the perfusionist's confession that he had given a contraindicated drug during surgery. Heparin was the drug that you ordered as the one in charge of the surgical team. And it is a decision that could most likely cost you your license to practice.

I turned and asked if he had researched the meaning of his name. Puzzled, he responded he had not and asked why. I did not feel compelled to enlighten him at this time. Zopyros was a Persian nobleman that feigned mortal wounds to gain the trust of his countrymen only to betray them. Strangely, I felt no satisfaction in troubling him.

CHAPTER 15

A Case of Malpractice

A man who is his own lawyer has a fool for his client.
-early 19th

I had taken a position on the second row of the visitor's section in Judge Kent's courtroom; a strategic position where I could observe the defendant's mannerisms. He was well coached. He donned a conservative suit and tie. His legs uncrossed and his hands were placed on his lap; he had the look of a victimized servant, a man who had sacrificed himself to rescue a desperate person that was destined to lose everything. His attorney's opening statement insisted he was an honorable man, a good man, and the accusations of the plaintiff were unfounded and based on a theory put forth in a book filled with conjecture and half-truths. The attorney hammered home the point that 'They' are trying to find a scapegoat for unsound medical decisions. And that the need for legal malpractice counsel is because of 'Them' and their lack of Informed Consent. It is 'Them' and 'They', not the defendant that is at fault.

The courtroom was an intimate setting. The opponents sat within close proximity - so close that whispers could be heard despite efforts to keep them confidential. Wood veneer lined the walls. Overstated, wooden desks and uncomfortable pews that

242

made ones back hurt throughout the day agitated the tension of the participants. Opposite the jurors box on the Defendant's side of the courtroom was a large projection screen. This screen would facilitate the presentation of evidence and support material. The Bench was elevated to place the judge in a position of authority and above that was the Great Seal of Alabama. Flanked on either side of the Bench were the flags of the United States and Alabama. Behind the Bench was a door where the judge would appear and retire. And beyond the door one could see bookshelves lined with legal journals. Frosted windows reached to the ceiling on one side of the courtroom. The windows served to remind me life goes on with sounds from the street below.

The judge read the charge. Claims made by Dr. Zopyros against Damian Goretti accused him of committing conscious acts of misrepresentation; and that he acted negligently and with mal-intent with respect to that representation. And that those acts and failures to act fell below a reasonable standard of care for lawyers in like circumstances. The consequences of those actions resulted in the loss of the doctor's license to practice medicine. And consequently, the forfeiture of the opportunity to practice medicine resulted in a loss of an annual income of over $500,000.

My mind wandered as the volleying of facts and fabrication bounced from one side of the isle to the other. My agenda was simple; start a fight and stand back. I didn't really care who would win; in my mind they lost when they crossed me. The trial would drag on for several weeks. The local press, with a little baiting from me, found it to be an engaging human interest story. Even though I had orchestrated an event that would seemingly have long lasting effects, my emptiness still remained. Throughout the saga my feelings of uncovering the truth was tempered by compassion for those that were being affected. Something deep within me sensed a higher calling, one that transposed my desire for retribution to that of reconciliation. And the courtroom activities served to remind me of the effects of a life that still lives on; in the hearts of some and in the minds of others.

AFTERWORD

The mother's heart is the child's schoolroom.
Henry Ward Beecher

───────────

Mother died on the afternoon of the full moon prior to Easter; the Lenten Moon. The early Christians used this astronomical occurrence to mark the beginning of a time fasting and prayer; a season spent in mournful respect for the death of Christ. This time of solemn devotion and sacrificial lifestyle continued until the next full moon; the Egg Moon. The Egg Moon marked the end of the mourning and fasting period and signaled the beginning of spring and new growth; a new beginning, a rebirth.

My time of mourning and self denial began on the day of her death; my Lenten Moon. And my period of solemn devotion and singularity continued until I experienced my new beginning; my Egg Moon on the day of accountability. On that day I called heaven and earth to stand before those who had with reckless abandonment acted wantonly against my mother. Their admonishment: When given the option of life or death chose life that we all may live. It was not an act of vengeance; the infliction of punishment in return for a wrong that was committed: Retribution. It was a reckoning; a settlement of a debt; a reconciliation of how and why.

I am my mother's child; a life that was produced by her body. Although, she is not with me, I feel I am the fruits of her labor. This struggle has caused me to come to the realization that the true womb of a mother is her heart. And her children are reborn daily unto her good works. If that is true, I'll have many rebirths, scores of days to live on this earth to honor her and her good works. I owe it to that life that lives on in the hearts she left behind, and when you think of it that way, to do that is not really to die. And I finally have reason to smile and I hope mother is smiling, too.

I will see her again.

CONCLUSION

———————

Guilt was an emotion that caused me to become a person I am not. And guilt was a constant companion and nemesis for me until I evolved. The manifestation of guilt as regret and despair robbed me of my existence, my now, as I lived my life in the past – reliving decisions and experiences as if the next recollection of events would provide a different outcome. This is by definition a type of insanity. And as if to balance this guilt, I created fantasies of justice and resolution and looked to the future for salvation. I planned a course of action and awaited a set of events and decisions that would provide closure; a legal redemption that by anyone's definition would not change reality. So, the past and the future dominated my thoughts as the years, days and moments of my quest passed with feelings of agony and anticipation. There was not a time that my troubles did not dominate my present, or a moment that my hope was absent; hope that was dependent on others understanding my pain and troubles of which I had no control.

Reflecting on my experience I now realize that at any given moment, if I were to have ask myself a question – a question that focused on the inventory of my problems at that instance, two responses would have been appropriate. One is that I have a problem and can't affect any change at the time, so set the problem aside. And the other; I have a problem and I can take an action to resolve it, so take action. My inappropriate retort to the former question to not set aside the problem deprived me of what was an opportunity to experience my life and its intent. That experience was an out of control thought process that did nothing but consume my moments of Now with worrisome notions. The later would have focused my attention on a task at hand, an opportunity to perform a corrective action, an appropriate utilization of talent and industry. One is a defining moment, the other a waste of time. My evolution has raised my level of consciousness that Now is the most important time in my life. And there has never been a time in my life when Now did not exist.

This evolution has also taken me from a perspective that death is a closed door - an end of the road so to speak - to a realization that it is simply a transition. My deep seated fear was that nothing awaited me on the other side; nothing in terms of what I know as reality. The ending of relationships and the erasing of important memories was a radical concept that troubled me. Whether the extremes were an eternity of singing and lounging in a lavish paradise or the complete cessation of consciousness, neither provided a sense of security or accomplishment or peace. Death is simply the wiping away of the fog from a mirror to expose one's true self - one's true existence after a lifetime of props and staging.

Fear created a shortsightedness that caused me to focus on the temporal while missing the spiritual. And fear temporarily blinded me to the ultimate sacrifice that was made by one who had made so many accommodations in my life. That temporary blindness threatened to cheat me of an opportunity; an opportunity to affect the path of many lives. And to have done so would have dishonored a life that was lived with integrity and a death that was graced with dignity. In all of my efforts I still felt emptiness until I stopped focusing on the past – and on me - and realized that separateness is the exact opposite to human existence. We are all interconnected, we are one. What I do to myself, I do to all. What I do for all, I do for me.

I have come from a place in my life where I sought peace by my actions to a place where I am at peace with my actions. From a place where I looked for things external to define me to a place where I define those things external. I have experienced an awakening that I Am, instead of trying to be. I am God's greatest feeling – I am in fact, God feeling. I am God's way of experiencing creation. And it is within that framework that the jurisdiction exists for my efforts in pursuing my passion of affecting change in the consciousness of my opponents; to elevate their awareness of the spiritual and their responsibility to their highest calling. Guided by my thoughts; my soul's instructions. And lead by my words; the interpretation of those instructions. I was then enabled to perform the necessary deeds and actions to facilitate change. Extreme efforts so that what has happened to me will not happen to another.

My newfound freedom has been a conversion from a concept that we are bodies with souls to the awareness that we are souls with bodies. And what makes us who we are survives the body. The energy that Is, continues and never diminishes – it transitions. And continues to exist in many lives; as we have lived before, we will live again.

I have learned that Revelation is a virtue. Revelation is being honest: Forthcoming with what is known and candid with what is not. Revelation is being responsible: Owning that which is done and accepting that which is not. Revelation is what we expect from those we trust; politicians, business associates, religious leaders, our partners and our doctors; and something we should expect from ourselves. The awakening of the need for Revelation - full and complete disclosure is the next revival of the human experience. This awakening will have as its evangelist one's higher self – one's soul. The ability and willingness to listen to our soul's instruction will provide us direction as to what we should do – the soul's intent. Only then can one stop living life and begin to create it.

These are the things I have learned from a life that has ceased to exist in a body but whose energy is strong and vibrant. And now, in the Now, at this moment, as I contemplate my problems, I am without worry or regret. For I am either fully capable of addressing what confronts me or I am not currently able to affect any change; but I am comfortable with both. I do not dwell on things of the past, nor do I wait for future promise of a better existence. Simply put, I am. And that best serves what I want to be - me, a living legacy of my Mother.

ABOUT THE AUTHOR

Von Goodwin is a business consultant, personal coach and the author of books and articles revealing the role of the individual in creation. Since 1985 he has worked with individuals to rediscover ancient wisdom to enrich their personal lives. And he has conducted and participated in over 3,000 seminars, workshops, consulting and coaching sessions with companies and staffers to redirect their focus from key performance standards defined by industry to becoming more aware of the value of collective consciousness. In addition to those appearances, Von has been the featured presenter at twelve universities imparting the understandings of the ancients to the students of the present. He has been a pioneer in breaking down barriers of limiting bureaucracy replacing them with a vision of possibilities.